Evidence-Based Practice for the Helping Professions

A Practical Guide with Integrated Multimedia

Leonard E. Gibbs
University of Wisconsin–Eau Claire

BROOKS/COLE
CENGAGE Learning

Australia • Brazil • Japan • Korea • Mexico • Singapore • Spain • United Kingdom • United States

BROOKS/COLE
CENGAGE Learning

Evidence-Based Practice for the Helping Professions: A Practical Guide with Integrated Multimedia
Leonard E. Gibbs

Executive Editor: Lisa Gebo

Assistant Editor: Alma Dea Michelena

Editorial Assistant: Sheila Walsh

Technology Project Manager: Barry Connolley

Marketing Manager: Caroline Concilla

Marketing Assistant: Mary Ho

Project Manager, Editorial Production: Stephanie Zunich

Print/Media Buyer: Vena Dyer

Permissions Editor: Sue Ewing

Production Service: Peggy Francomb, Shepherd, Inc.

Text Designer: Jeanne Calabrese

Copy Editor: Jeanne Patterson

Illustrator: Natalie Dato

Cover Designer: Roger Knox

Cover Image: PhotoDisc

Compositor: Shepherd, Inc.

Cartoons courtesy of Cyndee Kaiser

© 2003 Brooks/Cole, Cengage Learning

For product information and technology assistance, contact us at **Cengage Learning Customer & Sales Support, 1-800-354-9706**

For permission to use material from this text or product, submit all requests online at **www.cengage.com/permissions** Further permissions questions can be emailed to **permissionrequest@cengage.com**

Library of Congress Control Number: 2002104360

ISBN-13: 978-0-534-53923-8

ISBN-10: 0-534-53923-8

Brooks/Cole
10 Davis Drive
Belmont, CA 94002-3098
USA

Cengage Learning is a leading provider of customized learning solutions with office locations around the globe, including Singapore, the United Kingdom, Australia, Mexico, Brazil, and Japan. Locate your local office at:
international.cengage.com/region

Cengage Learning products are represented in Canada by Nelson Education, Ltd.

For your course and learning solutions, visit
academic.cengage.com

Purchase any of our products at your local college store or at our preferred online store **www.ichapters.com**

Printed in Canada
6 7 8 9 10 11 10 09

To Mom and Dad,
who repeatedly demonstrated their willingness
to pay a price for ethical principles,
and to my students,
who I hope learn the same from me.

Contents

CHAPTER 2

Become Motivated to Apply the Current Best Evidence to Practice   25

CHAPTER 3

Pose a Specific Question of Importance to Your Client's Welfare 53

CHAPTER 5

**Treatment Effectiveness Research: Evaluating Study Quality
and Applying Results to Practice   147**

CHAPTER 6

Meta-Analysis: Evaluating Review Quality and Applying Findings to Practice   185

CHAPTER 10

Teaching Others   250

Foreword

The helping professions have been struggling to improve the quality of practice through a knowledge base substantiated by research and empirical evidence. While many of us would argue that expenditures for research are not nearly adequate, major investments have been made in building the knowledge base, and in building the right kind of knowledge base. But the uptake in practice has been modest. Professor Gibbs is a visionary. He has understood this problem and provided a reasoned, practical, and, yes, empirically based methodology for its remedy. This volume is a major achievement.

Over 30 years ago, I wrote "at this point in the history of the social work profession, it is clear that social work practitioners neither read, write, or utilize research" (Seidl, 1980). At that time, I urged that much of the research that had been done in social work was not useful to practitioners, that it dealt with variables over which clients and practitioners had no control, lacked time and space compatibility, or had little or no bearing on the problems of clients or the work of practitioners. While there is still a long way to go, the last three decades have seen great strides in the quality of the research literature and great strides, through computer databases, in the practitioner's ability to retrieve the information needed to practice effectively.

Professor Gibbs now tells us how to integrate research evidence into practice using electronic means to integrate current best evidence into practice decision making. Building on his own work in critical thinking, scientific reasoning, practice, and research methodology, as well as the work of others engaged in conceptualizing, utilizing, and teaching evidence-based practice,

Gibbs provides an open-ended blueprint for capturing useful research, assessing its quality, and applying the knowledge gained to the problems and concerns of clients.

While a good deal of deserved credit has gone to David Sackett and his colleagues (1997) for the rise in evidence-based medical practice, in particular, and evidence-based practice, in general, Gibbs laid out substantial groundwork in his earlier book, *Scientific Reasoning for Social Workers* (1991). For example, Gibbs addressed the following issues in the 1991 volume: how to ask a specific question about a method's effectiveness (including 11 ratable criteria), using on-line computer procedures to locate evaluation studies (including logic for constructing searches), how to evaluate studies to guide practice systematically, and experimenting to judge a method's effect. Professors Gibbs and Sackett are moving in the same direction, and the work of each supports the other. The present volume makes the previous work all the more relevant and usable.

Unlike some critical-thinking writers, Gibbs understands the social responsibility of the helping professions to address problems equipped with the best possible evidence. Perfect evidence—proof—is rarely if ever available. Gibbs would have us do an honest assessment and then the best we can with what we have. He also recognizes the positive role of client values, wishes, and concerns and profession's ethics, policy, and practice wisdom in decision making. He would move us away from the wishful-thinking claims that occasionally get made to knowledge and skill we can substantiate. He understands the need for practice skills and would like to add the skills of evidence-based practice to the list.

The text is successful in teaching us how to pose specific questions for which an answer may be sought, how to search efficiently and quickly for the best evidence using primarily electronic means, how to appraise the quality of the evidence and the implications for action, and how to take action and monitor what happens. Professor Gibbs provides us with a tool to do what we do much better.

Professor Gibbs is a practical man, and the present volume echoes his practicality. He is a down-to-earth man, and this is a down-to-earth book. His illustrations and examples are rich and to the point. The book's many messages are delivered with warmhearted humor and a precise but friendly writing style. Most important, however, Gibbs comes to terms with what may be the most pervasive problem in practice: doing the right thing, not doing the wrong thing, and finding out what the right thing may be. This is a timely and needed contribution.

Fredrick W. Seidl, MSW, Ph.D.
Emeritus and Dean Emeritus
Professor, School of Social Work
State University of New York at Buffalo

Preface

Because practitioners' reasoning determines what they do, and because what they do profoundly affects clients' lives, this text was written to help busy practitioners to make better judgments and decisions as they go about their life-affecting work. My motivation arises from experiences that I share with many in practice. I too have sweat over how to help a potentially suicidal person. As many in community mental health and in corrections, I too have agonized over whether an individual might be violent toward others, weighing the client's potential loss of freedom against what might happen to others. I wrote my doctoral dissertation and did a series of studies regarding how to match alcoholic clients with treatment partly because of a practice experience.

This text applies equally well to practice and to research methods courses in the helping professions, but its lessons can be applied to enrich any course in the helping professions where it makes sense to solicit a real question of practical significance from someone in practice. (Please see Exercise 3-2 at the end of chapter 3 to see how such questions might enrich any course.) This book could be used as a primary or supplementary text in research or practice, but it does not follow conventional outlines for either course. It follows emerging patterns of reasoning in articles and texts regarding evidence-based practice and clinical reasoning. Because references to the term *evidence-based practice* have been increasing almost exponentially for the past 5 years in the helping professions (see Figure 1.3), this text probably represents changes in the format for research and practice texts to come. Consequently, this text should help readers to serve on interdisciplinary teams that will increasingly apply principles of evidence-based practice.

Many examples in each chapter will demonstrate how, in real time, as problems arise, practitioners can pose questions of practical importance and search electronically for the best and most relevant evidence as a guide. This text is designed to help busy practitioners to avoid becoming overwhelmed by masses of information and, rather, to sift quickly and efficiently for the current best evidence. Searching does not ensure that the best evidence will always help to chart a clear course. Often no strong evidence can be found, but still a thorough and competent search that finds nothing of value *is* a finding.

Evidence-based practice is not a cookbook approach. Evidence-based practice encompasses practice experience, a commitment to placing the concerns of the client first, and a determination to utilize the current best evidence to guide decision making. Evidence-based practice is not a panacea: it is a tool. Evidence-based practice will augment but not replace interpersonal skill and practice experience.

Examples in this text come from a wide range of disciplines and settings, including social work, psychology, medicine, nursing, education, child welfare, geriatrics, mental health, social services, and corrections. I teach social workers primarily, but my students solicit questions from across all helping professions. Examples from practice illustrate:

- Learning how to pose questions regarding your practice so specifically that you can search for an answer
- Learning how to search efficiently and quickly through electronic bibliographic databases for the best evidence
- Critically and systematically appraising the evidence to determine its relative quality and implications for action
- Taking action and collecting data to monitor what happens
- Learning how to avoid common errors in reasoning about practice
- Teaching others how to follow the process of evidence-based practice

Chapter 1 defines evidence-based practice by concept, example, and operation. The second chapter seeks to motivate the reader to turn to current best evidence through three examples from practice. Chapter 3 demonstrates how to pose a specific, answerable, well-built question from practice. I call them Client-Oriented, Practical, Evidence-Search (COPES) questions. These questions concern effectiveness, prevention, risk estimation, description (including qualitative studies), and assessment. Learning how to pose these questions represents an essential first step toward getting an answer electronically. Chapter 4 demonstrates how you can practice applying efficient search procedures to locate the current best research relative to COPES questions. This chapter includes access to this text's Web site. Chapter 5 through chapter 8 provide six scales for critically appraising evidence regarding each of the aforementioned question types. Chapter 9 gives examples of the kinds of data that one might collect in practice to evaluate actions taken in practice. This chapter relies heavily on the "scientist-practitioner" model. And finally, chapter 10 discusses obstacles to evidence-based practice within organizations, issues in implementing it, and strategies for teaching it to others.

This text's format and exercises support but do not require a "hands-on" style of learning. If you are in practice, you might follow this text's exercises as models, but insert your own questions from your own practice. I think this text's lessons can be learned most effectively if you practice along at a computer terminal that has access to the World Wide Web.

This Book's Web Site

Many bibliographic databases are free and accessible for practice; many are not and can be accessed best through a university system. This book's Web site was written with Eamon Armstrong (a physician), Josette Jones (a nurse), and Donna Raleigh (a programmer). The Web site can be located at this address: www.evidence.brookscole.com. The Web site's grid lists professions horizontally and client types vertically with intersects marking Web sites specific to both. This Web site will be updated frequently. Please offer suggestions for updating it in the site's suggestions option.

This Book's Three CD-ROM Programs

This book's three CD-ROM programs have several uses. They might be used as a pretest before viewing their scoring keys (in chapter 2). The reader may appreciate getting immediate feedback right after taking the HITTT, the CITTT and the MITTT as tests; so the keys to these measures are in chapter 2. To take the tests, follow their instructions to record your responses on a file so you can score them against a key. The Hospital Interactive Team Thinking Test (HITTT) was recorded on an active Neurosciences Ward at Luther Hospital in Eau Claire. The HITTT best demonstrates the steps of evidence-based practice and has been used to vividly define evidence-based practice for social work and for Eamon Armstrong's medical audiences at professional workshops. The script for the HITTT was written by an interdisciplinary health care team at Luther. Because the HITTT demonstrates steps in evidence-based practice, it should probably be viewed first.

The Courtroom Interactive Testimony Thinking Test (CITTT) was recorded in Judge Wahl's courtroom. Barbara Gorman, who wrote most of the script, has thousands of hours in the "hot seat" giving testimony as an expert witness for the Eau Claire Public Defender's Office. Barbara intended that the CITTT would help to prepare for effective testimony as well as serving as a test of reasoning.

The Multidisciplinary Interactive Team Thinking Test (MITTT) was made in a classroom at the Lowes Creek Early Learning Center in Eau Claire, Wisconsin. Unlike the first two, the MITTT's actors are not professional actors; however, they are all professionals in the roles they play in real life (school social worker, speech therapist, special education teachers, school nurse, etc). The MITTT's team really does make judgments and decisions about special needs children—they thought up many of the MITTT's fallacy examples. My wife Betsy wrote the script in collaboration with her colleagues.

This Book's Instructors' Manual

This book is supported by a complete and detailed Instructors' Manual that includes: Suggestions for teaching EBP, answers to exercises, example course outlines, and multiple choice items.

Acknowledgments

This book has involved many dedicated people. Most just gave their time and expertise without thought of compensation. I think the majority did so because they share my passion for helping practitioners to reason more effectively in their vital work. As you read this work, please think of the many who made this book possible.

My thanks to: Eileen Gambrill, a true friend and powerful intellect who has helped me to sharpen my reasoning; Tom Endres for bringing dead audio back to life; Kay McBride for a review regarding efficacy of evidence-based practice; Kathy Finder for helping me with Outline and Word; Magdalena Paulow for locating references and for reading chapter 3; Karen Pope and Mimi King, Betsy Richmund, Richard Bell, and Dan Norstedt for reference help; Holly D. Verschay for library help and transcribing the HITTT; Donna Raleigh for Web site development; Bruce Dybvik for camera work and images; Eamon Armstrong for Web addresses and his modeling evidence-based practice; Christian S. Rushmann, AV Director, Luther Hospital, Eau Claire; Herman Schultz, Anthony Schieffer, and Jason Stoelting for programming; Mike Wick for locating Herman Schultz and for giving him an independent study to work on the program; Allie Shaul for a search regarding effectiveness of programs to improve interdisciplinary teams; Rich Grinnell for archive work to locate early empirical works; Dick Schoek for help searching for evidence-based literature regarding computers in human services, Rich Dirks, Copyright Officer at UWEC; Amy Wellbourn for database searching; to my colleagues and friends in the Department of Social Work at the University of Wisconsin–Eau Claire, including Diane Brandt, Pat Christopherson, Gloria

Fennell, La Vonne Cornell-Swanson, Rupa Gupta, Al Koeller, Carol Modl, Darlene Tempski, Don Mowry, Rick Ryberg, Kent Smith, Steve Tallant, and Nick Smiar who endured the inconvenience of my being on sabbatical and who helped to provide the inspiration to write this book; Mike Subkoviak for statistical help; Ron Satz, Provost & Vice Chancellor, for help with permissions; The University of Wisconsin–Eau Claire Summer Research Program for support for the HITTT, the CITTT, and the MITTT; and funds from Brooks/Cole–Thomson Learning and the UWEC Office of Research and Sponsored Programs.

Hospital Interactive Team Thinking Test (HITTT)

Producer: Leonard Gibbs, Department of Social Work, University of Wisconsin–Eau Claire. Authors: Leonard Gibbs, Department of Social Work, University of Wisconsin–Eau Claire; Eamon C. Armstrong, M.D., Lehigh Valley Family Practice Residency Program, Allentown, Pennsylvania; Joan Werner, School of Nursing UWEC; and Terry Allen, Department of Music and Theatre Arts, UWEC. Programming and Student Researcher: Herman Schultz. Script Writing: Eamon Armstrong, Bonnie Nierenhausen, Karen Woodie, Leonard Gibbs, and Terry Allen. Director: Terry Allen. Videotaping: Bruce Dybvik, UWEC Media Development Center. Acting: Terry Allen (Dr. Langdon); Paul Calenberg (Oliver the Occupational Therapist); Katherine Grosskopf (Nancy the Nurse); Donald E. Hoff, M.D. (Mr. Anderson the Patient); Jeanne Kussrow Larson (Chris the daughter); Richard Nimke (Dr. Myers); and Lynsey Ray (Sandy the Social Worker). Consultant: Peter Chambers, M.D., Marshfield Clinic. Library Services: Luther Midelfort Library Services, Ginny Wright and Becky Henning. Program Design Consultant: Susan Harrison, Department of Computer Science, UWEC. Hospital Settings: Neurosciences Unit and Library at Luther Midelfort Hospital in Eau Claire, Wisconsin. Administrative Help: Pam Wold, Dean Mathwig, and Terrance Borman of Luther Midelfort in Eau Claire and Jeanette Wiseman and Lisa Gebo of Brooks/Cole Publishers. Diagrams: Gene Leisz and Donna Raleigh. Technical Help: Lee Anna Rasar. Funding Support: University of Wisconsin–Eau Claire's Office of University Research and Internal Grant Programs, and UW–EC Department of Social Work. Editing: Leonard Gibbs, Thomas Video, and Terry Allen. Disclaimer: The script for the HITTT, the CITTT, and the MITTT were written and acted for professional education purposes only. They were written by members of helping professions and acted for realism, but any resemblance to real people is purely coincidental.

Courtroom Interactive Testimony Thinking Test (CITTT)

Authors: Leonard Gibbs, Department of Social Work; Barbara Gorman, Client Services Specialist, Office of Wisconsin State Public Defender; Joan Werner, School of Nursing; Terry Allen, Music and Theatre Arts. Directing and Acting:

Terry Allen, Prof., Music and Theatre Arts (Judge). Programming: Jason Stoelting and Anthony Schieffer (on the MITTT). Script: Barbara Gorman, Eau Claire Public Defender's Office; Terry Allen, Music and Theatre Arts at UW–EC. Acting: Joel Aggerholm (Peter Gilbertson), Anna Lee Brenna (Patti Wolf), Brad Calli (Mr. Black), Jennifer D'Lynn Westlund (Ms. Jones), Tony Duerkop (Donald Smith the Defendant), Peter McCain (Clerk of Court), and Rebecca Multz (Susan Higley). Videotaping: Bruce Dybvik (UWEC Media Development Center). Program Design Consultant: Susan Harrison, Prof., Computer Sciences Department. Courtroom Setting: Hon. Eric J. Wahl, Branch 2, Eau Claire County Court. Funding Support: University of Wisconsin–Eau Claire Office of University Research and Internal Grant Programs, UWEC Department of Social Work.

Multidisciplinary Interactive Team Thinking Test (MITTT)

Authors: Leonard Gibbs, Betsy McDougall Gibbs, and Joan Werner. Acknowledgments for Acting: Barb Breen, Jackie Brown, Bob Jankowski, Mary Mcfarlane, Joel Strayer, John Strei, Barb Thiel. Photography: Bruce Dybvik. Production: Ann Dybvik and Betsy McDougall Gibbs. Production: Anthony Schieffer and Jason Stoelting (Programming). Funding: Office of University Research (Internal Grant Program of the University of Wisconsin–Eau Claire) for a grant by Leonard Gibbs, Betsy McDougall Gibbs, and Joan Werner with Anthony Schieffer. Reliability Checks: members of the Methods of Social Work Research Class at the University of Wisconsin–Eau Claire.

For ideas, comments, or help, please contact me at lgibbs@uwec.edu

Evidence-Based Practice: Definition and What It Offers to You and to Your Clients

1

Overview

This chapter defines *evidence-based practice* (EBP), starting with a detailed example from nursing home practice, then by general concept describing its major features, and finally by an operational definition that defines its seven steps. This book's chapters follow steps listed by Sackett, Richardson, Rosenberg, and Haynes (1997, back cover), with the exception of the first step regarding motivation. You will be able to observe these steps in action (by enclosed CD-ROM) as a hospital interdisciplinary team goes about solving a simulated problem to help an 80-year-old man. Please do take time to watch the Hospital Interactive Team Thinking Test (HITTT) option on the CD when you get to the section of this chapter that requests it. The HITTT will define vividly what this book is about. The HITTT demonstrates an integration of practice skill, a concern for clients' wishes, and use for current evidence better than just text ever could. A team of professionals including nurses, social workers physicians (a whole medical team) actors, and production people all put their hearts into the HITTT. Hopefully, such care in definition will help you to see accurately what evidence-based practice is and how it might fit your practice.

You also can become more familiar with the feel of evidence-based practice by doing the exercises that accompany this and all chapters. This text's exercises reflect almost 20 years of experience teaching how to pose specific practice-related questions and to search electronically for the relevant, current, best evidence (Gibbs & Johnson, 1983; Gibbs, 1990, 1991; Gibbs & Gambrill, 1999, pp. 235–252).

Later exercises include access to this book's Web site: *Evidence-Based Practice for the Helping Professions*. The Web site can be located at this address:

www.evidence.brookscole.com

This Web site was developed to help locate the current best evidence relative to practice questions across the helping professions.

This chapter concludes with arguments to consider regarding why you might want to adopt evidence-based practice now as a valuable aid to your practice. The chapter argues that EBP is consistent with ethical codes and with continual efforts in the helping professions to make research relevant and useful to practitioners as they go about their life-affecting work. You may want to consider EBP now because reference to it seems to be growing almost exponentially in the literature of the helping professions. Consequently, your collaboration with other professions may require some knowledge of EBP procedures, particularly if your work involves interdisciplinary teams.

Definition by Detailed Example

Susan Montgomery (personal communication, January 18, 2001) took her undergraduate social work field placement at a 70-bed nursing home because she regards aging as a ". . . fascinating part of peoples lives that can be made better if we know how to help them." Susan was impressed with the nursing home from the start. The nursing home's location in a small community led to an atmosphere that seemed to permeate the home making it a ". . . homey place where the staff knew the names and faces of each resident and were concerned about their well-being. It seemed like a healthy place for someone to be." The nursing home's philosophy was to maintain the best quality of life for its residents and their family members with the greatest independence for residents.

As Susan became more acclimated to her new duties, she took on more and more responsibilities. These included helping new residents and their families with the admission process, including the Patient's Bill of Rights, Durable Power of Attorney, and Advance Directives; meeting residents for one-on-one talks to attend to residents' emotional and informational needs; and keeping family members informed about residents. Susan worked on a team beside other disciplines to coordinate services. She attended weekly care team conferences regarding residents (the care team included a social worker, a physical therapist, a nurse, a speech therapist, an occupational therapist, a dietary coordinator, an activity director, care aids, residents, and their family members), and she worked out plans for discharging residents back into the community.

Susan was unprepared for one thing about her placement: she did not expect to see so many residents so deeply affected by dementia. About a third of the home's residents suffer from some form of dementia—most of these from Alzheimer's disease and most in its later stages. Some wander about the home, but their Wander Guard bracelet buzzes an alarm if they try to walk out a door. Later-stage dementia affects residents individually. Some cry that they are lost. For some, their minds fly back to a time long ago; they may ask to speak to someone long dead or may think they need to go outside to work in the barn. They lose their own identities and, sadly, cannot even recognize their own children or beloved spouses. They die locked away in their own world, unable to say good-bye to those whom they loved. Some residents enter the home clearheaded and progress into dementia. In its early stages, those affected recognize their slipping mental capacity and sometimes hide it or make light of it. For example, Susan first noted one of her favorite clients' confusion at lunch in the dining room. The client had asked a staff member to accompany him to his room "so he could talk on the way," but he appeared confused about where to go when the staff member could not walk with him. Susan realized that he had become spatially confused and really wanted the staff member to take him to his room. Susan's heart went out to family members trying to communicate through their loved one's fog of confusion. Susan herself felt a bit uncomfortable with her own uncertainty about how to effectively relate when such residents spoke out to her, and she noted a discomfort among staff who occasionally avoided such residents.

Susan's empathy for clients, for their family members, and for fellow staff members and her concern for her own need to know more led her to pose important questions. She said, "It's straining to watch people go through this." Susan resolved that if she could find enough good quality evidence to answer her questions, then she would share what she found with others. She identified several central issues. She wanted to know how to communicate with family members about the progression of dementia regarding what they might expect. She wanted to know about the typical emotional toll on family caregivers and on professional caregivers, and she wanted to know what might help both with their emotional burdens while giving care. She wondered what services would best support caregivers' quality of life, and she wondered about the relative efficacy of interventions that might help confused residents to feel less anxiety and to exhibit less confusion.

These issues led Susan to pose these and other related questions:

1. Regarding *family caregivers* helping demented aged persons, what do surveys reveal about the caregivers' emotional reactions to being a caregiver?
2. Regarding *professional caregivers* helping demented aged persons, what do surveys reveal about the caregivers' emotional reactions to being a caregiver?
3. Regarding family caregivers helping demented aged persons, which method of support for caregivers will result in the best quality of life for the caregivers?
4. Regarding aged residents in a nursing home suffering from severe dementia, which form of behavioral treatment will result in the residents' lowest level of confusion or anxiety?

The first two questions are *description questions;* the last two are *effectiveness questions.* Other question types include *prevention, assessment,* and *risk.* To answer the preceding questions and other related ones, Susan searched electronically using skills for evidence-based practice that she had ". . . learned in the research class and in internship." Susan used a computer to log on to an earlier version of this book's *Evidence-Based Practice for the Helping Professions* Web site. Links within that Web site took her to databases most likely to contain evidence specific to her questions. Though Susan searched in MEDLINE (medicine), CINAHL (nursing and allied health), and ERIC (education), she found her best and most relevant evidence in PsycINFO (psychology) and SWAB (social work abstracts). Within each database, she quickly homed in on the best evidence using terms called MOLES that Susan said ". . . easily weed out the weaker evidence" (Montgomery, 2000, p. 7). Some of the articles were available directly as full-text articles; some were not and had to be retrieved through interlibrary loan at her university library.

At the same time that Susan searched for evidence, she began screening the evidence for its quality based on information in abstracts. Some she rejected for weaknesses in experimental design (a topic in chapter 5 of this text), some for obvious biases. Later, she applied rating scales to help her to decide which studies were strongest and therefore most credible to answer her questions [I am not evaluating whether Susan found the best possible evidence here; rather, I am just reporting on what Susan did.] Regarding Susan's first question about the emotional reactions of family caregivers, Susan found an exploratory study based on interviews and scales of depression and grief administered to 100 nonrandomly chosen caregivers of demented persons— 83 women and 17 men (Walker & Pomeroy, 1996). This study indicated that, among the caregivers studied, "anticipatory grief," rather than depression, best described family caregivers' emotional state (p. 247). Susan found a study that examined factors associated with grief among 60 couples (half were male caregivers and half were female, and half gave care in the home and half in a nursing home) (Rudd, Viney, & Preston, 1999). This study used qualitative scales—anxiety, sadness, anger, and guilt. It reported that family caregivers experienced the greatest anxiety, sadness, and guilt if giving care in a nursing home but experienced the greatest anger if giving care in the home, with wives being the most angry among home caregivers. The study's authors speculated that female caregivers were most angry because, after a life of caregiving responsibility, the females had looked forward to growth and freedom. Susan concluded that "[T]hey're [caretakers] experiencing a feeling of loss even though the person is still living with them." Susan's second question concerned the emotional reaction of professional caregivers to clients with dementia. Susan found an article about factors associated with burnout (i.e., ". . . frequent irritation and anger with patients, withdrawal from work or absenteeism, staff turnover, low productivity, job dissatisfaction and loss of creativity . . .") among geriatric nurses (Duquette, Kerouac, Sandhu, Ducharme, & Saulnier, 1995, p. 444). This study of 1545 respondents among

1990 nurses surveyed indicated that hardiness (i.e., enjoying a challenge, commitment, and a determination to control problems) was substantially the most important factor in avoiding burnout over work support and coping methods. Susan also uncovered useful evidence regarding her third question, including a review (Toseland & Rossiter, 1989) and two randomized trials (Montgomery & Borgatta, 1989; Ostwald, Hepburn, Caron, Burns, & Mantell, 1999). Regarding Susan's fourth question, better evidence sheds little light on which behavioral method would most help caregivers. [Susan chose to ignore drug treatment for confusion related to dementia, a limiting of the range of treatments to consider, possibly because she is not qualified to administer pharmacological treatments.] Three meta-analyses summarize evidence regarding the effectiveness of reminiscence therapy, validation therapy, and reality orientation therapy as ways to assist in orienting and reducing stress for dementia clients. For reminiscence therapy and for validation therapy, the Cochrane Library found, respectively, just one (total n = 15) and two studies (total n = 87), both with no statistically significant treatment effects for either (Spector, Orrell, Davies, & Woods, 2000a; Briggs, 2000). The Cochrane review of reality orientation therapy (RO) found six randomized trials (total n = 125) with the following conclusion:

> There is some evidence that RO has benefits on both cognition and behavior for dementia sufferers. Further research could examine which features of RO are particularly effective. It is unclear how far the benefits of RO extend after the end of treatment, but and [sic] it appears that a continued programme may be needed to sustain potential benefits. (Spector, Orrell, Davies, & Woods, 2000b, p. 2)

Susan decided to share her information in a 50-minute in-service presentation that she titled: "The Experience of Loving Someone with Dementia." She thought that the presentation would be useful, stating "I had read that knowledge would help them [caregivers] with their stress. . . . I thought it would be the more professional and responsible thing to do" (Montgomery, personal communication, 2001). To advertise the in-service, she placed bulletins by the staff time clock and in the nursing home newsletter and contacted families of residents who might be interested.

Susan began the presentation by describing her deep personal reasons for being interested in dementia and how she enjoyed working with the staff and residents. She described how she had searched for evidence and briefly described her best evidence as it related to topics that included formal descriptions and definitions of dementia, the burden of being a caregiver, methods for helping caregivers, and evidence related to behavior-management techniques for helping those with dementia. Her presentation related to both the experience of caregiving and current best evidence.

Susan used qualitative and quantitative approaches to evaluate her audience's reaction. Ten staff members and ten family caregivers attended her presentation in the nursing home's chapel, including the nursing home administrator and Susan's field instructor. At the end of 50 minutes, Susan was concerned ". . . that they would just get up and leave . . ."but they didn't.

All remained for at least 10 minutes of discussion, mostly about their experiences as caregivers. Seventeen of eighteen (94%) made statements at posttest that Susan's content analysis was interpreted as positive regarding their global reaction to her presentation. Though five (28%) did not take her pretest and posttest (because they came in late), six (33%) in attendance indicated that they felt their knowledge had increased on Susan's eight-item self-designed Likert type of scale; four (22%) felt there had been no change, and three (16%) felt they knew less. Susan interpreted "less" to mean that her talk (including some inconclusive research) had made some question their initial knowledge (Montgomery, 2000, p. 11).

Flushed with her success, Susan scheduled a time after a regular staff meeting to demonstrate an electronic search to department heads. Nine agreed to come. She set up a modem-equipped portable computer in her supervisor's office. To avoid surprises, Susan tested the computer's phone-line connection with the *Evidence-Based Practice . . .* Web site mentioned earlier. Her equipment included a data projector that displayed her searching on a blank wall for all to see. Unfortunately, her thorough preparation was defeated by something beyond Susan's control—the server was busy when Susan tried to connect with the databases! Susan said in her typical positive way, "They understood because I explained that it was a matter of the Internet being too busy [the university's access] . . . and they appreciated it because they said it was a good start." In retrospect, Susan said that the demonstration might have gone better if she had solicited a question and practiced searching it first; but she could not have overcome the Internet access problem at the time.

A Conceptual Definition

Here is the essence of evidence-based practice: *Placing the client's benefits first, evidence-based practitioners adopt a process of lifelong learning that involves continually posing specific questions of direct practical importance to clients, searching objectively and efficiently for the current best evidence relative to each question, and taking appropriate action guided by evidence.* Following is an examination of this definition's concepts, one by one, in order of their appearance in this definition relative to what Susan Montgomery did.

Placing the client's benefits first . . . Susan appeared motivated by a genuine concern for the welfare of her clients and their caregivers. She made reference to how "straining" it was to watch caregivers struggle with their loved ones' dementia. She compassionately described the effects of dementia on clients and their caregivers and made reference to her own discomfort at not knowing more about dementia. At first impression, Susan's placing these client concerns above her own needs—including what personal needs she might have had for prestige, influence, and personal gain—may seem only natural. But what if her field instructor and her colleagues had *not* respected sound evidence as a guide for practice? What if others in the nursing home had placed greater weight on tradition, reverence for authority, illogical thinking, dogma, and speculation? A negative reaction would have forced her to draw deeply on wellsprings of her courage to follow evidence-based practice in less-favorable circumstances. Chapter 2 addresses these motivational issues.

    . . . *evidence-based practitioners adopt a process of lifelong learning* . . . Evidence-based practice is a problem-solving *process*, not a collection of truths. The process that Susan demonstrated can generalize, as you will see through many examples in this text, to many settings and to many types of clients. Electronic databases make it increasingly possible to keep up-to-date right from the office. This book takes you, step by step, through the *process* of EBP.

    . . . *that involves continually posing specific questions of direct practical importance to clients* . . . Susan posed four questions of central importance to clients and to their caregivers. Her questions had immediate practical value and concerned matters of central importance to the whole caregiving team. Her questions were also specific, well-built ones that contained elements essential to conducting an electronic search. Each question listed the client type (i.e., caregiver for demented aged persons, resident in a nursing home suffering from dementia), proposed course of action (i.e., what do surveys reveal, form of behavioral treatment), and intended result or relevant finding (i.e., family caregivers' emotional reactions, level of confusion or anxiety). Learning how to pose well-built questions from your own practice or from others in practice comprises the lesson for chapter 3.

    . . . *searching objectively* . . . When Susan searched for evidence, she avoided backward reasoning: she did not begin with a conclusion that she wanted to support including only supporting evidence. To the contrary, precisely because she placed the welfare of her clients above her own self-interests, she sought, with equal determination and thoroughness, that which *refuted* and that which *supported* her hunches. She valued *knowing* over supporting her own ideas. Results of the Cochrane reviews regarding the efficacy of behavioral treatments for dementia are mixed but still included here.

    . . . *and efficiently* . . . Susan has learned how to search efficiently in electronic databases for evidence. Her techniques include determining the most appropriate databases for each question, identifying terms that mark her subject, applying terms that we call *MOLES* to locate the best evidence, and applying efficient search logic to narrow the evidence. You will experience applying these techniques to this book's Web site in chapter 4.

    . . . *for the current best evidence relative to each question* . . . After Susan made her first pass through the evidence, reading abstracts and full-text articles, she then applied objective standards for rating evidence quality. While Susan conducted her search, she kept these standards in mind; but, once she narrowed her evidence to a few sources, she rated the sources on a rating form to determine which was the strongest. These rating forms and their background explanations appear in chapters 5, 6, 7 and 8.

    . . . *and taking appropriate action guided by evidence.* Susan took action by making a compassionate and well-informed presentation to 20 people in the nursing home's chapel. Chapter 5 discusses guidelines for interpreting evidence to see if it warrants taking action, including indices such as *number needed to treat* and *positive predictive value*. Susan evaluated her effort through a pretest and posttest to see how her audience had reacted, and she also took action by setting up an unsuccessful demonstration. Respectively, all of these final steps are covered in chapter 5 through chapter 10.

Additional Conceptual Definitions

The term *evidence-based* as applied to the helping process appears to have been coined by a Canadian medical group at McMaster University and originates in medicine (Evidence-Based Medicine Working Group, 1992). The group at McMaster says that evidence-based medicine (EBM) is ". . . the conscientious, explicit and judicious use of current best evidence in making decisions about the care of individual patients" (Sackett, Rosenberg, Gray, Haynes, & Richardson, 1996). I like Eamon Armstrong's (1998) definition because it refers to the process of lifelong learning. He says, "EBM is a process of lifelong problem-based learning and 'information mastery' that enables physicians to keep up-to-date while improving their clinical behavior and patient outcomes" (p. 3).

An Operational Definition: Steps of Evidence-Based Practice

Up to this point, evidence-based practice has been defined by example and by general concept. This leaves *operational definition* as the one remaining way to define EBP. An operational definition describes specifically the steps, the procedures, and the activities that one follows to make the concept specific. The seven steps that follow, except for the very first and last, are the steps for EBP that have been defined by the team at McMaster University in Ontario, Canada (Sackett et al., 1997, p. 3). Please note these steps carefully. They represent the organization of this book. Each step is demonstrated in this book's HITTT program on the CD-ROM.

1. *Becoming motivated to apply evidence-based practice (chapter 2).* Your motivation toward EBP will probably come first from the heart, from your dedication to do no harm, from your determination to make better judgments and decisions, wherever possible, in collaboration with your clients. Your second source of motivation may come from your practical nature. Evidence-based practice, as defined in this book's chapters, harnesses technological advances that can allow you, the practitioner, to consult the current best evidence quickly from your office, in real time, as events happen, soon enough to guide your actions.

2. *Converting information needs into a well-formulated answerable question (chapter 3).* Such questions are formulated specifically enough to guide a computer search; are vital to the client's welfare; concern a problem that has some chance of a solution; concern frequently encountered problems; and, ideally, are formulated in collaboration with the client.

3. *Tracking down with maximum efficiency the best evidence with which to answer the question (chapter 4).* This requires electronic access to biblio-

graphic databases and skill in searching them efficiently and quickly enough to guide practice.

4. *Critically appraising the evidence for its validity and usefulness (chapter 5 through chapter 8).* This implies applying a hierarchy of evidence that applies to each of several question/evidence types.

5. *Applying the results of this evidence appraisal to policy/practice (chapter 5 through chapter 8).* This implies deciding whether the evidence can validly apply to the decision at hand based on whether your clients are similar enough to those studied, access to interventions as described in the literature, and weighing of anticipated outcomes relative to indices (e.g., number needed to treat, practical matters, and the client's preferences).

6. *Evaluating performance (chapter 9).* This can imply record keeping, including using measures, qualitative studies, and single-subject or group study designs.

7. *Teaching others to do the same (chapter 10).* Teaching others the process of evidence-based practice will become easier, because more practitioners will have the necessary equipment—essentially the same as that required for E-mail—and because other disciplines will be adopting EBP too.

An Operational Definition Applied to the Hospital Interactive Team Thinking Test

Just a few years ago, those who read practice texts could only imagine what the author was talking about, but this is no longer the case. The CD-ROM that accompanies this text demonstrates steps in evidence-based practice. Before opening the CD-ROM and its HITTT file, please take a moment to read some background regarding the purpose and content of the CD-ROM.

The HITTT's Three Purposes

First, the HITTT serves to clarify an operational definition for evidence-based practice by demonstrating the steps listed earlier. This demonstration might have just as well defined EBP's steps in adoptions, child protective service, mental health, health, or any among a long list of other types of settings and client types; but hospital social work was chosen because it was familiar to the team who produced it.

Secondly, the HITTT demonstrates how an interdisciplinary team (occupational therapist, social worker, nurse, physicians, and client) may work together with evidence-based-practice steps to guide them. Following these steps may help team members to bond together more tightly and to help their clients more effectively, but this is only speculation. Social workers have participated in interdisciplinary teams to help a wide range of client types, including the following: drug abuse rehabilitation (Iles & Auluck, 1990); assessing children for mental retardation/developmental disabilities (Sands, 1989); hip fracture case management (Giguere & Lewis, 1994); emergency psychiatric care (Slaby,

Goldberg, & Wallace, 1983); and aged clients (Poulin, Walter, & Walker, 1994). My search for methods to remove barriers to effective interdisciplinary team functioning revealed the following types of efforts: learning how to send and receive clear messages (Kofpstein, 1994); using a pause-button technique where members could stop the team's action for discussion (Winitzky, Sheridan, Crow, Welch, & Kennedy, 1995); developing a team working contract (Toner, Miller, & Gurland, 1994); formalizing the role of devil's advocate (Heinemann, Farrell, & Schmitt, 1994); and role negotiations (Rubin, Plovnick, & Fry, 1975). However, I have not yet found literature about how an EBP approach increases team effectiveness; so speculation here that a team following EBP steps will help teams to be more effective is purely just that—speculation. Still the EBP approach in the HITTT might model a way to improve team performance. The topic seems well worth consideration by practitioners, given trends toward interdisciplinary cooperation. Collaboration on such teams requires skill. The Council on Social Work Education (CSWE) appears to recognize the importance of increased interdisciplinary collaboration on such teams in the future.

A recent study of accreditation across helping professions, conducted for the CSWE and funded by the Annie E. Casey foundation, studied the way accreditation standards affect interdisciplinary cooperation to help families. This study's conclusion stated:

> Social workers, teachers, nurses, counselors, psychologists, physicians, public administrators, and others must work collaboratively, understand each other's roles and expertise, be able to communicate, learn from each other, share resources, and plan together with the families. To collaborate successfully, these professionals must shift their thinking from the old paradigms of parallel play, silos of contact, and the competition that might occur with multidisciplinary models, to a team orientation and sustained dialogue for interprofessional education and cooperation. (Zlotnik et al., 1999, p. vii)

Finally, the HITTT was *intended for use as a realistic and reliable measure* of ability to reason critically and scientifically, a topic for chapter 2.

Background for the Hospital Interactive Team Thinking Test

This program's CD-ROM demonstrates a hospital team approach to helping an 80-year-old man (Mr. Anderson) and his daughter (Chris) to decide whether the father, who is experiencing symptoms of deepening dementia, should undergo surgery to remove a narrowing—stenosis or blockage of 65%—in his carotid artery, a large artery in the neck (see Figure 1.1).

Mr. Anderson's Condition

Mr. Anderson presently is not experiencing symptoms (i.e., asymptomatic) related to the blockage. Mr. Anderson's case is purely fictitious. For those interested, your instructor has a realistic and complete history and physical for Mr. Anderson. Box 1.1 contains an abbreviated version.

Figure 1.1

A narrowed
carotid artery
(located in the neck).
(Source: Gene Leisz.)

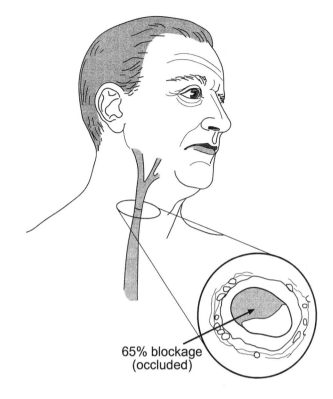

65% blockage
(occluded)

| Box 1.1 | **Abbreviated History and Physical** |

Identification
Mr. Malcolm Anderson is an 80-year old widower.

Reason for Referral
Mr. Anderson is unable to take care of himself.

History of the Problem
History of Presenting Illness   Mr. A was brought to the hospital emergency room on a Sunday by his daughter Chris who had gone to her father's home to check up on him. She has been concerned about her father's declining health and his apparent lack of ability to take care of himself. On the day of admission, Chris found her father in bed at noon, unshaven and unkempt and wearing clothes that he had been wearing for at least 3 days, which smelt of stale urine. Apparently Mr. A's home was in a mess and he clearly had not had a proper meal since his last "Meals on Wheels" meal the previous Friday. Chris is the patient's durable power of attorney (DPA). She is Mr. A's eldest daughter and has been primary caregiver since the death of the patient's wife (her mother) 4 years ago. Chris lives in an adjoining town and tries to check on Mr. A at least once a week. She reports that she and her siblings have noticed a steady and gradual decline in their father's memory and global functioning over the past year. Their dad has had noticeable difficulties with most of his activities of daily living (ADLs) and to boot is no longer able to pay his bills and manage his finances. He is extremely unsteady on his feet and has had numerous falls of late, necessitating a number of doctor and emergency room visits. In addition to his forgetfulness, Mr. Anderson is moody with what appears to be a distinct change from his previously affable and easygoing personality. The patient's family and his family physician suspect that he has progressive

continued

Box 1.1 | continued

Alzheimer's-type dementia. Numerous informal family meetings have been held with the patient about his deteriorating health and to broach the issue of possible nursing home placement. On all of these occasions, the patient has become defensive, and angry and refused to leave his home, stating that he is perfectly able to care for himself. Chris states that she is now at the end of her rope and can no longer be solely responsible for her father's care and states that his care is taking its toll on her life and that of her immediate family.

Client's Perceptions
When asked why he came to the emergency room, Mr. A is adamant that there is nothing wrong with him. He states angrily that his daughter Chris and his other children are conspiring to place him in a nursing home and evict him from the home that he and their mother built so many years ago. He says he is feeling fine and would like to be taken home, adding that if Chris had not recently contacted the DOT [Department of Transportation] and had his license taken away he would have driven himself home. Further attempts to get a clear history from the patient are unsuccessful, and the remainder of the history is obtained from the patient's daughter Chris and old medical records.

Social History
Patient is a retired dairy farmer. He lives alone in the farmhouse on the outskirts of Augusta, Wisconsin, that he and his wife built 40 years ago. His wife of 55 years died of pneumonia 4 years ago. Mr. A has three sons and one daughter, each with their respec-

tive families. His youngest son lives in Illinois; the two middle sons live in the Madison, Wisconsin, area; and his (eldest) daughter Chris who is his DPA [durable power of attorney] and primary caregiver lives in Fall Creek, Wisconsin, a 15-minute drive from the patient's home.

Physical History
Illnesses/Conditions
1. Essential hypertension (high blood pressure)
2. Myocardial infarction (MI), 1988 [heart attack]
3. Type 2 diabetes (adult-onset diabetes)
4. Benign prostatic hypertrophy (BPH)
5. Osteoarthritis (degenerative joint disease) affecting especially both knees
6. Mild COPD [chronic obstructive pulmonary disease]

Previous Surgical History
1. Appendectomy, 1963
2. CABG [coronary artery bypass graft] 1988 subsequent to MI (?)
3. Bilateral cataract surgery, 1992

Strengths
Mr. Anderson is asymptomatic [does not have symptoms] related to his narrowed carotid artery. Though somewhat disoriented to time and place, he can cooperate with his care. His daughter lives close and can assist minimally in his care.

Present Decision
Given Mr. Anderson's present physical condition and dementia, should he have surgery [carotid endarterectomy, *endart* for short] to remove blockage from his carotid artery?

Note. Written by Eamon Armstrong and edited by Bonnie Nierenhausen, Karen Woodie, Terry Allen, and Leonard Gibbs.

The Health Care Team's Decision

When you open the HITTT, action begins in the patient's room when the surgeon (Dr. Langdon) urges Chris to make the decision to allow her father's surgery (because Mr. Anderson has been determined not competent to decide for himself because of his dementia). Next Chris discusses her concern that her father might be too frail to undergo the surgery with Sandy, the social worker.

Sandy then discusses Chris's concern with the nurse (Nancy) and family medicine physician (Dr. Myers). These three then go to the hospital library to pose the question regarding surgery more specifically and to answer the question electronically. Finally, the team of surgeon, social worker, family medicine doctor, nurse, occupational therapist (Oliver), and Chris meet to discuss their points of view so Chris can decide what to do in the best interests of her father.

Instructions for the HITTT

Enclosed within the cover of this book you will find a CD-ROM. Follow instructions that accompany the CD-ROM to activate its program. (I had trouble by not clicking on the IAVA option in quick time.) When given the option, go to the HITTT program. Within the HITTT program, pick the option merely to watch the team's interaction, not to take the test. If you pick the former, you will be able to pause the action and to move around in the action as you wish. (Just drag the ball at the bottom of the screen.) Stop the action as often as you like. As you watch the action, refer to the steps presented earlier to see if the program demonstrates all of the steps for evidence-based practice. You might want to take notes in Exercise 1-1.

Potential Benefits of Evidence-Based Practice

I hope the definitions that have been provided have helped you to accurately picture evidence-based practice. This final section supports why you might consider incorporating some features of EBP into your practice. This section describes professional concerns and trends that support EBP now.

Evidence-Based Practice Incorporates Three Essential Elements

One feature of evidence-based practice concerns how it overlaps with other aspects of practice. Evidence-based practice concerns more than just the current best evidence. Figure 1.2 shows how EBP lies at the intersection of three elements of practice, including practice experience, the wishes of the client, and current best evidence (Haynes, Sackett, Gray, Cook, & Guyatt, 1996a, p. 196; Sackett, Straus, Richardson, Rosenberg, & Haynes, 2000, p. 1).

Evidence-Based Practice Harnesses Advances in Information Science as a Way to Integrate Research into Practice

Members of the helping professions do read professional literature, but they could do so much more efficiently. Kirk and Penka's (1992) survey that was mailed in 1988 to 500 randomly selected MSW-trained social workers—all respondents were members of the National Association of Social Workers—indicated that many social workers do read professional journal articles. Kirk and Penka's 276 respondents (56%) reported reading monthly the following

Figure 1.2

Three elements in
evidence-based
practice.

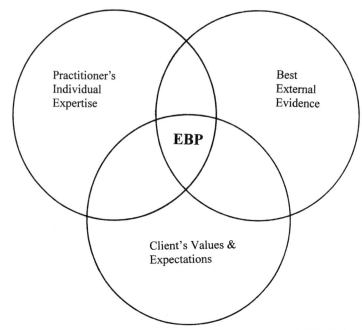

Note. From "Transferring Evidence from Research into Practice: 1. The Role of
Clinical Care Research Evidence in Clinical Decisions," by R. B. Haynes, D. L.
Sackett, J. M. Gray, D. J. Cook, & G. H. Guyatt, (1996b), *ACP Journal Club, 125*
(3), pp. A14–A16. Adapted with permission.

numbers of articles (pp. 413–414): one to three articles (43%), four to five
(24%), and six or more (25%). This means that 92% read at least one professional article a month.

Though social workers may read professional literature, they may make
little use of research literature to support their decision making in practice
(Kirk, 1979, 1990). Direct evidence about how little some social workers
apply research literature comes from a study by Rosen (1994). Rosen studied
73 professionally trained social workers for 6 months to study the reasoning
behind their decisions. To conduct his study, Rosen had the social workers
keep a log of their reasoning regarding an average of 2.07 clients per worker.
Coders then went through each log to classify rationales for decisions into
seven categories, including: theory/concept, value/assertion, policy, client wish,
instrumentality (relevant to some desired end), empirical evidence, and personal experience (p. 567). The coders agreed on their classifications from 82%
to 96% (the article did not say whether coding was done entirely independently). Coders classified a log entry as making reference to research if it mentioned any of the following: "any allusion to a research study, a research-based
generalization, naming a study or author, or simply stating 'research has
shown' " (p. 573). Coders found only 2 (.0025%) of 771 rationale responses
that made reference to research, almost nothing compared to theory/concept,

value/assertion, and policy with 183, 394, and 58 references respectively. Whether Rosen's findings generalize to other locations is not known. Rosen did say that "the workers were trained in Israel, where the curriculum content and emphases are similar to that of master of social work programs in the United States and also include 2 years of practicum" (pp. 565–566).

If reasons could be understood for practitioners not consulting research literature to guide practice decision making, those reasons could be addressed in training. A survey of nurses found that their most common obstacles to use of literature were an overwhelming volume of information, ignorance of searching techniques, lack of time, and problems with library hours (Bunyan & Lutz, 1991). A search of the Social Works Abstracts database for (read* research) June 25, 2001, yielded three documents, all speculative without data. Kirk and Berger (1993) speculate that practitioners may not read research because it investigates trivial problems, is flawed, misinterprets results, and buries its findings under technical language.

One problem may be the sheer volume of literature. How could a practitioner sort through even a small fraction of it? A study in 1963 reported that scientific knowledge had then been growing at an exponential rate since the 18th century, doubling about every 15 years (Price, 1963, pp. 6–7). At that time, the number of professional journal articles had been increasing at about a half million a year.

Until just recently, keeping up with research evidence as a way to guide practice has been extremely difficult, but advances in information technology and information literacy hold promise as a way to integrate research into practice. Recently, about half of the University of Minnesota-Minneapolis field instructors had access to E-mail in their agencies (Maura Sullivan, personal communication, November 2, 1999). With such access comes access to the Internet and to electronic bibliographic databases, and these resources are expanding in their availability and efficiency. Lynch (1997) estimated that there were 130 World Wide Web sites in 1993 and 650,000 sites in 1997 (p. 53). The speed and, therefore, the amount of information that can travel electronically leaps ahead. Alcatel, the present world leader in sending signals via optical cable, has just quadrupled the previous speed record. Alcatel, in collaboration with a European Internet provider called Jupiter Network, has sent information at 40 gigabits per second (40 billion bits per second) (M2 Communications, Ltd., M2 PRESSWIRE, 2000). By 2004, the Internet within the United States will have the capacity to carry over 80 terabits per second (1 terabit = 1 trillion bits) (Stix, 2001, p. 81) and new optical switches will form the ". . . .linchpin for networks that transmit trillions of bits each second" (Bishop, Giles, & Das, 2001, p. 88).

This speed will provide faster access to an increasing number of databases. Approximately 6300 databases are now available on-line, and another 7500 are available in portable form (e.g., CD-ROM). There are 2900 on-line services and vender distributors of database products (Faerber, 2000). The ready availability of information in these databases, coupled with increased speed for access to them, supports evidence-based practitioners.

Evidence-Based Practice is Consistent with Professional Goals and Ethics

The *Code of Ethics* of the National Association of Social Workers (January 1, 1997), lists the following three principles:

- "Social workers' primary responsibility is to promote the well-being of clients" (section 1.01). "Social workers respect and promote the right of clients to self-determination and assist clients in their efforts to identify and clarify their goals [with notable exceptions regarding harm to self and to others]" (section 1.02) (i.e., Concern for Client's Preferences).
- "Social workers practice within their areas of competence and develop and enhance their professional expertise" (section on Ethical Principles, Value: Competence) (i.e., Professional Expertise).
- "Social workers should critically examine and keep current with emerging knowledge relevant to social work and fully use evaluation and research evidence in their professional practice" (section 5.02) (i.e., Research Evidence).

Please take a look at Figure 1.2 again. The three elements from the *Code* appear as elements in evidence-based practice.

Evidence-Based Practice Can Help to Resolve an Age-Old Division Between Research and Experience as Guides to Practice

Note how the model for decision making in evidence-based practice in Figure 1.2 shows how EBP lies at the intersection between practical experience and research. The intersection between experience, the client's preferences, and current best evidence has important implications for resolving a tiresome debate regarding the place of evidence in practice. The helping professions have been locked in an empirical practice debate for decades (Witkin, 1996). "Extreme empiricists box themselves into positions that reduce complex social environments to a set of relatively understandable but context-stripped measurable events. Practitioners at the other extreme resist the valuable albeit partial knowledge that is communicated through such measurable events and mistake the immediacy of the individual experience for the efficacious 'knowledge' of what to do about problems" (Bloom, 1995, p. 3). The three elements in Figure 1.2 offer an honorable way out for both sides: Always place the client's concerns first; apply the current best evidence where it can answer important questions, but rely on experience—and admit that you are doing so—when strong evidence cannot be found.

All three elements (see Figure 1.2) were evident in the HITTT dramatization. Initially, the team heard Chris's concerns about her father's surgery. The whole team became involved in the decision-making process that included drawing on the team's experience working with frail older persons. This experience, and Chris's concerns, led to posing an important question and a search for evidence to answer it. The team located the current best evidence and shared it with Chris in terms that she could understand.

Evidence-Based Practice Is Consistent with Efforts to Integrate Research into Practice

Social work has a long history of commitment to conduct, locate, and synthesize research evidence as a guide for practice going back to the turn of the century (Reid, 2001, pp. 36–53). Fischer (1978) stated in *Effective Casework Practice* that eclectic practitioners should use methods "where the evidence indicates that such application has a substantial chance to produce successful outcome . . ." (p. 67). Grinnell (1978) stated in the first successful research methods text for social workers that ". . . professional decisions should be derived from the best knowledge base possible . . ." (pp. 3–4). Martin Bloom (1975), then at the School of Social Service at Indiana-Purdue University, may have been the first in any discipline to construct an electronic database containing evaluation studies for practitioners. Bloom's pioneering work antedates even the experimental "Databank of Program Evaluations" (Wilner et al., 1976) and anything I have seen about evidence-based practice. Recently, one of the most popular practice texts for social workers states: "Research is important to social work practice. Research informs and supports intervention approaches, identifies theories and programs that are more likely to be effective, and helps workers ensure that the client is helped, rather than hurt, by what workers do (Kirst-Ashman & Hull, 1999, p. 20).

Integrating research into practice surely has been a priority, and the scientist/practitioner model has been its vehicle. As a practical way to integrate research into practice, the scientist-practitioner model includes the use of single-system designs to structure and to evaluate our intervention and to monitor client performance against standardized, rapid-assessment measures (Wakefield & Kirk, 1996, p. 83). This model of scientist-practitioner (Bloom, Fischer, & Orme, 1999), as one who collects data right in practice and uses rapid-assessment instruments to evaluate practice, though sound in principle, has run into practical problems with implementation (Wakefield & Kirk, 1996). Busy practitioners often cannot conduct single-system studies in their practice. Surveys of MSW-trained social workers report these percentages of single-subject design use: 0% (0 of 9 respondents) (Welch, 1983); 10.3% (28 of 276 respondents) (Penka & Kirk, 1991); 40.4% (48 of 119 respondents) (Gingerich, 1984); 26% (46 of 177 respondents) (Marino, Green, & Young, 1998); and 75% (134 of 179 respondents, but fewer than 10% were social workers) (LeCroy & Tolman, 1991). Apparently, no surveys exist of BSW-trained social workers regarding their use of single-subject design use. Rubin (1992) reviewed research regarding research in BSW programs. He stated: "We do not know how many graduates of BSW programs with the strongest curricula on practice evaluation are actually evaluating their social work practice after graduation" (p. 381).

Recently, some have turned to qualitative studies as a vehicle for integrating research into practice (Tutty, Rothery, & Grinnell, 1996), but a persistent problem still remains: Will qualitative designs be any more practical and less time-consuming to implement in practice than single-system designs have been? Evidence-based practice may help here.

Figure 1.3

Number of
documents for
Evidence-Based
by discipline.
(November 9, 2001)

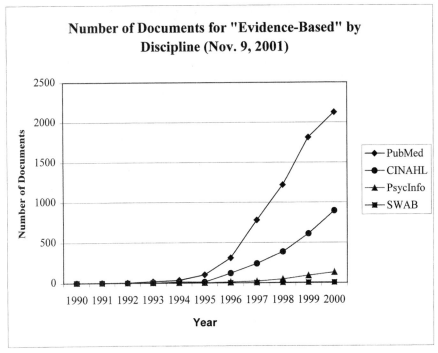

Number of Documents for "Evidence-Based" by Discipline (Nov. 9, 2001)

Source: Gibbs and Gambrill, 2001

Evidence-based practice may take less time to answer practice questions. The average length of time to conduct an electronic search can take 7 minutes, 6 seconds (Gibbs & Johnson, 1983, p. 131) and 5.5 minutes (Gibbs, 1991, p. 178). Searching electronically through bibliographic databases can uncover excellent evidence. In a review of nine nonrandom studies that compared the thoroughness of electronic versus manual searching across multiple disciplines (pharmacy, biology, business, research methods, and general interest), electronic searches recovered equal quality evidence faster (Gibbs, 1991, pp. 168–169). Furthermore, the quality of evidence retrieved by electronic means may overshadow the quality of what practitioners can learn by doing their own studies. They may not have the resources to implement sophisticated experimental designs nor the means to control bias with their limited resources.

Evidence-Based Practice May Provide a Common Ground Across the Helping Professions

Electronic access to information may ultimately rival the impact of the printing press on intellectual history. Few aspects of culture are not affected by advances in information technology, including the helping professions. This electronic revolution in literature for the helping professions can be tracked by noting the number of references to the term *evidence-based* in the medical (Medline), nursing and allied health (CINAHL), psychology (PsycINFO), and social work (Social Work Abstracts or SWAB) databases. Figure 1.3 shows that the burgeoning literature on the topic during the past decade indicates a sharp increase in references to the term *evidence-based* in about 1996 for all but social work. The total numbers of references to *evidence-based* in February 2001 accounted for 5750, 1934, 278, and 9 documents, respectively; in November of 2001, the figures were 8805, 2785, 440, and 18 documents, respectively. Social work will likely follow this trend.

Given an increasing interest in evidence-based practice, all in the helping professions need to at least become familiar with EBP, because they will probably encounter other helping professionals who are familiar with EBP procedures. A common understanding of EBP might help to bond professional helpers together with a common set of procedures, as the HITTT CD-ROM demonstrates.

Summary

Evidence-based practice is a *process*, not a collection of truths. This process involves posing specific questions of practical value to clients, searching electronically for the current best evidence, and taking action guided by that evidence. The process involves integrating the concerns and values of the client and the practitioner's experience and common sense, along with the best relevant research evidence. Because EBP integrates these three, it is not a cookbook approach to practice. Evidence-based practice is not a panacea either. In many instances, the current best evidence will be overruled by other concerns; but, still, the approach will foster the process of lifelong learning that can help practitioners to avoid stagnation and the chance that they will harm their clients. The process does not preclude applying interpersonal skills. It does not preclude using knowledge from other experience and that of others; nor does it preclude using single-system designs and measures to evaluate practice. Evidence-based practice holds promise for practice, because it is consistent with ethical codes and with attempts to integrate research into practice. Evidence-based practice harnesses advances in information technology, and it can provide a common set of procedures for diverse professions to follow together.

Exercise 1-1 EBP Steps of Evidence-Based Practice Demonstrated in the Hospital Interactive Team Thinking Test

Purpose

This exercise is designed to help you to become more familiar with the seven steps of evidence-based practice.

Background

The HITTT's 22-minute story of a hospital team's decision making is a dramatization, but it reflects a real type of situation, namely whether an 80-year-old man with moderate dementia should have surgery (carotid endarterectomy) to remove a 65% blockage in his neck's carotid artery. The decision requires all involved to weigh costs and benefits carefully. This kind of situation does in fact arise often and is dealt with presently by real health care teams. Though fictitious, the script was written by Bonnie Nierenhausen and Karen Woodie (both social workers on the neurosciences ward shown) in collaboration with a family practice physician, Eaman Armstrong (with assistance from our director, Terry Allen). True to reality, Karen and Bonnie generally do lead care team meetings in the same conference room shown in the HITTT when family members have raised concerns.

Instructions

Please follow these steps:

1. Read chapter 1 carefully and understand it fully, particularly the sections marked: "An Operational Definition . . ." and "An Operational Definition Applied to the Hospital . . ." These sections will clarify steps in evidence-based practice. Note that these steps may not happen just once exactly in sequence but, rather, may happen out of sequence and be revisited.
2. Watch the HITTT at least once. You may pause it to reflect and take notes by clicking on the Pause key. At this point, do not take the HITTT as a test.
3. As you watch the HITTT, record on the HITTT Steps Worksheet your observations demonstrating steps in evidence-based practice. Is each step demonstrated by action in the story? Did the team accomplish all seven steps, including Step 6?

The HITTT Steps Worksheet

1. Become motivated to apply evidence-based practice. What did professionals say and do that demonstrated their motivation to apply EBP?

_____

_____

2. How did they convert their information needs into a well-formulated, answerable question? What was their question?

_____

_____

3. How did they track down with maximum efficiency the best evidence with which to answer the question?

_____

_____

4. How did they critically appraise the evidence for its validity and usefulness?

_____

_____

5. How did they apply the results of this evidence appraisal to policy/practice?

_____

_____

6. How did they evaluate performance? Did they?

_____

_____

7. How did they teach others to apply evidence-based-practice procedures?

_____

_____

Exercise 1-2 Ethical and Practice Standards as Considerations in Evidence-Based Practice: Psychology, Social Work, Nursing

Purpose

This exercise is designed to help you to become aware of professional concerns regarding evidence-based practice. At first impression, these concerns may seem simple and straight-forward relative to ethical standards and practice guidelines, but first impressions can deceive. [In August of 1999, on Kodiak Island, I found myself between a huge sow bear and her three cubs to the front and behind us one of her former year's cubs; that experience can be *nothing* next to experiences interpreting EBP relative to Council on Social Work Education standards.)

Background

Evidence-based practice implies changing the way you make judgments and decisions in practice. It implies continually changing your methods as you encounter current best evidence. Evidence-based practice implies adopting a commitment to lifelong learning. It implies a new set of procedures for relating within agencies and among professionals serving on interdisciplinary teams based on current best evidence over what have often been patterns of reliance on blind adherence to authority and tradition. Change, no matter how beneficial, always brings discomfort. One way to deal with such discomfort is to go back to the basic roots of professional ethical codes and practice standards.

Instructions

Please follow these steps:

1. Read chapter 1 carefully to get the picture of what evidence-based practice is and to understand its potential benefits.

2. Examine the selected sections (noted in the "Ethics and Standards Work-sheet" that follows) from the American Psychological Association's *Ethical Principles of Psychologists and Code of Conduct,* the National Association of Social Workers' *Code of Ethics,* the Council on Social Work Education's *Educational Policy and Accreditation Standards,* and the International Council of Nurses' *Code of Ethics for Nurses.*

3. Please reflect on whether evidence-based practice fits ethical and practice standards across these disciplines.

Ethics and Standards Worksheet

The American Psychological Association's *Ethical Principles of Psychologists and Code of Conduct* (Draft 6, October 21, 2001) states:

"2.03 Maintaining Expertise. Psychologists undertake ongoing efforts to maintain competence in the skills they use. 2.04 Bases for Scientific and Professional Judgments. Psychologists' work is based upon established scientific and professional knowledge of the discipline.

1. Does this ethical standard apply to evidence-based practice? Please explain your answer.

_____

_____

_____

The *Code of Ethics* of the National Association of Social Workers (1999) states:

Section 1.01. Social workers' primary responsibility is to promote the well-being of clients. . . . 3.08 Continuing Education and Staff Development. Social work administrators and supervisors should take reasonable steps to provide or arrange for continuing education and staff development for all staff for whom they are responsible. Continuing education and staff development should address current knowledge and emerging developments related to social work practice and ethics. . . . 5.02(c). Social workers should critically examine and keep current with emerging knowledge relevant to social work and fully use evaluation and research in their professional practice. . . . 5.02(p). Social workers should educate themselves, their students, and their colleagues about responsible research practices.

2. Do these ethical standards apply to evidence-based practice? Please explain your answer.

_____

_____

_____

_____

3. How might implementing evidence-based practice in an agency lead to controversy regarding these standards?

_____

_____

_____

_____

Following are provisions of the Council on Social Work Education's *Educational Policy and Accreditation Standards* (2001):

> IV. F. Social Work Practice. . . . Practice content also includes identifying, analyzing, and implementing empirically based interventions designed to achieve current goals; applying empirical knowledge and technological advances; evaluating program outcomes and practice effectiveness. . . . . IV. G. Research. . . . The content prepares students to develop, use, and effectively communicate empirically based knowledge, including evidence-based interventions. Research knowledge is used by students to provide high-quality services; to initiate change; to improve practice, policy, and social service delivery; and to evaluate their own practice.

4. Do these educational standards apply to evidence-based practice? Please explain your answer.

_____

_____

_____

5. How might implementing evidence-based practice in an educational program lead to controversy regarding these educational standards? For example, might these educational standards be met if students are guided in their practice by the current best evidence, or do these standards require that students must do a small study including single-subject studies in their training.

_____

_____

_____

_____

The International Council of Nurses' *Code of Ethics for Nurses* (2000) states:

> 2. Nurses and practice: The nurse carries personal responsibilities and accountability for nursing practice and for maintaining competence by continual learning. . . . 3. Nurses and the profession: The nurse assumes the major role in determining and implementing acceptable standards of clinical nursing practice, management, research and education. The nurse is active in developing a core of research-based professional knowledge.

6. Do these ethical standards apply to evidence-based practice? Please explain your answer.

_____

_____

_____

_____

At least don't hurt em.—**William S. Middleton**
(personal communication, fall of 1974)

Become Motivated to Apply the Current Best Evidence to Practice | **2**

Overview

Anyone who follows the process of evidence-based practice as a guide to helping clients will quickly encounter muddled thinking that is in direct opposition to EBP. Muddled thinking puts clients at risk for harm. Your ability to quickly identify and label such thinking patterns will benefit your practice in two ways. First, you will be forewarned and forearmed so that you can respond more effectively for the good of your clients. For example, assume that you have found strong evidence that an agency practice probably is harming clients and someone objects, saying, "We have always done it this way." You may identify this argument as an *appeal to tradition* and label the argument as such. Second, understanding thinking patterns that oppose EBP possibly will help you to become more motivated to adopt EBP yourself; that is, by knowing how to identify common errors in thinking, you will adopt EBP that relies on principles of sound reasoning.

This chapter begins by defining generally what it means to reason scientifically about practice. Then it defines logical fallacies that stand in direct opposition to evidence-based practice. After becoming familiar with logical fallacies conceptually, you will have an opportunity—using this book's CD-ROM—to take three tests of ability to spot logical fallacies. The simulations on CD-ROM include the HITTT, which you have already seen; testimony by expert witnesses under hostile cross-examination in a courtroom interactive Testimony thinking test (CITTT); and a meeting of professionals in a school's individual education plan team, as shown in a multidisciplinary interactive team thinking test (MITTT). All three of these are illustrations of situations that you may encounter in your practice, or you might have already encountered these situations.

The three exercises and the final section on quack reasoning all demonstrate fallacious reasoning that violates principles of evidence-based practice. *I hope that these three exercises will vividly demonstrate why you might turn to EBP, as operationally defined in the HITTT, the CITTT, and the MITTT to avoid failing to help or even harming your clients.*

Scientific Reasoning

Science is an "objective, logical, and systematic method of analysis of phenomena, devised to permit the accumulation of reliable knowledge" (Lastrucci, 1967, p. 6). *Scientific reasoning* is a *logical,* data-based, systematic process for posing specific questions and for answering them through a process of observation and experimentation. This chapter applies logical thinking to practice. Chapter 3 deals with posing questions, and later chapters deal with other aspects of scientific reasoning. Those who apply logical thinking to practice try to avoid common fallacies or errors in reasoning. *Fallacious reasoning* means "faulty in logic" (McKechnie, 1983). Eileen Gambrill and I call such errors, where applied to practice, "practice fallacies" (Gibbs & Gambrill, 1999, p. 151). For more on practice fallacies, you may consult our book, *Critical Thinking for Social Workers: Exercises for the Helping Professions,* which goes beyond this chapter's brief treatment of practice fallacies.

Why learn how to spot practice fallacies? One reason concerns the problem of learning transfer. Ideally, a strong association or correlation should exist between knowledge of research methods and the ability to reason critically and analytically about practice. That is, hopefully, practitioners' knowledge of research methods translates to well-reasoned judgments and decisions in their life-affecting work. For example, a research student who knows about how surveys, representative samples, and sound measures are necessary to make generalizations should not be taken in by a single, emotionally gripping case example.

To test this idea that knowledge of research methods transfers to sound reasoning about practice, colleagues and I administered a measure of critical thinking about the Scared Straight Delinquency Prevention Program (PRIDE1) and a 60-item measure of knowledge of research methods (Kirk-Rosenblatt Research Knowledge Scale) to research methods students in social work and psychology at four universities (Gibbs et al., 1995). The PRIDE1 presented videotaped evidence that lies in direct opposition to scientific thinking. The videotape was a nonstop assault on the emotions—full of case examples, glittering generalities, vague terms, emotional appeals, appeals to status, and other such trash—all presented with strong visual appeal to support the assertion that the Scared Straight program prevented delinquency. Though PRIDE1 presented human service propaganda in direct opposition to scientific reasoning, an average of 45% of the respondents to PRIDE1 said they would refer one of their clients to the Scared Straight program based on its content! We found, in five replications in research methods classes at the baccalaureate and masters degree levels, *no statistically significant association* between research knowledge and ability to think critically on the PRIDE1! In one university, we even found a negative correlation. This experiment suggests a serious, learning-transfer problem from knowledge of research methods to making judgments and decisions in practice.

A concern for an apparent lack of association between research knowledge and the ability to reason critically and scientifically is one reason that these exercises have been designed for you. As you do these exercises, first try to understand the fallacy from its definition. Then, later, as you watch the video, imagine how you yourself may encounter these fallacies and may respond to overcome the fallacy for the good of your clients.

Exercise 2-1 The Hospital Interactive Team Thinking Test

Purpose

As you may recall from chapter 1, the HITTT has two purposes:

- The HITTT can motivate you to apply principles of evidence-based practice by demonstrating how it can help to oppose muddled thinking that can harm clients.
- In chapter 1, the HITTT demonstrated the steps of evidence-based practice. Here, in Exercise 2-1, the HITTT will help you to test your ability to spot practice fallacies that can disrupt team cohesiveness and functioning.

Background

The HITTT tests your ability to spot fallacious reasoning about a realistic life-affecting situation in a hospital setting. At issue is how best to help Mr. Anderson, who is 80 years old, suffering from early dementia, and who also has a 65% narrowing of his carotid artery. Mr. Anderson has been admitted because his physical condition has deteriorated due to his not being able to care for himself independently in his home. The surgeon wants to perform an operation called a carotid endarterectomy that will remove the material that threatens to cause Mr. Anderson to have a stroke and possibly die. Chris, Mr. Anderson's daughter, calls on the team to help her to decide whether her father should have the surgery. (Mr. Anderson is a fictitious character.)

Expect to see some fallacious reasoning and some sound reasoning in the HITTT. The HITTT test option on the CD-ROM will pause to ask you for a reaction. Be prepared to examine the reasoning that *immediately* preceded the pause to determine whether it demonstrates no fallacy or demonstrates fallacious reasoning. Try to imagine how fallacious reasoning may present an obstacle to an evidence-based approach to practice.

How to Prepare to Take the HITTT

Please examine the following list of fallacies to get a clear idea of each fallacy's definition before doing the HITTT exercise. These fallacies may appear in the HITTT.

• *Appeal to numbers, popularity, widespread use, bandwagon:* The mistaken belief that if many people believe something, then that belief must accurately reflect the truth. Where applied to practice, those who adopt an intervention method or other practice procedure simply because others do so would demonstrate this fallacy. The distinctive features of this fallacy, where applied to practice, are: (a) a worker is pressured to adopt a method or to accept a conclusion about clients; (b) this pressure is based on the number of people who believe (implying that so many cannot be wrong); and (c) no balanced evaluation of research has been conducted. For example, the following reasoning demonstrates an *appeal to numbers* or *popularity*:

> Mental health counselors in increasing numbers are turning to practice standards or practice guidelines as a way to determine what they should do in their own practices. If so many counselors are turning to them, I shall also.

To avoid being taken in, one needs to examine the evidentiary basis for a belief before accepting or rejecting it. Those who develop practice guidelines need to follow the process of evidence-based practice to arrive at their guidelines. As motivation to avoid this fallacy, examine the history of the helping professions. This history is full of examples of widespread beliefs that were proven wrong. For example, it was common practice to treat premature infants with high levels of oxygen and many infants were born blinded (James & Lanman, 1976). Many practitioners joined the movement to treat persons with psychotic mental illness with heavy doses of neuroleptic medication, until it was discovered that such treatment could cause irreversible uncoordinated movements called "tardive dyskinesia" (Jeste & Wyatt, 1981). Always ask for the evidence before jumping onto the *band wagon*.

• *Uncritical documentation, merely citing, citing without evidence, citation only:* The mistaken belief that, if an idea can be documented by a source in an article, book, or other publication, then the idea must be true. *Merely citing* a source ignores the need to consider the credibility of the evidence that the source has cited. Can you think of an idea that cannot be documented somehow somewhere? For example, did you know that wolves have raised children? Here's documentation: Zingg, R. (1941). India's wolf children: Two human infants reared by wolves. *Scientific American, 164*(3), 37. Did you know that baboons have raised children also? Here's documentation: Foley, J. P. (1940). The "baboon boy" of South Africa. *Science, 91,* 291–292. In practice, *uncritical documentation* may arise by citing a study in a professional journal without discussing the study's methodology, or it might appear as a reference to supporting documentation without discussing the evidence in that documentation.

• *Appeal to status, appeal to authority, prestige (ad verecundiam):* Believing that, if an idea has been expressed by someone of high status, then that idea must be true. *Appeal to authority* is a "classical fallacy" (Chase, 1956), meaning that it has been described and understood for a long time. According to Chase, quoting a revered authority pushes the argument too far and "freezes mental activity" (p. 89). This fallacy is evident when the following happens: (a) someone claims that something is true about practice, (b) this claim is based purely on the authority's status, and (c) the authority does not refer to studies to support or to refute the claim. The fallacy relies on an attempt to "overawe an opponent" (Engel, 1990, p. 209). An example of *appeal to status* follows:

> Ann McKibbon of McMaster University spoke to us about how to apply methodological filters to searching for evidence regarding our practice. If a famous author from such a famous university says so, I will surely try using the filters.

Keep in mind that persons of high status are bound by the same rules for evidence along with everyone else. In the preceding case, one might ask whether the methodological filters find evidence as thoroughly as a hand search would, or one might ask which filters work most efficiently against what indices of successful searching. Understanding the *appeal to authority* fallacy particularly benefits practitioners tempted to uncritically follow a well-known charismatic leader, or guru, of the profession. To avoid this fallacy, resolve not to be taken in by prestige or status but, rather, look for that person's evidence and evaluate that.

• *Appeal to experience, personal experience, prior experience:* Believing that direct *personal experience* in practice with a method or practice procedure ensures that related conclusions are true over believing research evidence. Those who commit the fallacy often say: "From my experience I have learned that" or "From my experience I know that" (Gula, 1979, p. 71). This fallacy is evident in practice when (a) an assertion is made that something about one's practice with clients is true (e.g., that a treatment method works, that a risk assessment scale predicts accurately); (b) the person making the assertion does so purely on the basis of personal experience; and (c) no measures, records, data, or experimental evidence are offered to support the conclusion where such evidence exists. Dawes (1994, pp. 38–132) has examined the *appeal to experience* fallacy in depth to understand its mechanisms. An example of this fallacy follows:

> I'm not impressed with your meta-analyses of studies. For clients referred to Greene County Mental Health Services Clinic, it has been my experience that nicotine addicts reduce their smoking just as well using self-help materials (books, videotapes, and audiotapes) as they do in our Clinic's individual behavioral counseling and nicotine replacement therapy (nicotine gum, patch, or inhaler).

The preceding statement may well be true; but, without data, how can you know? If no data have been systematically collected directly at the Greene County Clinic, then studies done elsewhere may supply a form of data if findings from those studies can generalize to the clinic's clients. A search of the Cochrane Library found systematic reviews of randomized control trials and quasirandom studies regarding the treatments listed in the statement. The Cochrane reviews use *odds ratio* to compare the effectiveness of these treatments. To calculate odds ratio (Greenhalgh & Donald, 2000, pp. 80–81) for those in treatment, divide the number who abstain from nicotine by the number not abstaining; for those in the control group, divide the number who abstain from nicotine by the number not; then divide the former by the latter. A value of one means no difference. Larger values mean greater effectiveness for those in treatment. The odds ratio for self-help materials was 1.23 (95% confidence interval 1.02 to 1.49) (Lancaster & Stead, 2001b); the odds ratio for individual behavioral therapy was 1.55 (95% confidence interval 1.27 to 1.90) (Lancaster & Stead, 2001a), and the odds ratio for nicotine replacement was 1.71 (95% confidence interval 1.60 to 1.82) (Silagy, Mant, Fowler, & Lancaster, 2001). These findings are based on a synthesis of 9, 11, and 100 studies, respectively, that met standards for inclusion in the review.

The *appeal to experience* fallacy involves elevating *personal experience* to the level of better evidence. The fallacy involves ignoring or not knowing that there is a hierarchy of evidence, which is the topic of this book's chapter 5 through chapter 8. In the absence of stronger evidence, personal experience may be all you have to go on; consequently, relying on experience then would not constitute a fallacy.

• *Vague question, not well-formulated question, question not specific, poorly formulated question, question not well built:* Refers to a question so imprecisely stated that it cannot be answered. Specific to concerns addressed here, a *vague question* refers to a question that does not specifically state the client type, the course of action being considered, an alternate course of action, and what you intend to accomplish. These four features of a specific *client-oriented practical evidence search* (COPES) or well-built question are described in much more detail in chapter 3. The following is a vague question:

> Which is the most effective treatment for depression?

The question states that the problem is depression, but for whom? Which treatments will be compared, against what outcome(s)? A more specifically stated COPES question follows:

> For a 37-year-old woman who is experiencing her first episode of depression 2 months after the birth of her first child, will cognitive behavior therapy or antidepressant medication most effectively reduce her symptoms of depression as rated on a depression scale (e.g., Beck depression inventory)?

Generally speaking, vague questions can lead only to vague and useless answers. Learning how to pose specific questions allows the chance to search for an answer in electronic databases. Specific questions are also essential to designing a study and testing hypotheses.

• *Vague quantifying adjective, vague term, vague adjective, meaningless term:* Refers to terms that imply the likelihood of an event but do so in such general terms that they convey no meaning. Here are such *vague quanti-*

fying adjectives: somewhat, generally, most likely, probably, certainly, not uncommonly, unlikely. An example of how such a term might appear in a case record follows:

- Jessica will *most likely* adapt to her new foster home and will *probably* not run this time.
- I seriously doubt that Kisha's foster home placement will fail. She will *almost certainly* adapt to and remain with the Bagji family.

This fallacy has been demonstrated empirically by asking practitioners to state in probabilities what such *vague terms* imply. For example, if your physician says, "Your headache is probably caused by stress, and it is *rather unlikely* that it indicates a tumor," what does this mean specifically? Do you know? Timmermans reported a survey of medical practitioners regarding the meaning of *rather unlikely* and other *vague quantifying adjectives* (1996, p. 4). He found that *rather unlikely* meant from 0% to about 30% likely in the minds of medical practitioners (p. 4). Some terms conveyed even less meaning. He found that practitioners rated the term *very likely* to mean from 40% to 100% likely (p. 4).

To avoid this fallacy, refer to specific probabilities taken from studies or from data based on experience with similar clients in the past. For example, you might say, "An average of 32% of female juveniles released from Right Correction Facility during the past decade returned to a correctional facility within one year of their discharge." Such precision conveys greater accuracy than saying, "Few return to Right Correctional Facility within one year of their discharge."

  • *Tradition, appealing to tradition, appealing to precedent:* Refers to the idea that a new procedure or idea should not be tried because it does not agree with what was done in the past. *Appealing to tradition* relies on the *tried and true* philosophy. The following reasoning relies on this appeal to tradition:

> Why would you want to teach our fieldwork students to evaluate the quality of risk assessment measures? We have never done so in the past, nor have other research methods texts done so in the past. Traditionally, risk assessment has not been included in our lists of necessary competencies. I think we should eliminate risk assessment from this fieldwork exercise.

Those who subscribe to the fallacy may say, ". . . but we have always done it that way!" To avoid this fallacy, examine the evidence. Sufficient evidence may support changing procedure; it may not. Let the evidence, fairly and thoroughly evaluated, decide what to change and what not.

Instructions for Taking the HITTT

To take the HITTT, click on the *Take Test* option. Then click on the HITTT pull-down option. Then read the instructions for taking the test. To start the test, click on the *Start* button. The program will pause periodically. If you think no fallacy occurred in the interaction that *immediately preceded* the pause, enter the words *No Fallacy* in the *Fallacy Name* box and leave the *Fallacy Description* box empty. If you think the interaction just before the pause contained a fallacy, then enter the name of the fallacy in the Fallacy Name box and define the fallacy and how it is evident in the Fallacy Description box. When you are confident of your answer, click on the *submit* button to continue the test. Take as long as you like to ponder your answer before recording it. In this sense, the video does not reflect reality—you will not have minutes to respond when a fallacy arises in your practice. You may have only seconds. On the other hand, the video is true to reality. You do not have the chance to go back and correct your actions, just as the video does not allow you to go back and fix your answer. When the HITTT stops, please record your answers. These answers can be accessed in a Word file that has been saved for you (ITTA Folder, media/hittt.mov). If you prefer, you may record your answers on the HITTT answer sheet in Figure 2.1. (A scoring key can be found at the end of this chapter in Table 2.2.)

Exercise 2-2 The Courtroom Interactive Testimony Thinking Test

Purpose

Members of the helping professions make judgments and decisions daily as they go about their life-affecting work. Consequently, efforts to improve reasoning in practice may help to improve service to clients. The courtroom interactive testimony thinking test (CITTT) was designed to

- Demonstrate the utility of evidence-based practice as a way to prepare for courtroom testimony
- Increase the chance that justice will be done based on sound reasoning and evidence
- Provide valuable lessons prior to serving as an expert witness so you can prepare substantively and emotionally for this stressful task
- Test your ability to spot practice fallacies that can affect courtroom testimony

Background

This program was designed to assist those in helping professions to better prepare for their testimony in a courtroom as an expert witness from an evidence-based and critical thinking perspective. Those in the helping professions frequently go into a courtroom assuming that the courtroom interaction will follow their own experience of dispassionately seeking the truth—let it fall where it may—about how best to help their client. They find to their amazement and sometimes to their embarrassment that the courtroom is an adversary procedure, whose advocates do not necessarily follow principles of logical evidence-based critical thinking.

Figure 2.1   The HITTT Answer Sheet

Instructions: At each pause, please state the name of the fallacy in reasoning or write *No Fallacy* and describe how the fallacy is evident if you name a fallacy. (Please write clearly in pen.)

Pause Number	Fallacy Name or *No Fallacy*	Description of How Fallacy Is Evident in Interaction or Left Blank If *No Fallacy*
1		
2		
3		
4		
5		
6		
7		
8		
9		
10		

How to Prepare to Take the CITTT

Look for the practice fallacies in the CITTT exercise. Please examine the following list of fallacies to get a clear idea of each fallacy's definition before doing the CITTT exercise.

- *Uncritical documentation:* Defined in the preceding HITTT exercise.
- *Leading question, leading the witness, suggestive question, suggestion question, loaded question:* Refers to posing a question in a way that implies the answer expected. A popular text on interviewing gives this definition for a *leading question:* ". . . to phrase a question in a way that leads the interviewee to provide an answer that the interviewer desires. . . . *Leading questions* make it difficult for interviewees to respond freely. They [interviewees] have to oppose the interviewer if they respond in a way that contradicts the answer that the question implies" (Kadushin & Kadushin, 1997, p. 249). *Leading questions* begin with a statement, not with an inquiry. Some *leading* or *loaded questions* follow:

> Your patient will be able to live independently in the community, won't she?
>
> You will not remain in a home with such a violent person, will you?
>
> You realize that you will not be getting any alimony payments, don't you?
>
> Your client clearly knew the implications of his behavior, didn't he?
>
> You suspected that your client presented high risk for another offense, didn't you?

Leading questions represent a slick courtroom strategy that tries to get the witness to support a particular argument. A witness cowed by the intimidating manner of a cross-examiner might feel compelled to agree with the "question." To counter leading questions, recognize their format and prepare to encounter them. Prepare for them by anticipating questions that might be asked. Recognize that you are free to disagree by stating your evidence. Review the facts of the case thoroughly and have your records well organized and available for ready reference. When questioned, take time to think and to organize a response in a thoughtful manner.

- *Stereotyping, stereotypical reasoning, hasty generalization, unsupported generalization:* Refers to a sweeping generalization made about an entire class or group of people. *Stereotyping* assumes that every member of the group has some set of properties (probably erroneously) identified with the class (Moore & Parker, 1986, p. 160). "The *stereotype* strips a person of his complexity and his individuality and reduces him to one quality" (Gula, 1979, p. 40). Studies of practitioners demonstrate that stereotypes based on attractiveness (Johnson, Kurtz, Tomlinson, & Howe, 1986; Nordholm, 1980), race (Cousins, Fischer, Glisson, & Kameoka, 1986), and sex (Kurtz, Johnson, & Rice, 1989) can affect practitioners' judgments. Some examples of stereotypical thinking follow:

FIRST SITUATION

AGENCY SUPERVISOR: I try to hire women to do hard-to-place adoption studies, because women have the necessary sensitivity to make more accurate judgments about such placements.

SECOND SITUATION

CHILD PROTECTIVE SERVICE WORKER: I have noticed that about 70% of our child abuse cases involve parents who don't know how to manage their child's behavior. I know our resources are too limited to offer parent effectiveness training to all of our cases, but we might be able to offer PET randomly to some of our families. The family court judge might go along with requiring PET for some families. We could conduct a randomized experiment to see if the PET training affected the severity and frequency of reabuse.

AGENCY SUPERVISOR: May I be a bit candid with you about this?

CHILD PROTECTIVE SERVICE WORKER: Sure.

AGENCY SUPERVISOR: You're a good worker. Still, I don't think women have the emotional makeup to do good studies. I think they tend to mix up their emotions with the demands that accurate data collection and analysis would require.

To avoid this fallacy, study the evidence. If an evaluation concerns an individual, then study the specifics as they apply to that individual. To counter the fallacy in the first situation, you could examine any data regarding the accuracy of risk assessments, the thoroughness of adoption studies, and actual performance by individual workers. To counter the second fallacy, deal with the methodological issues of designing and conducting the study. You might define the fallacy directly at the moment. You might wait until later and describe the specifics of your proposal in a meeting or in writing to gain support where others could address any stereotypical thinking.

• *Insufficient documentation, no data, inference not supported by observations, no documentation, poor documentation, unsupported inference, jumping to a conclusion:* Refers to the general problem that occurs when a witness draws a conclusion without sufficient documentation. *Insufficient documentation* can occur when the witness lacks any of the following: direct observations, specific records, facts and figures, direct quotes recorded at the time in the record, or a log of client contacts. Insufficient documentation may represent the greatest threat to professional testimony. An example of insufficient documentation follows:

PSYCHOLOGIST: I am pretty sure that my impressions are accurate based on my frequent contacts with Mr. and Mrs. Ahmed.

DISTRICT ATTORNEY: I have reviewed your files and find only two entries to document your contacts during the past 9 months. One was 8 months ago on June 15th for half an hour at the Dane County Court House, and the other was on August 12th for an hour with Dr. Hansen in his office. Do you have specific records, entries in case notes, or other Department of Human Services records to document your "frequent" contacts with Mr. and Mrs. Ahmed?

PSYCHOLOGIST: No, but I can assure you that I have seen them more frequently.

DISTRICT ATTORNEY: Can you produce written proof of your contacts?

To avoid this fallacy, keep careful records regarding your clients and know how to access records related to your clients. Review and organize those records carefully before testimony. Take your notes and carefully organized records that you may need with you to the courtroom.

• *Attack at the person, personal attack, at the man, at the person, discrediting the person (ad hominem):* Refers to a diversion from the issue by attacking the person. According to Chase (1956, 2, 61), when you try to state your case by diverting attention from the credibility of the argument and by *discrediting the person* who is presenting the argument, you argue at the person, or ad hominem. "The fallacy of personal attack is an argument that diverts attention away from the question being argued by focusing instead on those arguing it" (Engel, 1990, p. 188). The argument involves ". . . attempting to impugn the argument by denigrating one's opponent . . ." (Detlefsen, McCarty, & Bacon, 1999, p. 6). The ad hominem serves as an emotional diversion that can sidetrack an expert witness. A *personal attack* can unsettle the witness enough emotionally to cause confusion in the witness. This example demonstrates the personal attack:

DISTRICT ATTORNEY: Your vitae show that you were a registered nurse for about 4 years before you entered your doctorate work in nursing at Syracuse University. Is that right?

NURSE: That's right.

DISTRICT ATTORNEY: And while you were at Syracuse, you studied memory patterns in goldfish. Is that right?

NURSE: My dissertation concerned memory on a much broader scale; only a small part concerned memory in lower animals. I think it had important implications for human learning, particularly regarding how memory can be affected by aging.

DISTRICT ATTORNEY: And after your doctorate work, you then worked with sex offenders at Greenfield for 3 years. Is that right?

DEFENSE ATTORNEY: Your honor, at this point I object to further questioning because it serves no purpose here.

DISTRICT ATTORNEY: Your honor,—

DEFENSE ATTORNEY: Pardon me. If I might complete my position. If he wants to attack the credibility of the doctor, then that's totally inappropriate in a hearing like this. If he wants to have a hearing, that's fine, but this is a probable cause hearing. Let's stick to the facts of this case.

To avoid being taken in by the ad hominem, recognize the distinction between an argument *at the person* and an argument ad rem (at the thing). The latter refers to the need to argue to the facts. Often those lacking a strong argument will try to win by discrediting their adversary personally. If you can present the evidence (argue at the thing or at the issue) and avoid becoming emotionally rattled, you can most effectively counter the ad hominem argument.

• *Two-headed question, multiple-barreled question, two questions posed as one, multiple-headed question, double questions:* Refer to two questions posed as one. *Double questions* happen when the interviewer ". . . asks more than one question at a time." Or the interviewer asks one question and ". . . before the client can begin to answer, the interviewer asks a second question" (Kadushin & Kadushin, 1997, p. 254):

> Will you be able to cook your own meals, and will you be able to continue driving your own car?

> Do you think your client will be able to reliably take his Clausaril, and do you think he will present a risk for violence if he doesn't?

> Did you assess your client for the risk that he might become violent, and do you agree that, given what he has done, you should have taken action to prevent his violent behavior?

Double questions can pose a problem just because answering them with a *yes* or *no* provides an ambiguous answer. A single answer can entrap the witness later. A single *yes* might be construed to mean agreement to both questions. Be careful. Avoid being taken in by a double question by asking for clarification. For example, "You have asked me a double question. I am not sure which one you want me to answer."

Instructions for Taking the CITTT

To take the CITTT, click on the *Take Test* option. Then click on the CITTT pull-down option. Then read the instructions for taking the test. To start the test, click on the *Start* button. The program will pause periodically. If you think no fallacy occurred in the interaction that *immediately preceded* the pause, enter the words *No Fallacy* in the *Fallacy Name* box and leave the *Fallacy Description* box empty. If you think the interaction just before the pause contained a fallacy, then enter the name of the fallacy and define the fallacy and how it is evident in the preceding interaction. When you are confident of your answer, click on the *submit* button to continue the test. Take as long as you like to ponder your answer before recording it. In this sense, the video does not reflect reality—you will not have minutes to respond when a fallacy arises in your practice. You may have only seconds. On the other hand, the video is true to reality. You do not have the chance to go back and correct your actions, just as the video does not allow you to go back and fix your answer. When the CITTT stops, please record your answers. These answers can be accessed in a file that has been saved for you (ITTA Folder, media/cittt.mov). If you prefer, you may record your answers on the CITTT answer sheet in Figure 2.2. (A scoring key can be found at the end of this chapter in Table 2.3.)

Figure 2.2   The CITTT Answer Sheet

Instructions: At each pause, please state the name of the fallacy in reasoning or write *No Fallacy* and describe how the fallacy is evident if you name a fallacy. (Please write clearly in pen.)

Pause Number	Fallacy Name or *No Fallacy*	Description of How Fallacy Is Evident in Interaction or Left Blank If *No Fallacy*
1		
2		
3		
4		
5		
6		
7		

Exercise 2-3 The Multidisciplinary Interactive Team Thinking Test

Purpose

The multidisciplinary interactive team thinking test (MITTT) measures ability to reason scientifically about actions taken by a multidisciplinary team in a school. The MITTT was designed to

- Motivate you to apply principles of evidence-based practice by seeing how it can help to oppose muddled thinking that can harm clients
- Test your ability to spot fallacies in reasoning that can damage a team's ability to arrive at a well-reasoned conclusion
- Demonstrate the kind of problems and reasoning that members of individual education plan teams encounter in schools.

Background

Multidisciplinary teams meet universally in every school district within the United States. They are required by federal law as part of procedures for assessing whether schoolchildren and preschoolers have emotional problems and learning difficulties that can affect a child's learning in school. Such assessments must include an individual education plan (IEP) for each child with learning disabilities or emotional disabilities. IEP teams meet to make judgments and decisions about which children have problems and to decide which efforts will most likely help each individual child (Individuals with Disabilities Act Amendments of 1997). Teams must include at least one regular education and one special education teacher, a parent, and others that can include the following: school psychologist, school nurse, occupational therapist, physical therapist, speech therapist, and social worker. For children judged to need services by the IEP team, the team must meet annually to review each child's plan.

Actors in the CD-ROM's team meeting are not professional actors. They are real professionals who do meet regularly to discuss IEPs. The professionals shown interacting helped to develop the MITTT by describing common fallacies that they themselves have observed in team meetings, and they helped to edit the script for the MITTT. Any resemblance between Brian and a real child is coincidental.

How to Prepare to Take the MITTT

Look for fallacies in the MITTT exercise. Please examine the following list of fallacies to get a clear idea of each fallacy's definition before doing the MITTT exercise.

  • *Tradition, appealing to tradition, appealing to precedent:* Defined in the earlier HITTT exercise.

  • *Appeal to numbers, popularity, widespread use, band wagon:* Defined in the earlier HITTT exercise.

• *Appeal to experience, personal experience, prior experience:* Defined in the earlier HITT exercise.

• *Appeal to status, appeal to authority, prestige, (ad verecundiam):* Defined in the earlier HITT exercise.

• *Case example, single case, generalizing from a single case:* Refers to drawing a conclusion about other clients based on a few unrepresentatively chosen ones. *Case example* is a fallacy if, based on a single case or a few cases, a statement is made about what is generally true of a whole group (see Gibbs, 1991, pp. 239–253). Concluding that a rape crisis center's method is effective based on a detailed account of one woman's experience who went through treatment at the center or generalizing about all persons suffering from chronic pain based on one treated with acupuncture are examples of the case example fallacy. The case example often begins with the phrase "I knew a man who . . ." or some similar construction. Using cases to illustrate how an intervention may be conducted (e.g., demonstrating the *how to* of applying a treatment method) is not a fallacy if no generalization is made.

The "welfare queen" illustrates this fallacy well. Newspaper stories may carry a detailed description of a woman who claimed many nonexistent children, used many fictitious names, forged birth certificates, and defrauded the welfare system of hundreds of thousands of dollars. ("California Woman Earns 'Welfare-Queen' Title," 1981). Just reporting the facts of such a case would not constitute a fallacy. The fallacy occurs when stories generalize to all welfare recipients or to the entire welfare system from such cases ("She's Known as Chicago's 'Welfare Queen'," 1978). The author of this article said, "Atrocious things are going on in the welfare department, and the taxpayer is catching it. . . . If this Otis case doesn't prove to the taxpayer that something needs to be done, nothing will" (p. 28). This generalization from the case is what constitutes the fallacy.

One of the most important lessons that you can gain from this book concerns how describing single cases like the preceding one can support any prejudice. If an unethical or naive person wants to support a prejudice, a case can always be found to support the prejudice. Scientific reasoning can counter such prejudice. Related to the welfare queen example, quality control data from a survey of representatively chosen welfare cases refutes the fallacy. This survey found that the national error rate of AFDC overpayments was 13.8%, leaving only 5.8% of errors traced to the client; but, even among these 5.8%, the question of intent arose due possibly to the recipient's not understanding questions about eligibility (Family Support Administration, 1984, p. 23).

I like to think that people apply case examples to their generalizations not because they are mean spirited but because they are ignorant about why case example is so seductive. That is, they are not aware of social psychology and clinical reasoning studies that explain the fallacy's appeals. Research explains why case example appeals to the unwary based on its vividness, ignorance of the law of large numbers, and the need for sample representativeness.

Vividness of Case Example   Studies of how people reason demonstrates a relationship between the vividness of case material and greater generalization. That is, the more vividly the case material portrays a case, the more what is true of the case seems to be true of others. A study by Hamill, Nisbett, and Wilson (1980) randomly assigned 124 psychology students to 1 of 3 conditions. The first group read a derogatory case example about a person who received welfare and read survey results that countered the case example (like that given in the welfare queen example); the second read only the derogatory case material; and the third read no case material. Then the researchers measured attitudes toward people who received welfare. The students in both experimental groups had *equally more negative attitudes* toward people who received welfare than did the controls. It did not matter that one of the experimental groups had read the survey that refuted the derogatory case material. Apparently, the vivid details in the case material affected the students' attitudes regardless of the evidence. This effect of vividness of detail on generalization has been replicated in other experiments (Anderson, 1983; Oskamp, 1982).

Ignorance of the Law of Large Numbers   Case example also deceives by encouraging practitioners to ignore the law of large numbers. As a general rule, the *law of large numbers* states that samples that include successively larger and larger proportions of the population will generally represent that population more accurately. That is, the sample mean from the population will approach the population mean as the sample size increases, until finally the sample mean will equal exactly the population mean when the sample includes the entire population (Hays, 1981, p. 186). People seem to be ignorant of this fact, because they behave as though they generalize more from a few intimately known cases than they do from survey data. They seem to believe in the *law of small numbers*, meaning that they behave as though the smaller the sample the more accurately they believe it reflects the population (Abraham & Schultz, 1984; Tversky & Kahneman, 1971).

Belief in the law of small numbers has been demonstrated in two experiments (Tversky & Kahneman, 1974, p. 1125). In one, persons believed that samples of 10,100, and 1000 men's heights all estimated the height of a population with the same degree of accuracy. In the other, they believed that babies born in a small hospital would represent the sex of children in the population with the same degree of accuracy as would a sample in a larger hospital.

The belief in the law of small numbers can foster inaccurate generalizations about clients. For example, I recall an instance where I myself was taken in by the fallacy for a time. Our students had arranged a conference regarding issues in practice. One of the speakers at the conference was an extremely sincere and articulate woman who spoke about her work in hospice with dying clients. She told of one particularly poignant case of a dying, single-parent mother with two small children. I recall the tears welling up in my eyes and found myself agreeing with the speaker's argument that hospice is an effective and necessary service in hospitals. The speaker's case had so moved me emotionally that I had bought the argument for a moment, until I caught myself, realizing that only a sound evaluation study could address the general issue of effectiveness.

Ignorance of Sample Representativeness   *Representativeness* refers to the extent to which the characteristics of a sample taken from a population are typical of the characteristics of that population. The law of small numbers has already been explained as one way that a small sample may not represent the population. Other ways include self-selection of cases willing to volunteer to have their stories told. Volunteers for research tend to be better educated, of higher social class, more intelligent, higher in need for social approval, and more sociable than those not volunteering (Rosenthal & Rosnow, 1975, p. 195). Purposeful selection by those administering care is still another way that cases may be chosen unrepresentatively to prove a point.

Case example has occupied so much space here because it so often appears in practice literature as proof for an assertion about clients. You can read more about the mechanisms of incomplete or unrepresentative data that underlie case example in *How We Know What Isn't So* (Gilovich, 1991, pp. 29–48). To avoid this fallacy, resolve to seek stronger evidence from surveys, direct observations of many clients, and well-designed experiments.

• *Anchoring and insufficient adjustment, preconceived, not open to new data:* Refers to the tendency to formulate a quick initial impression of the likelihood of an event and then to hold to this initial impression despite evidence to the contrary (Tversky & Kahneman, 1982). Where applied to clients, this fallacy can cause serious misjudgment due to a preconceived notion that misrepresents the client's true nature (Kassirer & Kopelman, 1991, pp. 242–247). An example of *anchoring and insufficient adjustment follows:*

> **CHILD WELFARE CASEWORKER:** When I make a home visit, I can tell by first impressions. I use the sniff test. My nose can tell whether the home will be a clean safe environment for a child.

> **NURSE:** All I need to know is in the chart. If I see notes that a teenaged mother does not have insurance and does not list a husband, I know that she will not make rational decisions about the care of her child.

• *Groupthink:* Refers to the tendency of members of groups (possibly including evidence-based practice teams, multidisciplinary teams, human service work teams) to avoid sharing a dissenting opinion for fear of disrupting the group, causing disunity, or hurting the feelings of others. Janis (1971) says, "I use the term *groupthink* as a quick and easy way to refer to the mode of thinking that persons engage in when concurrence-seeking [seeking agreement] becomes so dominant in a cohesive group that it tends to override realistic appraisal of alternative courses of action" (p. 43). In other words, groupthink happens when members of a group are more concerned about getting along than they are about solving problems. Groupthink can deny the group the chance to critically appraise evidence that might be vital to helping clients. Groupthink undermines EBP because EBP requires that all strong evidence, *both negative and positive,* be searched out and included in any review. Ideally, a team following EBP principles would actively seek strong evidence regarding whatever problem it faces and would reward, rather than punish, those who present sound evidence, even if that evidence ran counter to team practices.

Consider an example of groupthink as it might apply to practice. A student who has been learning evidence-based practice has posed and searched for evidence regarding the following question: "If Mary, a 40-year-old chronic alcoholic, who has been in 3-day detoxification 5 times, but never in treatment, is committed for treatment, then will she be more likely to drink no alcohol than if she does not get into any treatment?" The student is attending a case conference at her agency where others are deciding what will be done regarding Mary's treatment.

FIRST GROUP MEMBER: I don't think it matters whether Mary gets into treatment. I think that treated alcoholics fare about the same as untreated ones do. I'm totally disillusioned by all the failures in alcoholism treatment.

SECOND GROUP MEMBER: Then we are all in agreement. We will not refer Mary for treatment.

THIRD GROUP MEMBER: That about sums it up. We're unanimous.

STUDENT (TO HERSELF): I wonder what their reaction would be if I summarized Emrick's (1975) review of over 300 evaluation studies finding that those treated fared better if they got into some treatment, any treatment, over no treatment. I guess I'll keep my mouth shut here.

Astute group leaders can take action to avoid groupthink. They can make actively seeking out and rewarding dissenting opinions a part of group procedure for the good of the group (Janis, 1982).

• *Straw man, diversion, misrepresenting an argument and attacking the misrepresented argument:* A form of diversion from the issue. Sometimes the argument is genuinely misunderstood and then attacked. Sometimes the argument is purposefully misrepresented and then attacked. In either case, the form of argument is a *straw man* argument because the arguer constructs a dummy or straw man, not the real thing, and then attacks the straw man. If you criticize a position that another did not really hold, and infer from your criticism that his real position is flawed, you have committed the straw man fallacy (Govier, 1985, p. 104). This interaction demonstrates the straw man:

AGENCY SUPERVISOR: I have a meta-analysis of studies indicating that level of funding generally has an impact on educational outcomes. May I show it to you? Meta-analyses are systematic reviews. Good ones state their criteria for including evidence; they rate the quality of the evidence, and they summarize the effect of programs relative to some index of effectiveness that makes sense. The evidence seems strong that level of funding does have an effect.

COUNTY BOARD MEMBER: Your argument doesn't hold water. We simply do not have the funds for the program. Just take a look at the budget for next year. Where are we going to get the funds?

To avoid the straw man fallacy, make certain that you understand what is being argued. Before reacting, rephrase what you have just heard in your own words and ask if your impressions are accurate. Then respond to the argument. If another misrepresents your position, take the earliest opportunity to clarify what you have just said.

Instructions for Taking the MITTT

To take the MITTT, click on the *Take Test* option. Then click on the MITTT pull-down option. Then read the instructions for taking the test. To start the test, click on the *Start* button. The program will pause periodically. If you think no fallacy occurred in the interaction that *immediately preceded* the pause, then enter the words *No Fallacy* in the *Fallacy Name* box and leave the *Fallacy Description* box empty. If you think the interaction just before the pause contained a fallacy, then enter the name of the fallacy and define the fallacy and how it is evident in the preceding interaction. When you are confident of your answer, click on the *submit* button to continue the test. Take as long as you like to ponder your answer before recording it. In this sense, the video does not reflect reality—you will not have minutes to respond when a fallacy arises in your practice. You may have only seconds. On the other hand, the video is true to reality. You do not have the chance to go back and correct your actions, just as the video does not allow you to go back and fix your answer. When the MITTT stops, please record your answers. These answers can be accessed in a file that has been saved for you (ITTA Folder, media/mittt.mov). If you prefer, you may record your answers on the MITTT answer sheet in Figure 2.3. (A scoring key can be found at the end of this chapter in Table 2.4.)

Avoiding Quack Reasoning

Those who want to avoid practice fallacies will want to draw a distinction between evidence-based reasoning and quack reasoning. A *quack* is "one who, with little or no foundation, pretends to have skill or knowledge in a particular field" (*Webster's New Twentieth Century Dictionary,* 1983, p. 1471). Usually, a quack is thought of as being "a pretender to medical knowledge or skill" (*The New International Webster's Concise Dictionary of the English Language,* 1997, p. 5940), but a quack can exist in any discipline. All practitioners need to be able to recognize features of quack reasoning. "The voice of the quack is not a harmless honk" (Miller, 1985, p. 1), because quack reasoning can harm clients. Table 2.1 contrasts quack reasoning and evidence-based reasoning.

Figure 2.3   The MITTT Answer Sheet

Instructions: At each pause, please state the name of the fallacy in reasoning or write *No Fallacy* and describe how the fallacy is evident if you name a fallacy. (Please write clearly in pen.)

Pause Number	Fallacy Name or *No Fallacy*	Description of How Fallacy Is Evident in Interaction or Left Blank If *No Fallacy*
1		
2		
3		
4		
5		
6		
7		
8		
9		

Table 2.1   Contrast Between Quack Reasoning and Evidence-Based Reasoning

Quack Reasoning	Evidence-Based Reasoning
1. Promises quick, dramatic, miraculous cures (Herbert, 1983). Some examples occur in this sentence: Quack language promises "fast working, inexpensive, painless . . . guaranteed . . . remarkable" results (Miller, 1985).	1. Tries not to extrapolate beyond the findings of the current best evidence. When discussing costs and benefits of a course of action, lists findings in terms that clients can understand (e.g., number needed to treat).
2. Speaks imprecisely and vaguely to describe the client and intended outcome (Herbert, 1983). "It really works! . . ." (Miller, 1985).	2. Speaks precisely in terms of probabilities when assessing risk (Gibbs, 1991, pp. 218–220) and in specific indices of treatment effect size when describing potential benefits of interventions (pp. 206–210).
3. Employs anecdotes and testimonials to support claims (Herbert, 1983).	3. Searches objectively in the current published and unpublished evidence to seek answers to specific practice-related questions (Cochrane Library Home Page, http://www.cochrane.org)
4. Is bound to particular dogma, theory, or beliefs and does not incorporate new ideas or methods based on their evidence (McCain & Segal, 1988, pp. 33–34).	4. Continually updates information regarding important questions with the most recent best evidence (Cochrane Library Home Page, www.nelh.nhs.uk)
5. Cries "foul" when asked to subject ideas to a test (Jarvis, 1987, p. 54; Jarvis & Barrett, 1993, p. 12).	5. Actively seeks criticism, counter evidence, and relies on more than one individual's independent rating of evidence to ensure accurate interpretations for evidence.
6. Joins cults that follow the techniques of a charismatic individual in which members consider themselves to be among the faithful (*Alternative Therapy*, 1986, p. 65).	6. Willing to take risks for adhering to evidence-based beliefs rather than following the dictates of the many and the powerful.
7. Uses the language and phrases of science but not the methodology of science: "research, researcher, scientific discovery. . . . clinical studies prove that . . ." (Miller, 1985, pp. 1–2).	7. Believes that no conclusion is better than the quality of the evidence regarding that conclusion, speaks of testing ideas and states findings tentatively, never "proves" beyond all doubt.
8. Claims that their methods have effects "such that they cannot be tested by normal approved methods of clinical trial" (*Alternative Therapy*, 1986, p. 71).	8. Bases claims on clinical trials. Rates the quality of these trials against criteria for a well-conducted clinical trial (Sackett, Straus, Richardson, Rosenberg, & Haynes, 2000, pp. 106–110).

Barrett (1993, p. 465) says that one way to avoid being taken in by a quack is to ". . . get good information when you need it." This book concerns just that. If you would like to get more information about quack reasoning, you can enter the word *Quackwatch* in your search engine and get to Stephen Barrett's Web site.

Summary

The preceding exercises intend to motivate you to apply evidence-based principles by showing rational, data-based, evidence-based practice in opposition to muddled thinking. The three exercises all place evidence-based practitioners in opposition to illogical thinking. This is not to say that evidence-based practitioners will not fall prey to illogical thinking; but, in its purest sense, evidence-based practitioners will gravitate to the best available evidence. Hopefully, the portrayals of evidence-based practitioners demonstrate that they apply their own personal experience, the current best evidence, and the concerns of the client.

Scoring the HITTT, the CITTT, and the MITTT

Apply the following criteria to scoring the HITTT, the CITTT, and the MITTT according to the scoring keys in Table 2.2, Table 2.3, and Table 2.4. You can get up to 4 points for each item or pause.

• *Scoring Column 2:* Use a dark colored marking pen to record a *0* or a *2* in each box of Column 2. For Column 2, give 2 points for *just one* fallacy name in agreement with the name in the key. If the proper response was *No Fallacy* in Column 2, give yourself 2 points in Column 2. If the proper response in Column 2 was *No Fallacy,* then give 2 points for either leaving Column 3 blank or for stating how the item is not a fallacy.

• *Scoring Column 3:* For Column 3, record a *0*, or a *1*, or a *2* in each cell in Column 3. Give 2 points for stating essentially what the key stated to describe the fallacy or to describe what was done to avoid the fallacy. A 2-point answer does not have to be worded exactly in the words of the key; but, if the answer says essentially the same thing as the key, then give it 2 points. Give 1 point for partial agreement with the key, for an answer that partially makes the point. Give 0 points for any argument that does not state a fallacy explanation at all in the key.

• *To compute the total score:* Total the scores for Column 2 and for Column 3, and record the grand total.

Table 2.2 | The HITTT Scoring Key

Pause Number	Fallacy Name or *No Fallacy*	Description of How Fallacy Is Evident in Interaction or Left Blank If *No Fallacy*
1	No fallacy	The respondent states in any way that there is no fallacy here. Any reference to a fallacy in this section gets 0 points in this box.
2	Uncritical documentation, merely citing, citing without evidence, citation only, appeal to status, appeal to authority, prestige, prestigious (ad verecundiam)	Either one or both of these fallacies: *Uncritical documentation* is present here because the surgeon merely cited the source and did not address in any way the study's methodology. *Appeal to status* is demonstrated by referring to the prestige of the *New England Journal of Medicine* but not to the article's methodology.
3	Appeal to numbers, popularity, widespread use, tradition, bandwagon	A standard of care can reflect a sound evidentiary basis, or it may not. Stating merely that one follows a standard of care ignores the evidentiary basis for that standard. One must critically examine the evidence that does or does not support the standard, regardless of how widespread the standard's use or how many accept it.
4	Appeal to experience, prior experience, personal experience	Experience can surely serve as a guide, particularly where the effects of a treatment are universally of great magnitude, but as in cases like that of Mr. Anderson, where the benefits of surgery are of a complex and variable nature, a harmful effect would be difficult to detect based purely on one's prior experience. The respondent needs to refer to the fallibility of personal experience as a guide or needs to refer to the need for research evidence to guide the decision.
5	Vague quantifying adjective, vague term, vagueness	What does ". . . substantially decrease. . . ." mean in specific terms? Does it reduce the chance of stroke by 50%, 10%, 5%? Chris cannot know specifically based on such a term. Any response that refers to vagueness here gets the full two points.
6	No Fallacy	They begin with a natural language question about the benefits of surgery but progress to Dr. Myers's well-built answerable question. They have begun to get interested in posing a question.

Table 2.2	Continued	
Pause Number	**Fallacy Name or *No Fallacy***	**Description of How Fallacy Is Evident in Interaction or Left Blank If *No Fallacy***
7	Vague question, not well-formulated question, question not specific, poorly formulated question	What does ". . . . benefit from surgery . . ." mean? Dr. Myers will demonstrate how this question does not make clear the "who," meaning the patient type, the "what," meaning carotid endarterectomy or no surgery with drugs like aspirin; nor does the question specify the outcome meaning stroke or death.
8	Uncritical documentation, merely citing, citing without evidence, citation only, did not examine study methodology, appeal to numbers, appeal to popularity, widespread use, band wagon	Either one or both of these fallacies. *Uncritical documentation* is present here because the surgeon merely cited the source and did not address in any way the study's methodology. A standard of care can reflect a sound evidentiary basis, or it may not. Stating merely that one follows a standard of care ignores the evidentiary basis for that standard. One must critically examine the evidence that does or does not support the standard. Blindly following a standard of care without examining the evidentiary basis for it is a form of *appeal to popularity or numbers.*
9	Appeal to experience, personal experience, Prior experience	Experience can surely serve as a guide, particularly where the effects of a treatment are universally of great magnitude; but, as in cases like that of Mr. Anderson, where the benefits of surgery are of a complex and variable nature, detecting a harmful effect based purely on one's prior experience would be difficult.
10	Tradition, appeal to tradition, appealing to precedent	Both ideas for 2 points (1 point each): 1. Simply because the procedure has always been done in the past does not provide sufficient evidence that the procedure should be used. 2. Evidence regarding the procedure's efficacy needs to provide the basis for the procedure's use.
Grand total (col. 1 + col. 2)	Total	Total

Table 2.3 | The CITTT Scoring Key

Pause Number	Fallacy Name or *No Fallacy*	Description of How Fallacy Is Evident in Interaction or Left Blank If *No Fallacy*
1	No Fallacy	The judge has merely started the facts of the case regarding Mr. Smith.
2	Two headed question, two questions posed as one, multiple-headed question, multiple-barreled question, double question	The prosecuting attorney, Mr. Black, asks both about Patti's experience as a probation agent *and* whether she has prepared a pre-sentence report. This question cannot be answered logically as posed with a "yes" or "no" answer.
3	Ad hominem, attack at the person, at the person, personal attack, at the man, discrediting the person	Instead of examining Patti's argument about why Mr. Smith presents a risk to others and should be in prison, Ms. Jones, the defending attorney, tries to discredit Patti personally. This diverts from the facts of the case.
4	No data, inference not supported by observations, no documentation, unsupported inference, insufficient documentation, poor documentation, jumping to a conclusion	Ms. Jones demonstrates that Patti has not done her homework to prepare documentation for the trial and to check that documentation for its accuracy.
5	Uncritical documentation, merely citing, citing without evidence, citation without evidence, citation only	Peter, the psychologist, makes an inference supported by documentation, but he cannot describe the source nor can he critique its methodology. No document is better than its methodology.
6	Stereotyping, stereotypical reasoning, hasty generalization, unsupported generalization	Here, Mr. Black draws an inference about "all sex offenders." He presents no evidence about this category of people to support his inference.
7	Leading question, leading the witness, loaded question, suggestive question, suggestion question	Here, Mr. Black attempts to intimidate the witness by making a statement daring the witness to disagree with him in response to his question. He is trying to tell the witness what to say.
Grand total (col. 1 + col. 2)	Total	Total

Table 2.4 | The MITT Scoring Key

Pause Number	Fallacy Name or *No Fallacy*	Description of How Fallacy Is Evident in Interaction or Left Blank If *No Fallacy*
1	No fallacy	The case manager (social worker) merely stated background and the purpose of the meeting.
2	Anchoring and insufficient adjustment, preconceived, not open to new data	The school psychologist uncritically accepted Tucker County's conclusion and did not try sufficiently to conduct her own investigation. The early childhood teacher corrected this error by investigating an alternate hypothesis.
3	No fallacy	Different points of view are presented. The special education teacher bases her inferences on behavioral observations in the home. The case manager makes an inference about the child's apparent attachment based on the special education teacher's observations in the home.
4	Case example, single case, generalizing from a single case	The first speaker (school psychologist) has recalled a case that involved a parent with criminal behavior and has generalized to Brian. The early childhood teacher, occupational therapist, and speech pathologist all counter the school psychologist's hasty generalization with their own specific observations.
5	Straw man, diversion, misrepresenting an argument and attacking the misrepresented argument	The school psychologist misrepresented what the others had said, and then she attacked the misrepresentation. The occupational therapist corrected this error by saying, "That is not what John said."
6	Relying on authority, appeal to status, prestige, appeal to authority (ad verecundiam), appeal to numbers, popularity, widespread use, bandwagon	The speech pathologist argues that Dr. Lovaas's method might help based on Lovaas's status, not on evidence regarding effectiveness. The occupational therapist supports Lovaas's method based on his reputation. The school psychologist corrects this error by questioning the idea of accepting a method based on the status of its originator. We all must follow standards for evaluating evidence regardless of our status.
7	Tradition, appealing to tradition, appealing to precedent	The speech pathologist states that the method should be tried because it has been in use since the 60s. The school psychologist corrects this error by stating that she is not convinced by the argument that the method should be used because it has been around for years.

continued

Table 2.4 | Continued

Pause Number	Fallacy Name or *No Fallacy*	Description of How Fallacy Is Evident in Interaction or Left Blank If *No Fallacy*
8	Appeal to experience, personal experience, prior experience	The early childhood teacher refers to her own experience with the method as evidence, but the school psychologist points to the need for better evidence regarding the method's general effectiveness.
9	Groupthink	The school nurse did not share a dissenting opinion during the conference regarding the possibility of a physical explanation for some of Brian's behavior because the nurse did not feel comfortable speaking out. The social worker (case manager) noted that the nurse should have shared her valuable opinion.
Grand total (col. 1 + col. 2)	Total	Total

You've got to be careful if you don't know where you're going 'cause you might not get there! —**Yogi Berra** *(1998)*

Pose a Specific Question of Importance to Your Client's Welfare

"If you don't know where you are going…"

Overview

Yogi's right. If you don't know where you're going, you just might not get there. Stated positively, if you can learn to pose a specific question, you have hope of finding a specific answer. This topic is *that basic* and the most important in this text. This chapter spends considerable time on learning to pose questions, because a well-built question is essential to all the other steps of evidence-based practice. The whole process of EBP depends on a good question. Other texts on EBP place posing a question first (Sackett et al., 2000, p. 13); and many write articles and whole chapters just about posing specific questions (Armstrong, 1999; Gibbs, 1991, pp. 109–133; McKibbon, Eady & Marks, 1999; Richardson, 1998; Richardson, Wilson, Nishikawa, & Hayward, 1995).

Problems caused by vague questions are discussed initially in this chapter to show why practitioners need question-wording skills. Then, what it means to pose a specific question is defined generally, first with reference to client-oriented, practical, evidence-search (COPES) concepts, then with reference to elements present in clear questions as stated in Table 3.1. This table includes five types of practice questions (effectiveness, prevention, assessment, description, and risk) and four features of a well-built question relative to each (client type and problem, what you may do, alternate course of action, what you want to accomplish). Do study Table 3.1 carefully to get the gist of this chapter's organization. Its examples will clarify the question types and criteria for clarity.

For each of the five question types, this chapter gives background regarding real practice situations and derives specific COPES questions regarding each situation. As you read each situation, try to put yourself in the practitioner's and client's positions. Practice posing your own clear answerable question from the case material, then read the sample question to see how well you did relative to criteria for a specific question. Doing so will prepare you for the three exercises at the end of the chapter.

This chapter's three exercises concern successively more complex questioning tasks. Exercise 3-1 gives you practice classifying and posing specific questions from case material. Next, Exercise 3-2 provides practice posing questions regarding real clients even if you do not have your own clients. Exercise 3-2 will guide you through the process of soliciting a question from a willing practitioner in any discipline, either by phone or by letter, and clarifying your question. Exercise 3-2 can supply you with a question that you can work on in later chapters (e.g., searching for related evidence, evaluating that evidence, deciding what action to recommend). Exercise 3-3 assumes that you are employed in an agency and have access to your own clients. This exercise guides you through posing a specific question from your own practice.

The Need to Pose Vital Questions

Practitioners seldom ask specific questions that are central to good judgment and decision making about practice. Typically, practitioners ask questions about how to administer a treatment, how much it costs, why other practitioners do what they do based on their experience, and so on. My collection of several hundred questions posed by practitioners yields none that meet rigorous criteria for clarity (Gibbs, 1991, pp. 109–133).

| **Box 3.1** | **An Example Regarding Post Troumatic Stress Disorder in Children** |

To illustrate questioning problems, an example from human service practice follows. On April 26, 2000, the Hospice Foundation of America presented a nationally televised program, "Living with Grief: Children, Adolescents, and Loss." The program was broadcast live via satellite across the nation, and more than a thousand observers were given the chance to submit comments directly by telephone to those running the program to be answered live by a panel of experts. The audience consisted of hospice workers, nursing home social workers, child-care workers, nurses, and many others. Public television's Cokie Roberts served as the moderator for the panel.

Cokie moderated as experts on the panel discussed their experiences in dealing with grief in their own lives and in their work with clients. One of the topics of the panel discussion concerned collective loss as experienced by large numbers of children, including school shootings and disasters such as a tornado, where children are exposed en masse to serious injury and death. Panel members gave anecdotal evidence from their own personal experiences and those of others and discussed ways to work collectively with such victims through crisis counseling.

Interestingly, though many questions were put to the panel by telephone from the audience, no one asked a clear, specific, answerable question regarding crisis counseling, though crisis counseling was a major part of the panel's discussion. Nor could I find such questions in documentation provided by the Hospice Foundation or evidence from randomized trials to evaluate crisis counseling methods for trauma victims (Corr, 2000; Sheras, 2000).

Being an evidence-based practitioner would imply first a predisposition to posing questions about the crisis counseling program in the interests of children and, next, once general questions are formulated, to posing these general questions more specifically in an answerable, well-built format. A question related to crisis counseling might be stated as follows:

> For children who have experienced a traumatic stressor (e.g. school shooting, natural disaster, exposure to serious injury and death), among those exposed to brief psychological counseling or not receiving such counseling, will the former experience fewer symptoms of post traumatic stress disorder?

Those who conduct grief and loss programs might be evidence-based. A systematic review of 11 randomized controlled trials in the Cochrane Database (one completed after the grief and loss program) discovered that individual debriefing did *not* reduce psychological distress nor did it prevent post troumatic stress disorder (Rose, Bisson, & Wessely, 2002). In one trial there was a statistically significant *harmful effect*. A search for such research must first begin with a specific question.

For example, following are general questions regarding the stress reduction program that demonstrate five types of questions that might have been put to the panel of hospice experts:

- Is crisis counseling effective? *(effectiveness question)*
- How can children be prepared to face a crisis so they will not be devastated emotionally? *(prevention question)*
- How can you predict which children will be most vulnerable in a crisis? *(risk/prognosis)*

- How can you tell which children are experiencing a serious grief reaction? *(assessment)*
- What proportion of children exposed to a crisis will experience a serious grief reaction? *(description)*

The audience might have begun with such general questions, then proceeded to pose more specific ones.

Importance of Learning How to Pose Specific Questions About Practice

Can you imagine any human progress that *did not begin* with purposeful, well-reasoned, evidence-based questioning? Orville and Wilbur Wright posed and answered questions regarding shapes of wings that would generate the greatest lift in their wind tunnel. AIDS researchers, in the early phase of the epidemic, questioned whether a virus was involved. Early political scientists wondered if the outcome of elections could be predicted based on survey results. All progress begins with a question. Learning how to pose specific, answerable, well-built questions presents great opportunities for improving practice. If you can learn to pose questions, you can help your discipline to avoid stagnation and dogmatic thinking.

Some reasons for learning how to pose specific questions about practice follow:

- Learning how to pose questions from practice is essential to improving practice, because if you never pose questions about what you are doing you can never change what you are doing on a rational basis.
- Learning how to pose a specific question can save time during an electronic search for the answer.
- Learning how to pose questions is essential to the process of lifelong learning that will continually improve your ability to serve clients. If the intent of education is to produce learners who are independent thinkers, then practitoners must have a predisposition to pose specific, answerable questions.
- Learning how to pose specific questions from practice is an excellent countermeasure against arrogance, because those who seek answers will discover how tentative the answers are and how much is not known.
- Learning how to pose questions can stimulate and excite you, because it will awaken your 'curiosity and delight in learning' (Richardson, 1998) [about how to serve clients better].
- Learning how to pose a well-built question can foster better communication with other practitioners who are familiar with the format for clearly worded questions (Richardson, 1998).
- Because a vague question can only lead to a vague answer, a specific question must be posed to ever hope to get a specific (useful) answer regarding practice (Yogi Berra says so).

Client-Oriented, Practical, Evidence-Search Questions (COPES)

Three Features of COPES Questions

COPES questions are worthwhile questions. COPES questions come directly from practice. COPES questions have three general features. First, they are questions from daily practice, posed by practitioners, that really matter to the client's welfare—they are *client-oriented*. (Here, the word *client* refers to an individual, to a group of clients, or to a community.) Generally speaking, COPES questions concern issues that are central to the welfare of the client and to those whose lives are affected by the client. For example, the accuracy and reliability of an assessment of a child to determine whether the child has autism would concern a matter of central importance to the child and to the child's parent. If the child has autism, then an effort might be made specific to that child's problem; but, first, the assessment presents a central problem. Another concern of central importance to a client might be that of a young woman who experiences feelings of panic in social situations. This problem presents a real problem for her. She thinks her quality of life will improve dramatically if she can get the problem under control; so the answer to a related question regarding the efficacy of treatments for her problem would be client-oriented. Regarding still another question, the effectiveness of group treatment for men who have abused their wives would be of vital importance for obvious reasons to the men, to their wives, and to their probation and parole agent who conducts the group. Regarding gangs, knowing which factors most frequently precede Hmong boys' joining gangs might help a community organizer and community leaders to design a gang-prevention program for them. All of these questions are *client-oriented*: they begin with a matter of importance to clients.

Second, COPES questions have *practical* importance in several ways. In addition to their central importance to the client and to persons affected by the client, COPES questions have practical significance if they concern problems that arise frequently in everyday practice. For example, if a child protective service worker takes telephone intake duty for at least one day a week and these telephone contacts generally require some assessment of risk, then asking a question about what types of clients present the greatest immediate risk for child abuse would have repeated practical significance. COPES questions also have practical significance if they concern the mission of the agency. For example, asking a question about how to match hard-to-place children with foster families most likely to meet the children's needs would be a question central to a foster care agency. A COPES question also has practical significance if knowing the answer concerns something within the realm of possibility. For example, a school psychologist searching for the answer to whether the Lovaas method will help a child with autism demonstrates a question that has no practical value if funds for the treatment are unavailable or if no one in the region can administer the treatment.

Third, COPES questions can guide an *evidence search*. To guide an evidence search, a question must be posed specifically enough to get an answer in an electronic search. The process of formulating a specific question begins with a somewhat vague general question and then proceeds to a well-built question. COPES questions generally fall into five types that all meet four criteria for answerability (see Table 3.1).

The term *COPES* was not my invention. In medicine such questions are termed a POEM (Patient Oriented Evidence that Matters) (Slawson & Shaughnessy, 1997). For many hours, my search went on without success for an acronym for practitioners aside from medicine that would get the features of a good question but would not be a *POEM!* One just would not come to mind, until I noticed two women doing crossword puzzles in their seats next to me during an airline flight. Between their comments about heroes of the soap operas and gum chewing, the women solved several complex crossword puzzles with incredible speed and efficiency. Their ability to discuss a television episode and to simultaneously solve a puzzle showed incredible verbal fluency. I wondered if they would mind directing their fine minds to the POEM acronym problem; they did, and they solved it in less than 10 minutes with *client-oriented, practical, evidence search (COPES)* (D. Brown, personal communication, September 16, 1999).

Five COPES Question Types and Four Features of Well-Built Questions

Table 3.1 provides the essence of this chapter. The five question types are on the vertical left. Across to the right next to each question type, the question is worded from left to right in a way that includes all four elements of a well-built COPES question. Do study the table for several minutes to get the most of the examples that follow the table.

Examples of General Questions and Related COPES Questions

Each of the ten situations that appear in Box 3.1 through Box 3.10 implies a COPES question or questions. Note how the situation is *client-oriented* in that it concerns a matter of importance to the client. Notice how each question arose logically out of a practitioner's concern for how to approach the problem in a *practical* way using available resources and skills, and notice too that the accompanying well-built question is posed so specifically relative to four criteria that it can guide an *evidence search*.

Each situation came from practice in an assortment of agencies and client types. All of the questions used in this chapter concern real clients, real members of the helping professions, and real practice issues, though the situations are modified slightly to protect confidentiality. None in this book are real client names.

Please note also that each of the five questions exemplifies one of the following five types: effectiveness, prevention, risk, assessment, and description. In the boxed situations, each question type is defined first; then, for each question type, two questions are given including a general question and a well-built

Table 3.1 | Five COPES Question Types and Four Corresponding Features of a Well-Built Question

Five Question Types	Four Elements in a Well-Formulated Question			
	Client Type and Problem	What You Might Do	Alternate Course of Action	What You Want to Accomplish
	How would I describe a group of clients of a similar type? Be specific.	Apply a treatment; act to prevent a problem; measure to assess a problem; survey clients; screen clients to assess risk.	What is the main alternative other than in the box to the left?	Outcome of treatment or prevention? Valid measure? Accurate risk estimation, prevented behavior, accurate estimation of need?
Example Effectiveness Question	If disoriented aged persons who reside in a nursing home	are given reality orientation therapy	or validation therapy,	which will result in better orientation to time, place, and person?
Example Prevention Question	If sexually active high-school students at high risk for pregnancy	are exposed to *baby-think-it-over*	as opposed to being exposed to didactic material on the proper use of birth control methods,	will they have fewer pregnancies during an academic year? Knowledge of birth control methods?
Example Assessment Question	If aged residents of a nursing home who may be depressed or may have Alzheimer's disease or dementia	are administered depression screening tests	or short mental status examination tests,	which measure will be the briefest, most inexpensive, valid, and reliable screening test to discriminate between depression and dementia?
Example Description Question	If members of a hospital team who are concerned about team functioning	take the preliminary checklist (clinical) team effectiveness test	or take the interdisciplinary team weekly inventory,	which measure will most reliably and validly reflect the team's ability to accomplish tasks?
Example Risk Question	If crisis line callers to a shelter for women who have been battered	are administered a risk-assessment scale by telephone	as opposed to practical judgment, unaided by a risk-assessment scale, being relied upon,	will the risk-assessment scale have higher reliability and predictive validity for violent behavior?

Note. This table follows *Evidence-Based Medicine: How to Practice and Teach EBM*, by D. L. Sackett, W. S. Richardson, W. Rosenberg, & R. B. Haynes, 1997, p. 29, New York: Churchill Livingstone. Adapted with permission.

or specific question. At each general question, you may want to practice posing your own COPES question before you read the example question. To do so, take a piece of paper and slide it down to cover the related, well-built question and try to pose it yourself before looking at the example. Doing so will help you to prepare for Exercise 3-1.

Effectiveness Questions: Definition by General Concept and Two Examples
Effectiveness questions (Box 3.2 and Box 3.3) concern the direct effects of an intervention on clients who share a particular problem and who have been exposed to the intervention (treatment).

Box 3.2	**Example of Effectiveness Question Regarding Long-Term Care for Residents of a Nursing Home**

Practice Situation
Older long-term-care residents of nursing homes often experience mental confusion due to Alzheimer's disease and other degenerative processes in their brains. Such confusion can cause wandering, disorientation, dizziness, and impulsive behaviors. Geriatric workers face a dilemma. On the one hand, behaviors related to mental confusion are serious—particularly because they can cause injuries including those associated with falling. To prevent injuries and harm to others and to protect medical devices used in the resident's treatment, various restraints are used to limit movement, including "mitts, belts, crotch/pelvis devices, sheet ties, ankle ties, geri chairs, wrist ties, fixed tray tables and lap trays, side-rails [on beds to keep residents from rolling out of bed onto the floor], and vests" (Hause, 1999, p. 3). Social workers, nurses, and administrators at a nursing home were faced with a

dilemma regarding restraints. Restraints have a negative side. Geriatric professionals, who generally value helping clients in the least restrictive possible environment, are reluctant to use restraints. Restraints are thought to aggravate a loss of steadiness and balance, problems of elimination, skin breakdown, obstruction in circulation, stress to the heart, and discomfort to the resident due to loss of personal control over mobility. The dilemma here concerned whether the nursing home practitioners should adopt a new policy that would eliminate restraints entirely. To help to resolve this dilemma, Erin Hause posed the following question.

General Effectiveness Question
"What happens to the number of falls among elderly nursing home residents when restraints are removed?" (Hause, 1999, p. 3)

Related COPES Effectiveness Question
Among aged residents of nursing homes with dementia (Element 1, *client type*), what is the effect of removing restraints (Element 2, *possible course of action*) relative to continuing to use restraints (Element 3, *alternate course of action*) on residents' rate of falls and injuries (Element 4, *intended result*)?

| Box 3.3 | **Example of Effectiveness Question Regarding a Probation and Parole Agent's Use of Cognitive Group Treatment** |

Practice Situation

Those who work with clients in the criminal justice system as probation and parole agents often observe that criminal offenders reason differently than nonoffenders. They note that clients who have committed a sexual assault, armed robbery, battery, or theft reason differently. Corrections workers note an impulsive thinking in many corrections clients, an inability to place themselves in the position of others including their victims, a difficulty reasoning about how to cope with stresses, and rationalizations for their behavior that insulate them against taking responsibility for their own behavior. Consequently,

group cognitive treatment programs have been developed to counter ineffective reasoning among their clients. The premise of such cognitive programs is that if offenders recognize their errors in thinking that they will also be less likely to commit new offenses. The general question that follows was posed by a probation and parole agent who was contemplating using cognitive group treatment methods with her clients.

General Effectiveness Question

"Will attending fifteen two-hour sessions of the Phase Two Cognitive Intervention Program effectively reduce criminal behavior among the offenders in the group [cognitive treatment]?" (Thibado, 1998, p. 1)

Related COPES Effectiveness Question

Among adult criminal offenders on probation, will a group cognitive intervention program compared to no such program result in a lower recidivism (reoffense) rate?

Prevention Questions: Definition by General Concept and Two Examples *Prevention questions* (Box 3.4 and Box 3.5 on page 62) concern the effectiveness of interventions (treatments) that intend to prevent the initial occurrence of a problem before it can happen.

Risk/Prognosis Questions: Definition by General Concept and Two Examples *Risk/prognosis questions* (Box 3.6 and Box 3.7 on page 63) concern the likelihood or probability that a particular type of client will experience undesirable consequences within a given interval of time.

Assessment Questions: Definition by General Concept and Two Examples *Assessment questions* (Box 3.8 and Box 3.9 on page 64) concern standardized measures or procedures to determine whether a client has a particular problem and/or strength and whether a client has benefited from an intervention (treatment).

Box 3.4	Example of Prevention Question Regarding an HIV/AIDS Program

Practice Situation

The worldwide acquired immune deficiency syndrome (AIDS) epidemic is well publicized, but many who work with young students are concerned about widespread ignorance and risky behaviors by teenage pupils in schools. The message of how human immunodeficiency virus spreads does not get to many at-risk youths who have multiple sex partners, often with tragic results. The prevention question that follows below comes from a Red Cross worker who wanted to effectively use local funds given to the Red Cross for HIV/AIDS education in area schools. The social worker wanted to use the funds to get the greatest effect possible from an HIV/AIDS prevention program in as many middle schools and high schools as possible in a 13-county area. The Red Cross staff member was looking for the least expensive and most effective program to prevent risky sexual behaviors that could lead to infection.

General Prevention Question

"What is the most effective way to educate youth about HIV/AIDS?" (Wiederholt, 1999, p. 3)

Related COPES Prevention Question

Among teenage school children, which HIV/AIDS prevention program will result in the highest percentage of condom use during sexual encounters? (This question may prematurely limit the inquiry. A more general question might concern the most effective way to prevent sexually transmitted diseases.)

Box 3.5	A Community Organizer's Question Regarding Preventing Hmong Boys' Joining Gangs

Practice Situation

Within a county of approximately 60,000 residents, there are 2300 Hmong refugees. Many Hmong families are under great stress trying to adapt to their new environment. Though about 95% of the Hmong in the area are employed, approximately 50% live below poverty level due to low wages and large families. Many of the Hmong elders, single parents, and recent arrivals to the United States are socially isolated. Though the leaders of the 13 local clans, local elders, and parents have managed to cope well with many stresses as their families adapt to their new culture, they are concerned that some boys of Hmong descent become isolated and turn to delinquent gangs for peer support. A youth worker employed as a leader working for the Hmong Mutual Assistance Association has become concerned about the extent of the problem and wants to initiate a program that will prevent young Hmong boys from joining the gangs. This youth worker's question follows.

General Prevention Question

"Which is the most effective way to prevent Hmong youth from joining gangs?" (Wood, 1998, p. 3)

Related COPES Prevention Question

Among Hmong and Asians less than 16 years old, which gang prevention program will most effectively prevent them from joining the gang?

Box 3.6	**A Protective Service Worker's Concern for Risk of Reabuse in the Child's Home**

Practice Situation

This question was motivated by the mission statement in the handbook of a county department of human services. That mission states: "The Department is guided by the following beliefs and principles: The well-being of the family and individuals enhances the well-being of the community. The family is the cornerstone of the community. Children are best protected and nurtured when families are strong" (Eau Claire County Department of Human Services, n.d.). The protective service worker who cited this statement worked as a protective service worker who served children who had been abused and their families. The worker felt torn in two directions. On the first, some children who had been abused/neglected had to be removed from their homes and placed in foster homes for a while to prevent further abuse and neglect; but, on the second,

after working with the families when the risks were judged acceptable, the children needed to be reunited with their families as soon as possible to allow them to live and grow with their natural family. So the question becomes, When are the family's problems sufficiently resolved and understood to risk reuniting them? This is a tough decision. If you are too conservative, children are unnecessarily kept from living with their families. If you are too liberal, children will be placed in their homes and abused or neglected again.

General Risk/Prognosis Question

"Is there an easy way to administer a quick, reliable risk scale with high positive predictive validity to determine if children should be returned to their natural homes from foster care?" (Troy, 2000, p. 5)

Related COPES Risk/Prognosis Question

For abused or neglected children placed in foster care by a protective service worker, which risk-assessment measure will provide the greatest predictive accuracy to predict reabuse when children are placed back into their homes with their families?

Box 3.7	**A Community Support Worker's Question Regarding Risk for Suicide**

Practice Situation

This question arose out of a tragedy. It comes from a staff member in a community support program (CSP) that serves persons with mental illness. The CSP workers make every effort to help persons with mental illness to live independently or in group homes where they have various levels of personal freedom. The CSP workers work intensively with their clients. They visit some daily. They assist their clients with living skills as teachers and with employment skills; they help them to locate jobs with the help of local supportive employment agencies, and they monitor their clients' behaviors for possible

drug side effects and behaviors that might harm others or themselves. Tragically, a CSP client jumped from a local building to his death. The young man had recently been diagnosed with schizophrenia and had joined the CSP caseload. Workers at the CSP were deeply affected by the tragedy, and one posed the following question related to the predictive accuracy of a measure used by the CSP workers.

General Risk/Prognosis Question

"How effective is the Brief Psychiatric Rating Scale at assessing suicide risk in the chronically mentally ill?" (Zenz, 1999, p. 2)

Related COPES Risk/Prognosis Question

Among persons with chronical mental illness, is the Brief Psychiatric Rating Scale compared to other suicide-prediction instruments as accurate at predicting actual suicide or suicidal behaviors?

| Box 3.8 | **A Protective Service Worker's Question About Shaken Baby Syndrome** |

Practice Situation

This question followed a protective service worker's visit to the hospital to remove an infant from the custody of its parents. The child had almost died in the hospital from its injuries. The infant had been shaken by its father so severely that a CAT scan revealed major brain damage including that from multiple strokes and resultant paralysis on the left side of the infant's body. The protective service worker wondered (through her tears) how accurately shaken

babies can be identified by specific behavioral or physiological signs to give a reliable and valid assessment. The worker was particularly concerned that shaken babies not go unnoticed and that they be identified early, before the child might be injured by another shaking.

Related General Assessment Question

"What is the most valid, reliable assessment tool for diagnosing shaken baby syndrome?" (Stamm, 2000)

Related COPES Assessment Question

To detect children with shaken baby syndrome, which assessment or diagnostic procedure will provide the most valid and reliable determination that the child has been injured by shaking?

| Box 3.9 | **A Hospital Social Worker's Question Regarding How to Screen for Dementia** |

Practice Situation

One of the principal duties of hospital social workers involves discharge planning for persons with physical and mental impairments who will need various forms of continued care, including nursing home placement. This question arose in response to a hospital social worker's experience with a client who was discharged from the hospital to her home. The hospital social worker noted that the client appeared preoccupied and confused before her discharge, but the doctor discharged the client without investigating the patient's confusion. The client returned to the hospital emergency room a few days

later due to an injury sustained in a fight with a family member over whether the client should go to the dentist. The hospital social worker became interested in a way to screen clients to determine whether the client has dementia so that this evidence might assist the medical team in its discharge decisions.

Related General Assessment Question

"What is the most valid, reliable, and rapid assessment measure for determining level of orientation for hospital/nursing home patients?" (Bloomfield, 1999)

Related COPES Assessment Question

For hospitalized aged persons suspected of having dementia, which rapid assessment measure will most quickly, reliably, and validly identify patients with dementia?

Description Questions: Definition by General Concept and Two Examples   *Description questions* (Box 3.10 and Box 3.11) most often concern surveys of client needs or client satisfaction but can include any kind of effort that involves observations of clients within a sample and generalizations made from that sample. Description questions can include qualitative studies that seek an in-depth understanding for client experiences and perceptions.

Box 3.10	**A Youth Worker's Question Regarding the Age When Racial Identity Takes Place**

Practice Situation
This question comes from someone who counseled children in a home for children near Durbin, South Africa. The counselor noted that great changes in South African society have been reflected in events in the children's home. Less than a decade ago, South Africans abolished Apartheid by democratic means and the Nationalist Party that had enforced racial segregation and repressive policies toward blacks lost its power. The African National Congress replaced these policies with ones that gave greater freedom to blacks, including their right to services previously denied to them. These policies affected the residents of the children's home by integrating black children into the previously all-white children's home. What concerned the counselor were the ways black children seemed to demonstrate racial identity problems when integrated for several years into the children's home. Zulu children learned English and Afrikaans and could not speak with their Zulu relatives. Some of the

children complained at having to be with blacks; they made statements that they were "really white" and screamed and cried when taken home by black relatives. Such events prompted the counselor to wonder at what age racial identity takes place with the idea that, if this age could be known, then it might be possible to initiate action at this age to help the children to retain their black racial identity.

Related General Description Question
"At what age do children develop racial awareness?" (Weber, 1999, p. 5)*

Two Related Well-Built Description Questions
Among children in integrated children's homes or orphanages, at what age do they first begin to see themselves as being either of white or black race?

Among children of black and white races who live in children's homes or orphanages, comparing blacks in all-black institutions compared to blacks in integrated institutions, at what age do children first see themselves as being black?

*A possibly more important question might be an effectiveness question regarding the effects of programs designed to foster or to negate racial identity. Questions of value that underlie any COPES question have not yet been discussed here.

| Box 3.11 | **A Special Needs Adoption Worker's Question Regarding Adjustment of Children Placed with Homosexual Couples** |

Practice Situation

This question was posed by a worker who does studies for special needs adoptions at a state agency. Such adoptions concern hard-to-place children (e.g., children with Huntington's chorea or Down's syndrome, older children, children with behavioral problems, older minority children). These children require a careful match between the child and prospective parents to best meet the needs of the child and to make sure the parents will have the stamina and sensitivity to care for the child. The social worker's concern arose when a homosexual couple applied to the agency to adopt a child. Homosexual adoptions are illegal in some states, but not in the state that employed the worker. This was the first application

from a homosexual couple that the social worker's agency had ever encountered. The social worker wondered what types of interpersonal adjustment problems, if any, the child would encounter if placed in a homosexual home.

Related General Description Question

"What social problems do[es] a special needs child frequently encounter with his/her identity and self-esteem because of the child's openly homosexual adoptive parent(s)?" (Scheithauer, 1999, p. 3)*

Related Well-Built Description Question

Among children with special needs who are placed in homosexual homes or homosexual homes, will there be any differences in the frequency and type of personal adjustment problems for the children?

*This question implies a particular direction for an answer and is therefore not a COPES question. Truth seeking implies an open mindedness to all possible answers to the question. This "let truth fall where it may" approach to seeking the answers to questions is discussed in depth in the next chapter.

Lessons Learned from Practitioners' Questions

Incredible Diversity of Questions

All of the 84 well-built COPES questions in Table 3.2 came from human service practitioners (e.g., social workers, teachers, nurses, physicians, psychiatrists, counselors, clinical psychologists). Students in research methods classes collected these questions as part of their assignment. Their assignment required them to ask practitioners for an effectiveness question to form the basis for their research methods assignment. Please read the questions carefully. They are fascinating in their diversity, and they tell a lot about real problems that practitioners encounter in their life-affecting work. Perhaps someday you may want to go beyond this work, and you may want to do a representative survey of practitioners regarding which questions matter to them most. Such a survey could support a rational basis for setting research priorities in the future.

Practitioners Pose Vague Questions

Note also in Table 3.1 how each question includes all four elements of a well-built question whose four elements appear in order from left to right. Note how, as you read the questions, they state first the client type, then the course of action being considered, then, where appropriate, an alternate course of action, and finally the intended result. Table 3.2's 84 questions came from a pile of hundreds that have been collected over two decades. Not one question was well-built relative to 12 criteria for a specific research question (Gibbs, 1991, pp. 109–133). Apparently, practitioners do not know how to pose specific questions. At least those providing questions for this table have not. All of the original practitioners' questions in Table 3.1 had to be reworded to make them well-built COPES questions. Therefore, another worthwhile area for research concerns how best to teach practitioners to pose specific questions about their practice.

Questions Concern Effectiveness and Other Issues as Well

All of the questions in Table 3.2 are effectiveness questions because I limited my research methods students only to this type of question. Practitioners should be encouraged to ask questions of greatest importance to their clients; so limiting my research students to effectiveness questions only, though defensible for practical reasons, artificially limited the task for practitioners. When given wider choices, practitioners will ask other types of questions. Limited experience with an evidence-based-practice assignment over a 4-year period (taught by Donald Mowry, Richard Ryberg, and myself) has shown that effectiveness questions account for slightly over half of the questions posed by the fieldwork students in their EBP exercise. The rest come from the remaining four question types. The numbers and proportions for each type of question during a 3-year period are as follows:

Effectiveness ($N = 35$; 53%)

Prevention ($N = 4$; 6%)

Assessment ($N = 15$; 22%)

Description ($N = 5$; 8%)

Risk/prognosis ($N = 7$; 11%).

Though limited, these data imply that practitioners may, when given the choice, ask effectiveness questions for about half of their practice questions. Another area for research concerns the need for surveys to discover which question types concern practitioners most in different settings.

Questions Need to Be Posed as Questions of Fact

All of the questions in Table 3.2 are ones of fact. All COPES questions meet criteria for being questions of fact, because they can be answered by making observations through a process of testing or verification, a process that would most commonly be called *doing a study*. Questions of fact can be posed in *if/then* format. In contrast, questions of value assume some underlying belief about what is fair and worthwhile in the world. Usually, questions of value contain the word *should*, either stated or implied, within them. Questions of value generally cannot be answered through a process of verification or by test; for an answer, they rely on what is in your heart. Each of the questions in Table 3.2 were posed because a human service worker had answered affirmatively an underlying related question of value including these: "Is it worthwhile to seek the answer to this question?" "Yes!" "Should we find out the answer to this question?" "Yes!"

Not Drawing a Distinction Between a Question of Fact and a Question of Value Causes Confusion

Another related lesson here concerns the fact/value distinction. Confusing questions of value with questions of fact can lead to unnecessary and unproductive argument. One of the biggest problems in practice arises when questions of fact are confused with questions of value. For example, assume that you have a great deal of your efforts tied up in an anger-management program and you value the program immensely because it concerns a matter of importance to you. You are concerned about violence among young people. You believe that such violence must stop. You believe in your heart that the young should treat each other with respect and kindness and that they should learn to manage their anger. Assume further that another practitioner asks the following question of fact related to your anger-management program: "If delinquent adolescents in an inpatient facility receive anger-management group therapy as opposed to no such therapy, then will the former have lower anger (State Anger Scale) scores?" You may become incensed and hurt that someone would pose such a question about the effectiveness of a program that you hold dear. You may say, "Don't you care about the problem of violence among adolescents? How could you ask such a question?" Your response would then demonstrate confusing a question of value with a question of fact. The practitioner posing the question of fact regarding effectiveness may share your values entirely but still want to know if in fact the anger-management program achieves its objective. Questions of value determine which questions of fact you try to answer. Questions of fact seek an answer to a specific question through a process of guessing and testing. This book cannot tell you which questions of fact to pose. This lies in your heart and in your profession's value base.

Questions Need to Be Posed So They Do Not Imply an Answer

One more lesson about posing questions is that all questions need to be posed so that they do not imply what the answer is expected to be. Question wording should imply an objective search for an answer. For example, does this question imply an objective search for an answer?: "If hard-to-place children are adopted into homes of homosexual couples as opposed to heterosexual couples, then, among the former, how much lower will their interpersonal adjustment scores be?" Such a question implies that it must be lower. To be worth your effort, you need COPES questions that are well-built, that are posed as questions of fact, and that are fair and objectively worded.

Please examine Table 3.2. Hopefully, the questions will serve as a model for effectiveness questions. You may want to read only those pertaining to a particular practice area, but so many are included here to demonstrate the incredible diversity of important effectiveness questions that practitioners can ask.

Table 3.2	Some Sample Effectiveness Questions
Setting	Question

Mental Health	If delinquent adolescents in an inpatient facility receive anger management group therapy as opposed to no such therapy, then will the former have lower anger (State Anger Scale scores)?
	If adolescent males who have physically assaulted women get S.T.O.P treatment as opposed to other treatments for the problem, then will the former have more positive attitudes toward women?
	If adolescents in a home for delinquent youths receive a token economy treatment or another treatment, then will the former have fewer aggressive, acting out behaviors?
	For an adult with Lesch-Nyhan syndrome living in a group home, which behavioral-management treatment program will result in more appropriate social behaviors?
	If emotionally disturbed adolescents in an inpatient facility who act out are given a time out or are given counseling immediately after their acting out, will there be a difference in future incidents of acting out favoring the former?
	If women with bipolar affective disorder who live in a group home are given weekly psychoeducation or not, then will those getting the education have more effective strategies for coping with their symptoms?
	If adult depressed outpatients are classified and matched with their drug treatment or are given drug treatment without matching, then will those matched have lower depression scores?
	If persons who have lost a spouse to death get individual counseling or attend a grief support group, will there be any difference in their depression and anxiety?
	If women at a refuge house for abused women participate in an abuse-education support group, will they experience higher self-esteem than if they do not participate?
	If depressed college students receive cognitive behavior therapy plus antidepressant medication or receive cognitive behavior therapy only, will the former have better academic achievement?
	If primary care givers for hospice clients get early supportive counseling or counseling after the caregiver's loved one dies, then will there be any difference in the care giver's coping skills?
	If couples planning to be married participate in a preparation for marriage training program or do not, then will the former report a higher marital satisfaction after marriage?
	If caregivers (loved ones) of those who have died of Aquired Immune Deficiency Syndrome participate in a grief support group or do not, then will the former have a higher index of grief resolution?

continued

Table 3.2 | Continued

Setting	Question
Mental Health (cont.)	Will an aged woman with Alzheimer's disease whose Haldol dosage is decreased, versus not decreased, then will she experience less confusion in the former?
	If chronic alcoholics treated as outpatients receive disulfiram or a placebo, then will the disulfiram group have less alcohol use?
	If criminal offender alcoholics are treated with alpha beta brain wave training, or with some other method, will the former have a higher rate of abstinence?
	If anorexia or bulimia clients participate in two forms of family therapy, which approach to family therapy will have the greatest effect on the eating disorder severity?
	If adolescents in a home for delinquent youths who have conduct disorders are exposed to an errors-in-thinking program or to a corrective-thinking program, then will the former have more positive attitudes and behaviors toward authority figures?
Health	If pregnant women in an unstable relationship get intensive social casework services, or do not get such services, will the former get better prenatal care for their babies?
	If adult clients in a group home who have epilepsy receive a vagus-nerve stimulator treatment plus antiepileptic drug or antiepileptic drug only, then will the former have less severe seizures?
	If women who receive a facelift plastic surgery operation and receive arnica or a placebo, will the former have faster wound healing?
	If pregnant women smokers participate in the Smokeless program, or an alternate form of smoking cessation program, which will have the least in smoking behavior?
	If outpatient women get breast cancer awareness education or not, will the former get more breast examinations?
	If residents of rural counties are exposed to advertisement for a mobile human immunodeficiency virus (HIV) unit's availability or not, then will there be a higher rate of HIV testing where the unit is advertised?
	If ear-nose-throat surgery inpatients get verbal instructions plus "teaching sheets" or just verbal instructions, then will the former experience fewer complications postsurgery?
	If breast cancer patients with the same breast cancer tumors get lumpectomy and chemotherapy or radical mastectomy, then will the former have a lower sickness-impact score?
	Among mothers with uncomplicated vaginal births, if some are discharged from the hospital within 24 hours and others are discharged after 24 to 48 hours, then will the latter have significantly higher infant health scale scores?

Table 3.2	Continued
Setting	Question

Health (cont.)	Among aged persons living in the community who have problems with independent living, if they receive Meals-on-Wheels nutrition brought to their door, or do not, will the former have greater physical health?
	For clients who have surgery for a myocardial infarction (heart attack) and receive their patient education about how to best participate in their treatment after discharge, or before discharge, will the former cooperate most fully in their rehabilitation?
Child Welfare	If families with delinquent children are treated in-home or are treated in the human services office, will the former have a greater reduction in delinquent, acting-out behavior?
	If children of mothers in a shelter home for abused women receive play therapy or nothing, then will the former have higher self-esteem?
	If unmarried adolescent mothers of small children are given parenting training or no parenting training, then will the former demonstrate better parenting skills?
	If parents of high-risk behavioral problem gradeschool children receive parenting skills training or no training, then will the former demonstrate better parenting skills?
	If communities are exposed to foster parent recruitment advertisements or not, then will those communities so exposed have more volunteer foster parents?
	If Hmong children participate in a building-bridges, peer-mentoring program or do not participate, then will the former have higher academic achievement and less social anxiety?
	If parents who have abused their children attend a parent-effectiveness-training program or a stress-reduction program, which will have a lower rate of re-abuse and a lesser re-abuse severity?
	For infants placed in homes for adoption, if some adoptions are open (biological parent knows identity of adopting parent) and some are closed (records sealed at least until child age 21), then will the latter experience fewer adolescent adjustment problems?
	If divorcing parents participate in a mediation group or do not, will those participating have a greater parenting issues awareness?
	If gradeschool children with behavioral problems participate in a school social skills training group or not, then will the former demonstrate better social skills in the classroom?
	If disadvantaged poor children with school behavioral problems in urban areas participate in a wilderness training program, or do not, then will the former have higher academic achievement?

continued

Table 3.2 | Continued

Setting	Question
Child Welfare (cont.)	If children in day care are served by a stable staff, or are served by staff with a high turnover rate, will the children in the former have a lower rate of behavioral problems?
	In investigations for child sex abuse, if investigators use techniques designed not to lead the child or use techniques that are not so designed, then will the former yield more accurate reports of what really happened?
	For victims of child sex abuse, which method of therapy will most effectively help the child to have healthy interpersonal relationships?
	For families with incest within the nuclear family, which method of treatment will most effectively prevent repeated incest where the child remains in the family?
Geriatrics	For aged persons who have problems living independently in the community, if they receive in-home respite care services or do not, will those so served be able to live longer within the community with a higher life satisfaction?
	If aged persons who live in a nursing home are exposed to a restraint-reduction program or are not so exposed, then will their rate and seriousness of injuries increase in the former group?
	For residents of a sheltered living home for aged persons who are medically able to participate in an exercise program, if some participate in a regular exercise program, and some do not, then will the participants report a better quality of life and generalized contentment?
	If aged residents of a nursing home with Alzheimer's disease are exposed to reality orientation therapy or to medication, will there be any difference in their level of orientation to time, place, and person?
	If aged persons without dementia just being admitted to a nursing home participate in a new admissions support group, then will they experience lower depression than those not participating in such a group?
	If aged residents of a nursing home who have dementia receive haloperidol or do not, then will the former's level of confusion be lower?
	If a floor on a nursing home with aged demented residents who wander has cloth panels placed over doorknobs, or does not, then will the residents' wandering in the former be lower?
	If aged residents of a nursing home with Alzheimer's disease are placed on a specialized Alzheimer's unit or are placed with other patients, then will the former show a higher social behavior rating score and better orientation to time, place, and person?
	If institutionalized elderly persons with pain receive Therapeutic Touch or a placebo, then will the former have lower reported pain?
	If aged residents of a nursing home who are not demented experience regular contact with a pet therapy dog or do not, then will the former report a higher client satisfaction?

Table 3.2	Continued
Setting	Question

Geriatrics (cont.)	For aged residents of a nursing home who experience seasonal affective disorder, if they receive ultraviolet light therapy or do not, will those getting the light therapy experience fewer symptoms of depression?
	If aged residents of a nursing home are exposed to aromatherapy or are not, then will those exposed report a score lower on a dissociative experiences scale (less confusion).
	If aged Alzheimer's residents of a nursing home receive tacrine or do not, will those treated report a better mental status on a mental status exam?
Education	If junior high school students are exposed to a violence-prevention program or not, then will the former demonstrate fewer violent behaviors?
	If behaviorally at-risk elementary schoolchildren participate in a peer counseling program or do not, then will the former have fewer incidents of violent acting-out behavior?
	If high-school students who have been identified as alcohol problem drinkers are matched with a peer mentor or not so matched, then will the matched group have higher academic performance?
	If high-school students with behavioral problems are given home schooling or are placed in an intensive in-school program, will the latter have higher academic performance?
	If parents of children in grades 1-3 whose children have had behavioral problems in the school participate in a parent effectiveness training, or do not, will the former have fewer behavioral problems in the school?
	If at-risk for pregnancy middle school children attend a drama pregnancy prevention class or not, then will there be a lower pregnancy rate in the former?
	If high school children with emotional problems participate in a peer support group, or do not, then will the participants have higher academic performance?
	If Hmong grade school children who have reading and language difficulties are paired with a peer mentor, or are not so paired, then will those paired have better English language test scores?
	If grade school children participate in charter schools or public schools, then will the latter have higher academic achievement scores?
	If grade school children participate in charter schools or public schools, then will the former have a lower understanding of democratic institutions and citizenship?
	If Hmong grade school students with English language difficulties get traditional bilingual education or get a total immersion bilingual program, will the latter's English vocabulary and reading scores be greater?
	If fifth graders with autism are educated in special classrooms for autistic children or are mainstreamed into regular education classrooms, then will the latter have a higher academic performance on standardized achievement tests?

continued

Table 3.2 | Continued

Setting	Question
Schools (cont.)	If Hmong children participate in an after school 4-H program or do not, then will participants have higher self-esteem?
	If parents of children with attention deficit hyperactivity disorder (ADHD) participate in a specialized parenting training program in the school, then will their children demonstrate lower behavior intervention rates in the classroom than children of parents not participating?
	If girls with behavioral problems at an elementary school are paired with a female teacher or with a male teacher, will those in the former group have fewer behavioral problems?
	If children in preschool and elementary schools are exposed to good-touch, bad-touch training or not, then will those so exposed demonstrate more abuse avoidance behaviors later?
Homeless Families	If homeless families are served continuously in the same shelter or are served by shelters in multiple locations, then will the former have lower stress levels?
	If homeless families participate in a problem-solving training and support group, or don't, then will the former have greater economic independence?
Professional Training	If students in helping professions training programs participate in didactic lecture training or in experience-based training to foster greater racial tolerance, will the latter have more positive attitudes toward diversity?
	If health care professionals participate in a stress management program, or do not, then will the participants have a higher index of general health?
	If female university students participate in an HIV/AIDS prevention program in an all female program, or in a mixed sex program, will the former report a greater intent to use condoms in their sexual contacts?
	If members of a hospital ward's multidisciplinary team participate in a team building program or not, then will the former experience higher team performance and team cohesion?
	For professional social work practitioners employed in human service agencies, which method of professional training will result in their greatest use of research to guide their every day decision making and ability to evaluate research results?
	If multidisciplinary teams serving preschool children undergo team building training or no such training, then will the former demonstrate more effective problem solving skills?
Corrections	If adult prison inmates are moved to a high population density prison or to a low population density prison, will there be a difference in the rate of violent behavior?
	If juvenile delinquents are exposed to a prison visit with hardened prisoners (juvenile awareness program) or not so exposed, then will the former have fewer and less severe delinquent behaviors?

Table 3.2	Continued
Setting	Question
Corrections (cont.)	If male sex offenders who have assaulted women participate in a behavioral treatment program involving aversive procedures, or do not, then will their penile plethysmography (sexual arousal) be lower if treated?.
	If males who have battered their wives or partners participate in a conflict-resolution-skills program or do not, then will their assault behavior be less frequent and less severe if treated?
Developmental Disability	If residents of a home for the developmentally disabled who have self-injurious behaviors participate in an intensive operant-conditioning treatment group or the standard treatment group, will the former have a lower rate of self-injurious behaviors?

Question Construction and Educational Policy and Accreditation Standards Regarding Diversity

The examples in Table 3.2 demonstrate that questions can reflect an interest in helping others specific to diverse groups (e.g., same-gender couples wanting to adopt, babies at risk for shaken baby syndrome, youths developing racial awareness, adolescent males who have physically assaulted women, abused women, and unmarried adolescent mothers). Ethical codes and accreditation standards across the helping professions stress the need to avoid discrimination and to serve disadvantaged groups. For example, the APA's *Ethical Principles of Psychologists and Code of Conduct* (2001) states:

> Unfair Discrimination. In their work-related activities, psychologists do not engage in unfair discrimination based on age, gender, race, ethnicity, culture, national origin, religion, sexual orientation, disability, socioeconomic status, or any basis proscribed by law.

The *Educational Policy and Accreditation Standards* of the Council on Social Work Education (2001) states:

> IV. Foundation Curriculum Content, B. Diversity: social work programs integrate content that promotes understanding, affirmation, and respect for people from diverse backgrounds. . . . Programs educate students to recognize diversity within and between groups that may influence assessment, planning, intervention, and research.

The International Council of Nurses' *Code of Ethics for Nurses* (2000) states:

Table 1 Elements of the Code: Nurses and People: In curriculum include references to human rights, equity, justice and solidarity as the basis for access to care.

The point here is simply that ethical concerns can lead to posing questions of particular value to serving disadvantaged groups. The evidence-based-practice process does not state which questions must be asked. That is up to each professional and to that professional's adherence to ethical principles; however, once the question is posed, the process implies a fair and honest look for disconfirming and confirming evidence and assessment of that evidence.

How Evidence-Based Practice Can Incorporate a Strengths Perspective

Do keep in mind the client's strengths while posing a COPES question. Champions of the strengths perspective advocate for an inventory of the client's assets and for these assets being emphasized in helping the client (Saleebey, 1992; Weick, Rapp, Sullivan, & Kisthardt, 1989). Keeping in mind the client's network of supporting relationships, religious beliefs, practical skills, loyalties, sense of determination, knowledge, and other personal qualities can sometimes determine which questions you ask and your chances of success.

A particularly poignant example comes to mind that demonstrates the strengths perspective. My father discovered that he has adenocarcinoma of the esophagus, a tumor at the base of his esophagus. Being evidence-based, he immediately searched MEDLINE and other databases regarding his prognosis and treatment. I searched also, and what we found was not particularly encouraging given the location, type of tumor, and its level of advancement. Dad was fortunate enough to encounter an evidence-based physician who asked him what his preference would be. (See Figure 1.2 for how EBP incorporates the client's preferences.) Dad's first thought had been to accept palliative care, because his first concern is for caring for my mother who is frail and who depends on him to do the housework, shopping, and driving. Dad asked his doctor, "What will keep me the strongest the longest so I can care for my wife?" Consequently, the COPES question became: For an 82-year-old man in with adenocarcinoma of the esophagus in good physical condition, would palliative care, surgery, or a combination of moderate chemotherapy and radiation result in the longest period of physical ability to do work? He and his doctor chose moderate chemotherapy and radiation. One of Dad's strengths is his determination to care for my mother. Understanding this strength helped his doctor to help him to choose his treatment. Incidentally, Dad's underlying value question concerned his priority—to stay strongest the longest, not necessarily to live the longest.

Exercise 3-1 Classifying a Client-Oriented, Practical, Evidence-Search Question and Posing a Well-Built Question

Purpose

This exercise is designed to give you experience determining question types—so that in later chapters you will be able to search electronically for an answer more effectively relative to search terms that match your question type—we'll call these search terms MOLES—and so that you will be able to apply appropriate criteria to evaluate the evidence you find. This exercise is also designed to give you practice posing a COPES question.

Background

The six situations listed in this exercise are from real practice. Each situation is accompanied by a general question that concerned the practitioner at the time the situation arose.

Instructions

Please state the question type—effectiveness, prevention, assessment, description, or risk/prognosis—in the space provided. Then state a well-built COPES question that clarifies the general question. Be sure to include all four elements in your well-built question, and do so from left to right. This includes (a) the client type, (b) what course of action you might take, (c) an alternate course of action, (d) and the intended result. If in doubt, consult Table 3.1 and Table 3.2.

Situation 1: Patients' Satisfaction with Their Discharge from a Hospital's Telemetry/Medical/Oncology Unit

Sweeping policy changes affect how much hospitals can be reimbursed for their services. The advent of diagnostic related groupings (DRGs) and Medicare changes limit how long patients can remain in a hospital and what services they can get there. The hospital worker who posed this question shares concerns with other health care professionals about problems that arise when patients must be discharged hurriedly. Typically, the Telemetry/Medical/Oncology Unit serves cancer patients, including others that have respiratory, cardiac, and diabetic conditions. Many of the unit's patients are in their mid 70s to 90s and have physical and mental limitations. Discharges from the unit can be complex and stressful under such time pressure and can include an assortment of levels of continued care that involve plans for independent living with family assistance, visiting nursing (often with physical therapy), meal service to the home, and nursing home placement. The hospital staff was used to working on discharges under time pressure, but one case in particular raised a question about how satisfied the patients and their families must be with the whole discharge process. The patient was an elderly woman who died 6 hours after lengthy and complex arrangements had been made to discharge her to a nursing home. The staff and family knew the woman was dying. The social worker wondered what the family must think about the hospital's "discharge them sicker quicker" policy (Redig, 1998).

General Question   How satisfied are patients with the way they were discharged?

Question Type _____

Related, Well-Built COPES Question _____

_____

_____

Situation 2: A Crisis Situation Concerning a Mental Health Client

This situation arose out of a mental health counselor's concern that a 17-year-old male client might commit suicide. The client was admitted to the mental health ward of a hospital by a county sheriff. The officer explained that the client had followed a young woman on the highway flashing his lights and yelling at her to stop her vehicle. The officer pulled both over to the roadside for questioning. The young woman said that her boyfriend in the other car had held a gun to his head and said, "I have no reason to live anymore." The social worker who did the admission discovered that the client was despondent over breaking up with his girlfriend. She had started college and had told him that she ". . . . wanted more space." The client demanded his ring back and other things he had given her. He then pointed the gun at himself and followed her when she fled in her car. This case led the counselor to wonder if he could find guidelines to evaluate the probability that such clients would commit suicide (Du Bois, 1998).

General Question   How can I better evaluate suicide potential?

Question Type _____

Related, Well-Built COPES Question _____

_____

_____

Situation 3: A Mental Health Interdisciplinary Team

Those in the helping professions need to coordinate effectively to save on scarce resources, to avoid duplicating effort, and to focus their efforts in concert toward helping clients. Effective interdisciplinary teams should serve these ends. One such team is on a behavioral health ward at a hospital in a medium-size community. The team is composed of social workers, psychiatrists, psychiatric nurses, and psychologists, as well as the client and the client's key family members. Team meetings involve these persons meeting around some critical issue. Typically, the team meets to discuss treatment on the unit including how to stabilize the client's medications, physical condition, and counseling needs. Unfortunately, costly hospital treatment time is short; so teams must spend a great effort around discharge from the hospital to implement a plan for care that will most benefit the client. A staff member involved in this team noticed problems with the team's communication, task completion, and cooperation. The team member wondered if a measure, or measures, existed that could be applied to rate the team's performance, a measure that the team's members might fill out themselves. The team member hoped that such a measure could help the team to determine its weaknesses and strengths so it could communicate about these areas to improve them (Svik, 1999).

General Question   Is there a good measure that could give us some feedback about how we are doing as a team?

Question Type   _____

Related, Well-Built COPES Question   _____

_____

_____

Situation 4: Potential for Violence in a School

A counselor who worked in a gradeschool (ages 4–11) and in a high school in the same rural community became concerned about the potential for violence within the schools. She observed children fighting on the playground or in the gym and also observed bullying behavior including pushing, tripping, name-calling, and hurtful teasing. The counselor says, "Students should feel safe at school" (Andres, 2000, p. 2). Others recognized the potential for serious violence and turned to the Second Step Violence Prevention Curriculum for use in grades 1 through 3. The counselor wondered if evidence could be found about the program's ability to forestall violence.

General Question   Will the Second Step Violence Prevention Curriculum really prevent violence in later grades?

Question Type   _____

Related, Well-Built COPES Question   _____

_____

_____

Situation 5: Teen Living Skills Group

A child welfare worker at a county human service department became aware that several of her adolescent male and female clients seemed to face the same types of problems in their efforts to survive adolescence. All had been found to be physically abused and/or neglected. These clients faced choices about pregnancy, drug and alcohol use, how to react to physical abuse and neglect, and how to approach their schoolwork. The child welfare worker wondered if starting a group counseling or group treatment program would help these adolescents. The worker wondered if a most-ffective method was available for effective group counseling to teach teens living skills (Nehring, 1999).

General Question   What is the effectiveness of a support group for teenagers?

Question Type _____

Related, Well-Built COPES Question _____

_____

_____

Situation 6: Decision Making Regarding Discharge from a Nursing Home

During the past 20 years, a trend has been for those admitted to nursing homes to go back into the community to live entirely independently or somewhat independently. Placement back into the community involves a difficult decision. On the one hand, staff at the nursing home support the resident's wish to live independently; but, if the resident moves back into the community without sufficient strengths and resources, the community placement fails. For example, one 92 year-old resident of a nursing home was admitted to the nursing home after a long hospital stay. He was injured in an auto accident when he pulled out from a stop sign one foggy morning into the path of another automobile. His injuries required prolonged physical therapy before he could return home. At what point, given his mental status, extent of rehabilitation, and family support, would he have the best chance to remain in the community when placed back there? A social worker evaluating him recognized that a more fair and objective way may be available to assess the likelihood that such residents would be able to make it in the community after discharge (Schneider, 1999).

General Question   Is a way available to estimate the likelihood that a resident will fail in community placement?

Question Type _____

Related, Well-Built COPES Question _____

_____

_____

Exercise 3-2 Asking a Human Service Worker for a Client-Oriented, Practical, Evidence-Search Question

Purpose

This exercise assumes that you do not have access to your own clients. The exercise is designed to inspire your learning by posing a question regarding a real client question. This exercise is also designed to help you to gain experience discussing a real question regarding practice with a human service worker (e.g., psychologist, physician, social worker, teacher, nurse, physical therapist, counselor).

Background

This exercise assumes that you are not a practitioner, nor are you an intern in a human service agency, but you would still like to gain experience posing a well-built COPES question of real practical value. Doing this exercise can enrich any course, because a real question from practice carries with it the authority, urgency, and interest that only real life can bring. Well-built COPES questions can concern the topic of any course in the helping professions and can therefore serve as the first step in writing an evidence-based-practice paper for any course. This paper can end with a COPES question, or it may also include the next steps in EBP that are described in following chapters (searching for an answer electronically, evaluating the evidence that you find, and determining what to do in practice based on the best evidence). For 20 years, my students have called members of all the helping professions to solicit questions and to take their papers all the way through planning a study and suggesting action based on the best literature.

Be prepared for some difficulty in soliciting questions from others. Because learning how to pose questions regarding practice does not constitute a standard part of education for practice in any helping profession, doing this exercise presents a difficult though important challenge—if you never learn to pose specific questions, how could you ever hope to get a specific and useful answer?

Many practitioners have never seriously thought to pose specific questions about the effectiveness of their methods, nor seriously wondered if there might be a more accurate way to evaluate risk, nor wondered about the inter-rater agreement of persons doing independent assessments. My students report that some practitioners are struck dumb by the almost unworldly event of being asked to help pose a question. Be prepared to encounter a blank look (perhaps the blank stare of a walleyed pike) or a puzzled tone of voice when soliciting questions from practitioners. Sometimes practitioners assume that if they help you to pose a question, then they are committing themselves to doing a study and all the inconvenience and time that entails. It may help to reassure them that you are only planning a search for the current best evidence and may *plan, but not execute,* a study and that you will search the literature to see if it suggests a specific action.

Do prepare thoroughly before soliciting your questions from practitioners, regardless of their discipline. Review the concepts in this chapter so that you can clarify for others what a COPES question is, what the five question types may be, and which four elements of a question you need to state. Some practitioners "open the flood gates" when asked. They spew out many vague questions in rapid succession, mixing questions of value and questions of fact, all in a jumble; and, when asked for clarification, they insert still more questions and elements of questions. Such gushy cooperation can induce paralysis in a questioner's mind as effectively as can a walleyed look. To counter the open-flood-gate problem, try to focus on a single topic of importance; listen carefully and reflect feelings as questions of value come forward; try to solicit COPES questions that include all four elements of a well-built question.

Instructions

Please follow these steps:

1. Read chapter 3 carefully to fully understand (a) what constitutes a COPES question, (b) what marks each of the five types of questions, and (c) what you need to know to fill out all four elements in a COPES question.
2. Read the following letter carefully to understand fully what it asks. Ultimately, all you need are the details in the bottom boxes of the table at the end of the letter.
3. Decide whether you will call a human service worker to give an initial explanation for what you want and then send the letter or whether you may explain the letter's contents and simply fill in the boxes for your respondent.

Letter to a Human Service Worker to Solicit a Question

To:

From:

Re: (a) A request for a question of importance to you in your practice; (b) My promise to share my evidence-based practice paper with you regarding your question's answer

Date:

I would be most grateful if you can help me to start my evidence-based-practice (EBP) assignment by posing an important question from your practice. I promise that if you will help me to get started with a question, I will share a copy of my assignment with you that states a specific search question and results of a search for an answer to your question.

Evidence-based practice refers to the practitioner's integration of the current best evidence, practical experience, and the wishes of the client. Evidence-based-practice involves being able to pose a specific, well-built question, knowing how to electronically locate the current best evidence regarding the question weighing the evidence located, deciding what to do based on the evidence, and observing what happens. My EBP assignment will involve only your helping me initially to pose a clear question, nothing more from you.

I am looking for questions that can augment and extend what practitioners already do that might, if answered accurately, allow them to give better services to a wide number of clients. Questions may concern effectiveness of services, preventing problems, assessing risk, assessing clients and outcome, and determining need or satisfaction with services. I am looking for questions that have central importance for your clients—here the term *clients* refers to individuals, small groups of clients, and communities. A well-formulated client-oriented, practical, evidence-search (COPES) question meets the following general criteria (after Sackett et al., 1997):

- The question concerns a real problem of importance to your clients.
- The question concerns a problem that affects as large a number of clients as possible, so knowing the answer would likely affect many clients.
- The question concerns a problem that will likely arise again with other clients.
- The question is likely answerable by searching current best evidence in the literature.
- The question concerns something of practical significance that you can do something about.
- The question is posed specifically enough to guide an electronic search for its answer (my task).

The following table gets the essence of what I need. If you can decide on a type of question and can write its four elements in the bottom boxes, I will have my question. I may, with your permission, need to call you again to clarify your question. Otherwise, again, I promise to share my EBP assignment with you on its completion.

Five COPES Question Types and Four Corresponding Features of a Well-Built Question

	Four Elements in a Well-Formulated Question			
Five Question Types	Client Type and Problem	What You Might Do	Alternate Course of Action	What You Want to Accomplish
	How would I describe a group of clients of similar type. Be specific.	Apply a treatment; act to prevent a problem; measure to assess a problem; survey clients; screen clients to assess risk.	What is the main alternative other than in the box to the left, if any?	Outcome of treatment or prevention? Valid measure? Accurate risk estimation, prevented behavior, accurate estimation of need?

continued

Five COPES Question Types and Four Corresponding Features
of a Well-Built Question—Continued

	Four Elements In a Well-Formulated Question			
Five Question Types	Client Type and Problem	What You Might Do	Alternate Course of Action	What You Want to Accomplish
Sample Evaluation Question (Read across columns.)	If disoriented aged persons who reside in a nursing home	are given reality orientation therapy	or validation therapy,	which will result in better orientation to time, place, and person?
Sample Prevention Question (Read across columns.)	If sexually active high-school students at high risk for pregnancy	are exposed to *baby-think-it-over*	as opposed or to being exposed to lecture material on the proper use of birth control methods,	will they have fewer pregnancies during an academic year? Knowledge of birth control methods?
Sample Assessment Question (Read across columns.)	If aged residents of a nursing home who may be depressed or may have Alzheimer's disease or dementia	are administered depression screening tests	or short mental status examination tests,	which measure will be the briefest, most inexpensive, valid, and reliable screening test to discriminate between depression and dementia?
Sample Description Question (Read across columns.)	If family members of patients with stroke diagnosed with aphasia meet in a hospital support group	and receive a short client-satisfaction questionnaire of all support group participants,		which will the family members list as their area or areas of greatest and least satisfaction?
Sample Risk Question (Read across columns.)	If crisis line callers to a shelter for women who have been battered	are administered a risk-assessment scale by telephone	as opposed to practical judgment, unaided by a risk-assessment scale, being relied upon,	will the risk-assessment scale have higher reliability and predictive validity?
Determine your question type; then insert elements of your question into the spaces to the right. Be specific. Question Type:	Please fill in.	Please fill in.	Please fill in.	Please fill in.

Note. This table follows *Evidence-Based Medicine: How to Practice and Teach EBM*, by D. L. Sackett, W. S. Richardson, W. Rosenberg, & R. B. Haynes, 1997. New York: Churchill Livingstone. Adapted with permission.

Exercise 3-3 Posing a Well-Built, Client-Oriented, Practical, Evidence-Search Question from Your Own Practice

Purpose

This exercise assumes that you have access to your own clients. The exercise is designed to help you to construct your own COPES questions so that you can practice classifying them and formulating them.

Background

This exercise assumes that you are a practitioner in a helping profession, or you are in training in a human service agency, and you would like to gain experience posing a well-built COPES question. You may want to do this exercise only to practice posing COPES questions. You may want to go on and use your question to begin the next steps in evidence-based practice (searching for an answer; evaluating the evidence you find; taking action based on the evidence, if evidence warrants doing so; evaluating the result; and teaching others to do so).

Instructions

Please follow these steps:

1. Read the concepts in chapter 3 carefully, thinking of how you might apply them to posing your own COPES question. Think about which aspects of your work with clients have the greatest importance (e.g., concern that among your sex offender probation caseload that sex offenders will abuse another preschooler). Keep in mind the limitations of your time and resources. Knowing the answer to your COPES question should imply that you might take action differently in your practice regarding an important matter.
2. Fill in the information in the following table.

Elements for Asking Your Own Well-Built COPES Question

Background: How did your need for information arise? (Do include client perceptions.)

Describe your client(s) (distinguishing features including strengths and problem).

State generally what you would like to know.

State what you might do differently if you knew the answer. (If nothing, then do not search for an answer.)

What type of question are you posing?

    Effectiveness (effect of intervention) [ ]

    Prevention (forestall initial occurrence of problem) [ ]

    Assessment (evaluate client problem, strengths, outcome) [ ]

    Description (client's perception of needs, satisfaction [ ]

    Risk/prognosis (chance of undesirable event) [ ]

Course of action you are considering (e.g., try intervention or prevention program, measure, survey, evaluate risk)?

Your alternate course of action?

Your intended result (e.g., outcome, more accurate assessment, survey result, accurately predict behavior)?

Your well-built COPES question (include four elements see bottom line of table in Exercise 3.2)?

Note. This table follows *Evidence-Based Medicine: How to Practice and Teach EBM,* by D. L. Sackett, W. S. Richardson, W. Rosenberg, & R. B. Haynes, 1997, New York: Churchill Livingstone. Adopted with permission.

Exercise 3-4 Should This Question Be Asked?

Purpose

This exercise is designed to help you to apply the criteria for a COPES question to see if, in fact, the question meets all of its criteria.

Background

Members of a small evidence-based-practice seminar and I went to meet with two hospital social workers at their office on the hospital's neurosciences ward. The purpose of our meeting was to practice soliciting COPES questions from practitioners. The hospital social workers told the seminar that they had noted many head and spine injury cases involving teenage drivers in recent weeks. These cases were particularly tragic, because the teenagers were competent kids with every chance to live a long, full and productive life.

Instructions

The hospital social workers posed several questions, among them this question:

If high-school teenagers participate in a drunken driving prevention program as opposed to not doing so, will their participant's incidence of drunken driving arrests and serious injuries in traffic accidents be lower among participants?

Is this a COPES question? Does it meet *all* of the criteria for a COPES question? Why, or why not? Please write your conclusion and your reason here. (Hint: Review the criteria for making the question client oriented)

Yes [ ] No [ ] Why, or why not?

_____

_____

_____

_____

_____

There is a principle which is a bar against all information, which is proof against all arguments and which cannot fail to keep a man [or woman] in everlasting ignorance—that principle is contempt prior to investigation. **—Attributed to Herbert Spencer**

4 | Locate the Best External Evidence to Answer Your Question

"Don't bother me with the facts, my mind is made up."

Overview

By the end of this chapter, you should be able to follow steps for conducting an electronic search for the answer to your client-oriented, practical, evidence-search (COPES) question in an appropriate database. You should be able to locate these databases through the World Wide Web, through your local university library, through your agency's account with a database vendor, and through this book's own Web site: *Evidence-Based Practice for the Helping Professions.*

To accomplish these objectives, this chapter begins by discussing critical assumptions. The first concerns the spirit of searching for truth, let it fall where it may, for the good of the client over the professional's own personal and professional needs. This spirit implies absolutely that you one *searches for evidence and counter evidence with the same vigor.* Failing to do so can only produce an artfully concealed lie. This chapter also addresses essential equipment and database access issues. Then the chapter walks you through the steps for searching including the following: (a) beginning with a specific COPES question, (b) clarifying its key terms to guide the search, (c) selecting appropriate evidence quality filters called MOLES that will dig for you in any database, (d) planning a search strategy, and (e) and then executing that strategy. This chapter relies on specific examples and ends with exercises.

If you read this chapter and follow along at your computer by performing the electronic operations demonstrated, you will probably learn this material much more effectively than if you merely read along. A hands-on approach will help you to do the exercises at the end of the chapter.

Assumptions

You Have the Ability to Pose a COPES Question

This chapter assumes that you have read the previous chapter and that you can pose a client-oriented, practical, evidence-search (COPES) question. With your COPES background, you will be able to pose specific, answerable, well-built questions. You can ask factual questions that may be answered by evidence. You can also avoid asking questions that might not serve the client's best interests.

You Are Committed to Searching Fairly and Honestly for Disconfirming and Confirming Evidence

That the practitioner conducting a search does so fairly and honestly, looking for the best evidence, constitutes the second assumption for this chapter. This commitment means searching with equal diligence for evidence that refutes a favored view and evidence that supports it. The reason for a commitment to truth seeking should be evident in this chapter's banner quote. Indeed, this book is based on the assumption that the searcher values the client's welfare above the practitioner's own need for personal power, status, and income. *Always look first for that which disconfirms your beliefs; then look for that which supports them. Look with equal diligence for both. Doing so will make the difference between scientific honesty and artfully supported propaganda.*

Be prepared to pay a price for such intellectual honesty. Your commitment to truth seeking does not always win friends and arguments within a human service agency. Honest searchers must be willing to pay a price for their honesty, because they care more about their clients than they do about their own self-interests.

For example, a school nurse might have the impression that children with attention-deficit/hyperactivity disorder (AD/HD) will learn more effectively if they take medication for their disorder. The school nurse might have argued so with conviction in a school staff meeting. In other words, the school nurse argued that children who have a persistent pattern of unusually low attention and unusually high activity (AD/HD) will learn more effectively if they take stimulant medications that paradoxically will calm their behavior in the classroom (e.g., Ritalin, Adderall).

To document this point, the school nurse conducted a World Wide Web search. The nurse searched for the answer to the following COPES question: If gradeschool children with AD/HD take stimulant medication, as opposed to taking no medication, will those on stimulant medication learn academic skills more effectively over the course of their education? Assume that the school nurse, following procedures demonstrated in this chapter, located a systematic review of studies on the topic at this site: www.ahrq.gov.

The nurse then telephoned the authors for a copy of the review. This review was commissioned by the Agency for Health Care Policy and Research and was conducted at McMaster University's Evidence-Based Practice Center (*Treatment of Attention-Deficit/Hyperactivity Disorder*, 1999). The review lists the databases and search terms used to locate studies and sources searched. Those who did the review located 2405 citations that included 92 research reports and 78 studies that met criteria for inclusion in the review. This analysis listed strengths and weaknesses of the studies including small sample size and that 97% of the studies did not describe how subjects were randomly assigned. The review concluded: "The studies available provide little evidence for improvement in academic performance with stimulants, even though MPH [methylphenidate] treatment appears to produce consistent behavior improvement" (p. 5). The authors also state essentially that the studies are too flawed and varied to compute an index of treatment effect size to compare the impact of treatments. They say, "Comparison or synthesis across studies was limited by the low quality of reporting and by the large number and heterogeneity of outcome measures and tests used in the studies" (p. 5). "Larger studies with more rigorous design and longer term follow-up [sic] are needed to establish the effectiveness and adverse effects of most interventions in both children and adults" (p. 6).

What should the school nurse do? Assuming that the Search was thorough, this evidence contradicts what was said at the school staff meeting. Should the school nurse present evidence that refutes a position that the nurse had supported earlier? Of course! This book's Preface stated why—those in the helping professions will value the welfare of their clients above their own personal needs. The school nurse would present the evidence to the educational team, because the welfare of children depends on it. Well-informed decisions by colleagues, parents, and children depend on it. Also as a team member, the school nurse would be just as ethically bound to present *positive evidence* that supports the school's approach to teaching reading by the phonics method (Rayner, Foorman, Perfetti, Pesetsky & Seidenberg, 2002).

You Have the Necessary Equipment

This chapter also assumes that you have the necessary equipment. There are two ways to gain access to the Internet. *Direct access* means hard wired to a network, as is commonly the case in universities and government agencies. Access through this permanent connection will be provided by the institution, and the institution will generally provide training in how to use the equipment.

I hope that many reading this book will be individual practitioners in the helping professions who will want to get started searching through free electronic bibliographic databases and, possibly, through one or two database subscriptions. This section lists what these independents will need. Table 4.1 lists the items, characteristics, and expected costs for equipment necessary to get started as an individual or as a human service agency (such costs surely will change).

You Have Access to Electronic Bibliographic Databases

Finally, this chapter assumes that you have access to the necessary electronic bibliographic databases. Some of these databases are free; some definitely are not. Many sources on the Internet presently concern evidence-based practice in fields other than medicine, but more will become available with time. Databases will be described later. If you are curious now, you can take a quick look at this books EBP Web site, *Evidence-Based Practice for the Helping Professions* at: www.evidence.brookscole.com

The Brooks/Cole, Thomson Learning people maintain this Web site for our use and as their contribution to the helping professions. Consult Faerber (2000) for a listing and for descriptions of thousands of databases. Faerber's *Gale Directory of Databases* gets updated annually. Few listed in this volume concern EBP—thus, our book's Web site.

Steps in the Search Process

First, here are a few ideas to keep in mind regarding the search process. The essence of searching involves learning how to clarify terms in a well-built COPES question that will effectively mark documents in an electronic database. Once you have terms that clearly mark the topic, terms called MOLES (methodology-oriented locators for an evidence search) can be combined with the marker terms to quickly dig right down to the best evidence in the most appropriate databases. This whole process generally follows the steps listed in this chapter, and it can take just minutes. For some questions, you can find

Table 4.1 | Minimal Hardware Necessary to Conduct Electronic Searches

Item	Standard	Estimated Cost	Comments
Computer	Celeron System computer with 128 megabytes (MB) of random access memory (RAM), 20 gigabyte hard disk drive (GIG HDD)	Part of package	This allows graphics from Internet.
External monitor if computer not a portable	17-inch monitor with .28 dot per inch screen		
CD-ROM disk drive	8 X CD-ROM disk drive	Included in computer deal	
Modem	56,000 Kilobytes per second (KBps)	Included in computer deal	This will work for graphics available through the Internet.
Mouse	At least two click buttons	Included in computer deal	
Color Printer		Part of Package	
Total for Hardware		$600 buys all in preceding rows. (Wilson, T. Best Buy, Eau Claire December 21, 2001)	
Clean telephone lines	Low static, one-party line, call waiting disabled. Consult your Internet service provider (ISP) for minimal line standards	$305 per year including taxes (Myers, November 10, 2000)	Most telephone companies will check the line for you.
Internet service provider (ISP)		$240 per year	
Total for Internet and Telephone Access for One Year		$545 (Myers, November 10, 2000)	
Total for Software	Word Processing (e.g., Word) $150 and Antiviral program (e.g., Norton) $50	$200 (Wilson, T. Best Buy, Eau Claire December 21, 2001)	

Note. Based on items in *The Internet and Technology for the Human Services,* by H. J. Karger & J. Levine, 1999, New York: Longman, chapter 5.

your answer quickly enough to guide your practice. For example, one hospital social worker knew she would be seeing a client that afternoon that a doctor had listed in the record as having "thyroid storm." The social worker's search located information within a few minutes that described the client's condition. As with any new skill, it takes practice to search as quickly and as efficiently as she did. Also, keep in mind that even the most efficient searchers, who dig with mole-like power and determination, can still emerge with nothing to show for their efforts. A negative finding for a well-executed search reflects our state of knowledge, not the searcher's self-worth. A well-planned and executed search that finds nothing *is* a finding—it means we may not now know given the state of existing knowledge! In such cases, rely on your experience; be open with the client whatever the evidence.

Second, it may be impossible to complete each of the steps before going on to the next step, but the steps given generally follow one another. For example, the second step involves expanding the list of terms from your COPES question before planning a search strategy. Step 4 involves selecting the most appropriate databases. But these databases may have a thesaurus (list of synonyms that the database uses to identify a topic); so it may be most effective to look ahead to the appropriate databases (Step 4) to find effective search terms in the appropriate thesaurus for the database (Step 2).

Finally, the four steps that follow may make the most sense to you if you log onto your computer and actively follow the examples in this chapter. The INFOTRAC (College) database in this book's Web site will do to try the procedures, but the example immediately following was applied to the Social Work Abstracts (SWAB) database. You may not have access to SWAB because it costs money for a subscription.

Step 1: Formulate Your COPES Question

Rune Hellerslia works in child protective services (CPS) in a county human services department. He comes from Grimstad, a small village on the coast of Norway about four hours' drive south of Oslo. He has been shocked and saddened at cases of child abuse that he has encountered during his training. He and other CPS workers take turns answering intake calls to the agency. Intake work emotionally stresses CPS workers, because any call could require the worker to take immediate and decisive action to avert a crisis. Some calls present a serious situation that requires action. For example, a school official may call stating that a child has come to school with an injury and the child's explanation does not match the injury. A nurse at a local hospital may call stating that a 3-year-old child has a fracture and X ray has revealed previously healed injuries. These serious calls require immediate action. Some calls present routine low-risk problems. For example, a divorcing parent may call about a concern that the other parent may be allowing the child to watch the wrong kinds of television programs, may feed the child too much sugar, or may not be dressing the child warmly enough. Generally, intake workers get information from callers that relate to risk including the following indicators: who's in the home, drug or alcohol abuse, family support system, work history, prior abuse history, information regarding a history and severity of prior abuse, and the mental status and mood of the caller. If the intake call leads to an investigation, the CPS worker will go into these areas in more depth.

Rune's general question concerns the accuracy of such risk assessment. He says, "Another reason why I think it is worth answering my question is that I consider myself a caring person, who is concerned about the well-being of children. . . . To best serve the children of Eau Claire County, who are at risk of being abused, I want to make judgments and decisions about my clients as accurately as possible" (Hellerslia, 2000, p. 2). Rune wonders which factors are of greatest predictive value to indicate that a child will be abused later. He wants to make his risk evaluations more accurate. Rune's COPES question is as follows:

> If CPS intake workers administer a risk-assessment scale, or we rely on practical judgment, then will the risk-assessment scale have greater reliability and predictive validity? (Hellerslia, 2000, p. 3)

Step 2: Clarify Your COPES Question's Terms to Guide Your Electronic Search

If your COPES question has been formulated completely, it should list four elements of a well-built question from left to right as follows: client type and characteristics, course of action, alternate course of action, and intended result. These four elements from Rune's question appear across from left to right in Row 1 of Table 4.2. Note that for predict *, the * includes predicting, predict, predictive, predictable.

Client-oriented, practical, evidence-search terms may or may not work as markers in an electronic search, but they are a start. You may need to identify additional terms to more accurately mark documents for your search. You can identify these additional terms in several ways. One way involves thinking of synonyms from your experience and that of others (uncontrolled language or free text) that seem to mean the same thing. For example, in Rune's question, the client type and characteristics may be designated by these additional terms: abused children, child abuse, physically abused children, emotionally abused children, or child maltreatment. These and other terms have been added to Row 2 of Table 4.2.

Another way to identify terms to mark Rune's topic involves searching in a database's thesaurus for controlled language for like terms that identify the topic in the database. Doing so may reveal terms that one has not thought of. For example, MEDLINE has a thesaurus with its Medical Subject Headings that is called MeSH. You can get to MEDLINE for free and practice these steps at the following Web address: www.ncbi.nlm.nih.gov/entrez/query.fcgi, or you can get to it through this book's evidence-based practice Web site. A search for synonyms for the term *abuse* in the controlled language of MeSH appears in Figures 4.1, 4.2, and 4.3. This MeSH search netted two additional terms including *battered child syndrome* and *Munchausen syndrome by proxy*. These terms are part of the controlled language of MEDLINE; so they will work to identify documents well in that database; they may not work elsewhere. Terms located in this manner can also help to broaden your list of search terms that may work for any database.

Table 4.2 | Search Planning Worksheet

	Client Type and Characteristics	Course of Action	Alternate Course of Action	Intended Result	MOLES Relevant to Your Question Type
Row 1 Terms from Your COPES Question	CPS intake workers assessing risk	Risk-assessment scale	Practical judgment	Reliability of predictive validity for child abuse	
Row 2 Synonyms That You Can Imagine	Abused children, child abuse, physically abused children, emotionally abused children, child maltreatment			Greatest reliability, predictive validity, ease of use to predict abuse or reabuse	
Row 3 Controlled Language from a Thesaurus and MOLES (MOLES are further explained in Step 3.)	Child abuse Battered child syndrome Munchausen syndrome by proxy	Risk assessment Risk analysis Risk factors			Predictive validity, predictive value Receiver operat* ROC Sensitivit* Specificit* False positive* False negative* Predict* Prognosis*
Row 4 Terms Chosen and Combined in the Search (First combine terms with OR vertically in each column; then combine these sets with AND horizontally.)	Child abuse OR battered child syndrome	Risk assessment OR Risk analysis			Predictive validity OR positive predictive value OR receiver operating OR ROC

95

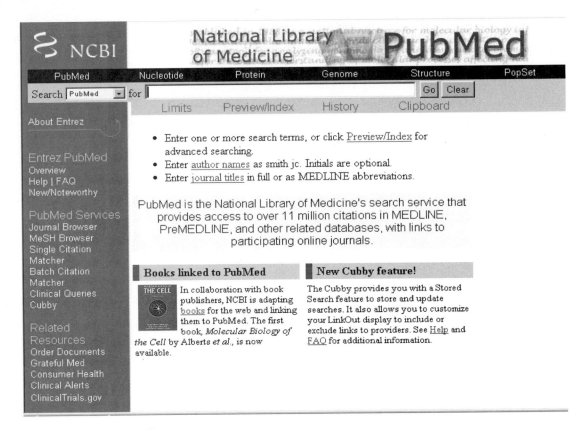

Figure 4.1

Select the term "MeSH Browser" from options on the left [assuming you are connected to PubMed as described here to follow along on your computer]. (All images from PubMed copyrighted in 2001, copied with permission.)

Figure 4.2

Enter the term "Abuse" and enter "Browse this term." (All images from PubMed copyrighted in 2001, copied with permission.)

Figure 4.3

Next, examine the
terms from
MEDLINE's MeSH
that also identify
child abuse.

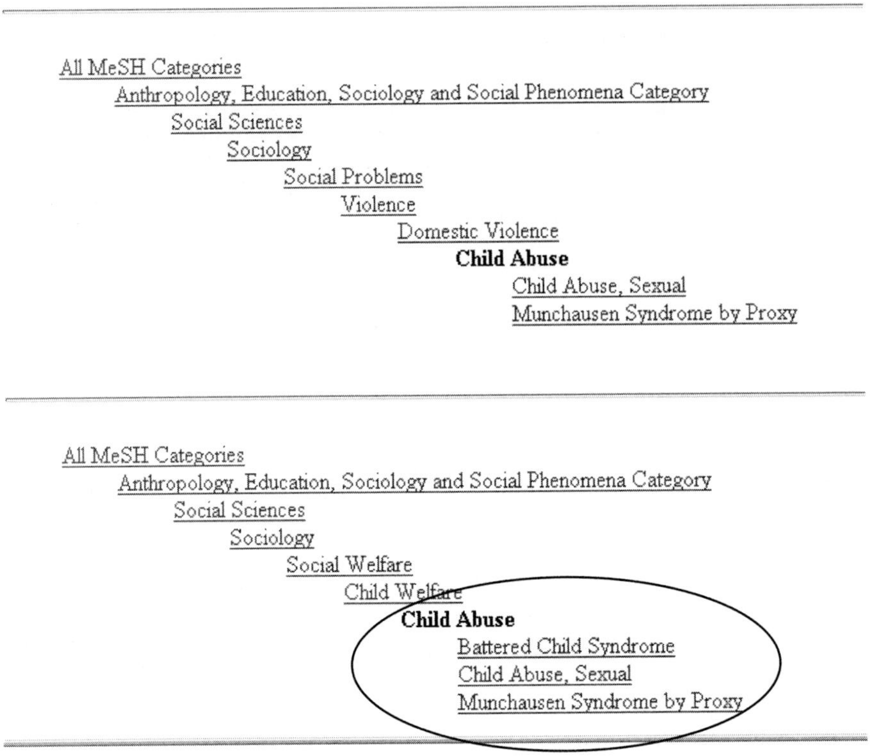

All MeSH Categories
    Anthropology, Education, Sociology and Social Phenomena Category
        Social Sciences
           Sociology
              Social Problems
                Violence
                  Domestic Violence
                    Child Abuse
                      Child Abuse, Sexual
                      Munchausen Syndrome by Proxy

All MeSH Categories
    Anthropology, Education, Sociology and Social Phenomena Category
        Social Sciences
           Sociology
               Social Welfare
                  Child Welfare
                  Child Abuse
                    Battered Child Syndrome
                    Child Abuse, Sexual
                    Munchausen Syndrome by Proxy

(All images from PubMed copyrighted in 2001, copied with permission.)

This same process was followed in the thesaurus for PsychINFO for *child abuse* and for the term *risk*. Terms for both thesauri are included in the first four columns of Row 3 in Table 4.2 marked "Controlled Language from a Thesaurus."

Figure 4.3 from PubMed has given you *Battered Child Syndrome; Child Abuse, Sexual;* and *Munchausen Syndrome by Proxy.* Still another way to identify useful search terms involves reading literature that clearly marks your topic. What terms appear in the text of that literature's text and abstracts? What terms appear repeatedly in such text? Place these additional marker terms across in Row 3 of Table 4.2.

Step 3: Select the Appropriate MOLES for Your Question Type

Rune's question is a risk/prognosis question. Therefore, the lowest far right box of Table 4.2 contains risk/prognosis terms called *MOLES.* MOLES are wonderful helpers! *Methodology-orienting locators for an evidence search* (MOLES) are terms that mark the best evidence for retrieval in *any* electronic

Mr. MOLE getting instructions

database. MOLES eliminate the need to rely on someone else to rank Web sites and databases for you. This is because MOLES will retrieve little or nothing from a database that contains weak evidence. MOLES provide a way to quickly sort through masses of weak information to get at the nuggets of useful evidence specific to each question type. The MOLES in Table 4.3 are arranged in descending order of their utility based on experience with them, though familiarity with the topic might require a different order. If you have no idea about which MOLES to apply, you might find it most useful to start with the MOLES at the top and to include others downward, because these terms have been arranged hierarchically downward according to their utility.

Table 4.3 lists MOLES specific to each of the five question types. MOLES have been found effective as a way to scan documents in any electronic bibliographic databases for concepts that describe better evidence. Elsewhere, MOLES have been called "terms to locate studies" (Gibbs, 1991, p. 175), or methodologic search filters (Haynes, Wilczynski, McKibbon, Walker & Sinclair, 1994, p. 448) or just "methodologic filters" (Sackett et al. 1997, p. 60). I favor the term *MOLES,* because real moles dig with wonderful efficiency through masses of material to locate choice bits.

Haynes and his coauthors (1994) demonstrated MOLES' effectiveness by going through ten journals for 1986 and 1991 to identify studies that concern the five question types. Once these studies were identified positively by laborious and slow hand methods so that these documents could serve as the "gold standard," Haynes and his team then applied their MOLES to electronic databases for the same journals for the same years to see how many of their "gold standard" studies were identified by the MOLES. Over all, the MOLES had a 93% sensitivity, meaning that they identified 93% of the studies that the hand search had identified (p. 447). This means that they missed 7% of the gold

Table 4.3 | Methodology-Orienting Locators for an Evidence Search (MOLES)

Effectiveness Questions	Prevention Questions	Risk/Prognosis Questions	Assessment Questions	Description Questions (with Qualitative Studies a Subset)	Syntheses of Studies (These work primarily with effectiveness and prevention questions but may work with others.)
random*	(random*	(risk assessment	(inter-rater	(random* select*	meta-anal*
OR	OR	OR	OR	OR	OR
controlled clinical trial*	controlled clinical trial*	predictive validity	inter-observer	survey	meta anal*
OR	OR	OR	OR	OR	OR
control group*	control group*	predictive value	true positive*	representative sample)	metaanal*
OR	OR	OR	OR	AND	OR
evaluation stud*	evaluation stud*	receiver operat*	specificity	(client satisfaction	systematic review*
OR	OR	OR	OR	OR	OR
study design	study design	ROC	false positive*	patient satisfaction	synthesis of studies
OR	OR	OR	OR	OR	OR
statistical* significan*	statistical* significan*	sensitivity	false negative*	needs assessment)	study synthesis
OR	OR	OR	sensitivtiy		
double-blind	double blind	specificity	OR	to retrieve qualitative studies:	
OR	OR	OR	predict*		
placebo	placebo)	false positive*	OR	qualitative stud* OR	
	AND	OR	receiver operat*	qualitative analys* OR	
	prevent*	false negative*	OR	content analys*	
		OR	ROC)	OR in depth	
		prognos*)	AND	interview* OR	
		AND	(assess*	in-depth	
		predict*	OR	interview* OR	
			diagnos*)	participant	
				observation OR	
				focus group *	

Note. The MOLES appear in rough descending order of their utility; so you might start with those at the top and, if you find few references, add more MOLEs downward with the OR command to enlarge the MOLES set. Also, some of the columns at their bottom include another set connected by the AND command. These additional terms generally mark the topic for their respective question type. MOLES reflect my search experience, ideas from Gibbs (1991), and ideas in *PDQ Evidence-Based Principles and Practice,* by A. McKibbon, A. Eady, and S. Marks, 1999, Hamilton, U.K.: B.C. Decker.

standard articles; so the reader would have to decide whether the laborious and time-consuming hand search would warrant the effort to find this additional 7%.

Step 4: Plan Your Search Strategy

Some general comments will help to understand what happens in Rune's search strategy. Any search will deal with several factors. First, an effective search strategy involves combining terms in Table 4.2 in a way that will net the best evidence quickly. Search efficiency first requires a judgment about which terms in Table 4.2 most clearly mark the major concepts. In any search, these major terms are combined according to principles of Boolean logic by relying on appropriate use of the terms OR, AND, and NOT. The searcher also needs to decide which fields in the document or record to search. The searcher can also shorten the search process by using truncation characters that will include all terms with the same root word (e.g., *abus** as a root will include abuser, abusing, abused, abusive). The following sections deal with each of these procedures regarding Rune's terms as stated in Table 4.2.

Selecting the Most Important Search Terms   Which terms are Rune's major ones? This involves a judgment based on familiarity with the topic. His judgments appear across the bottom row of Table 4.2. Working from left to right across the bottom row of Table 4.2, under the column *Client Type and Characteristics,* there are two major terms: child abuse OR battered child syndrome. The *Course of Action* column involves these terms: risk assessment OR risk analysis. The *Intended Result* column includes the following MOLES terms: predictive validity OR predictive value OR receiver operating curve OR ROC (i.e., receiver operating curve). Note that these terms are linked vertically within each column by OR. Under *Client Type,* the OR *widens the search* to include documents that include either child abuse OR battered child syndrome OR both. The same is true for risk assessment OR risk analysis and for the terms in the MOLES set. Generally, I construct a MOLES set first, then dip into it with topic-specific terms.

A Sample Search: How a Search Would Locate the SWAB Database Through a University Library and Would Search Rune's Major Terms   Each user will have different types of access to databases. Access to the earlier medical database was free through its Web address and through our book's Web site. Some will have access to electronic bibliographic databases through a university library. The following example demonstrates how such access would probably work at a university (see Figure 4.4 through Figure 4.17). Such access would probably begin with the university's home page as shown in Figure 4.4.

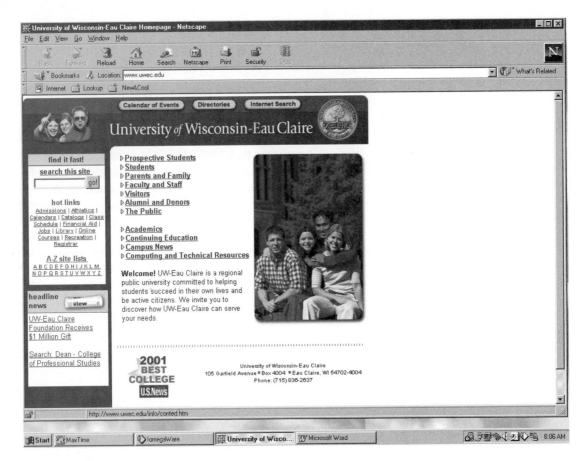

Figure 4.4

Access SWAB through a university home page, in this case by clicking the hot links button on the left marked "Library." Please follow along on your computer if you have access to SWAB. (All images from University of Wisconsin–Eau Claire library pages copyrighted in 2001, copied with permission.)

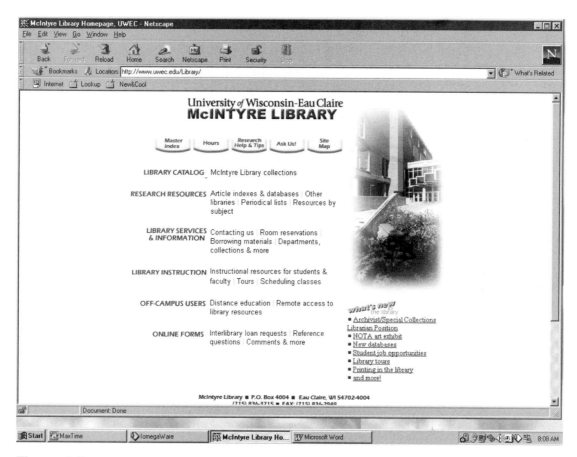

Figure 4.5

A university's library home page, which gives access to databases by clicking on the "Master Index" button at the upper left. (All images from University of Wisconsin–Eau Claire library pages copyrighted in 2001, copied with permission.)

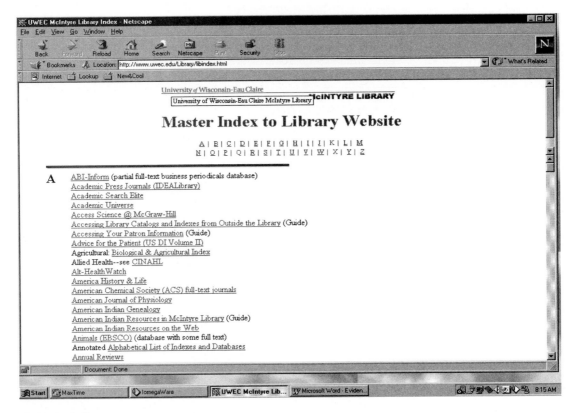

Figure 4.6

Selecting the SWAB database by clicking on the letter "S" in the alphabet. This particular university library lists its databases alphabetically from a master index. To locate the SWAB database, click on the letter "S" within the master index among the letters across the top. (All images from University of Wisconsin–Eau Claire Library Pages copyrighted in 2001, copied with permission.)

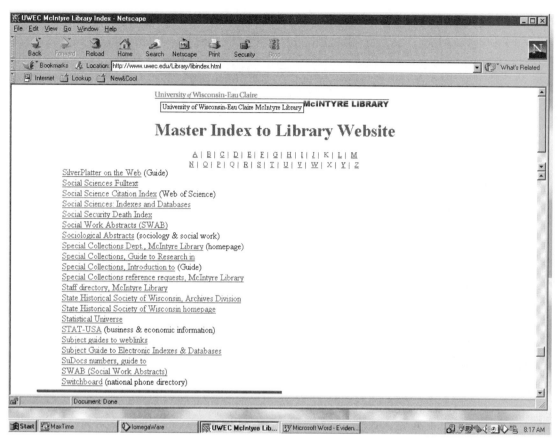

Figure 4.7

Selecting the SWAB database among documents starting in "S." (All images from Silver Platter copyrighted in 2001, copied with permission.)

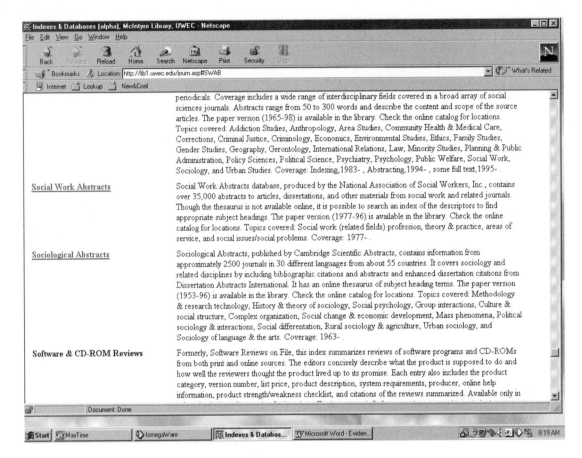

Figure 4.8

Description of the Social Work Abstracts: SWAB Database. The user clicks on the SWAB database to access it. The user then selects the SWAB database by clicking on "Social Work Abstracts." Once in the Social Work Abstracts, the user then searches for the term "predictive validity." (All images from Silver Platter copyrighted in 2001, copied with permission.)

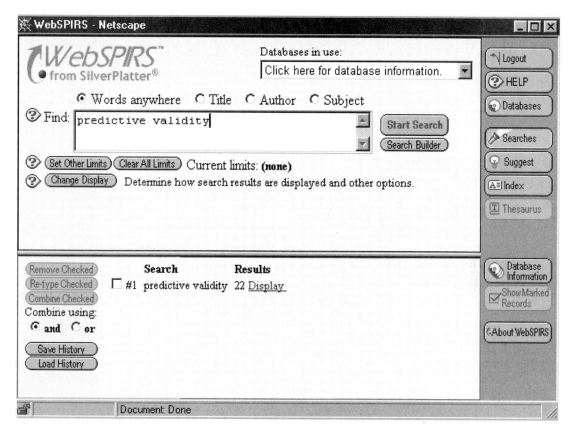

Figure 4.9

Searching for a single term in the SWAB Database. (There are 22 documents for the term "predictive validity" in the SWAB database.) (All images from Silver Platter copyrighted in 2001, copied with permission.)

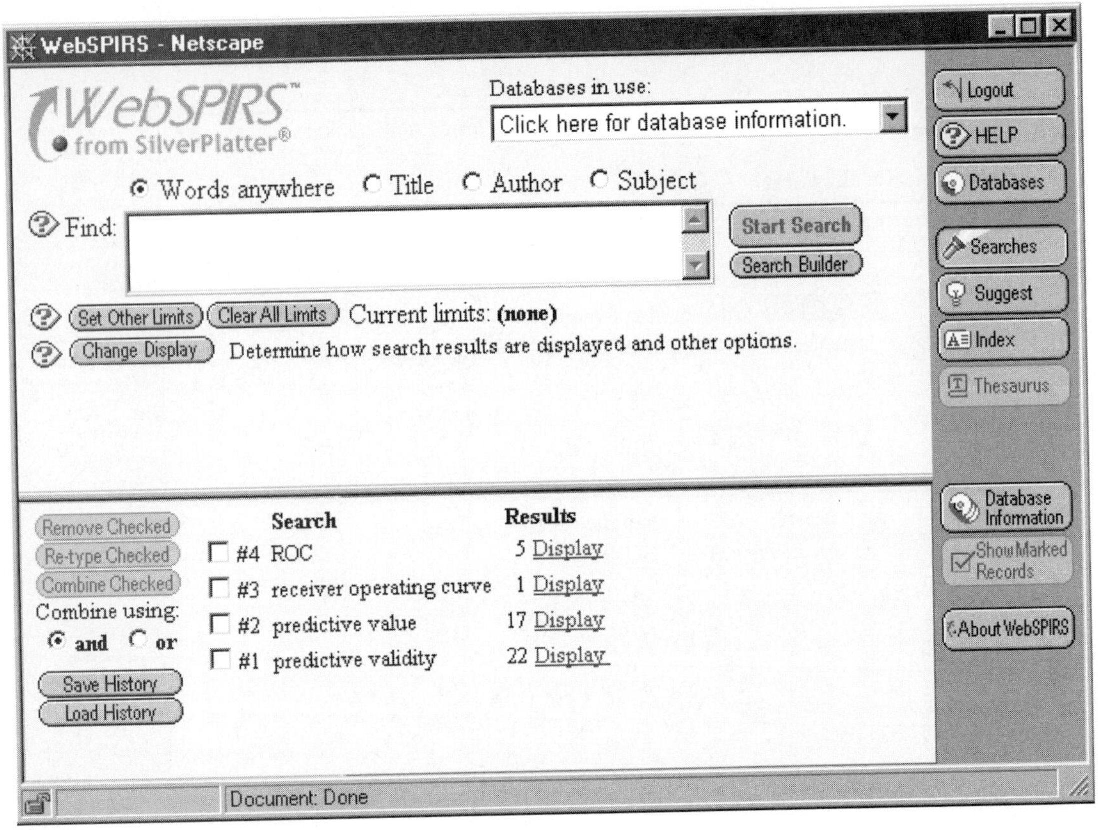

Figure 4.10

Number of documents for each of four MOLES terms. There are 22 hits for "predictive validity," 17 hits for "predictive value," one for "receiver operating curve," and five for "ROC." Here, Rune is constructing a set of MOLES terms that will include the best evidence. This set will be useful because he will then be able to dip into the MOLES set with terms that identify his particular risk question. (All images from Silver Platter copyrighted in 2001, copied with permission.)

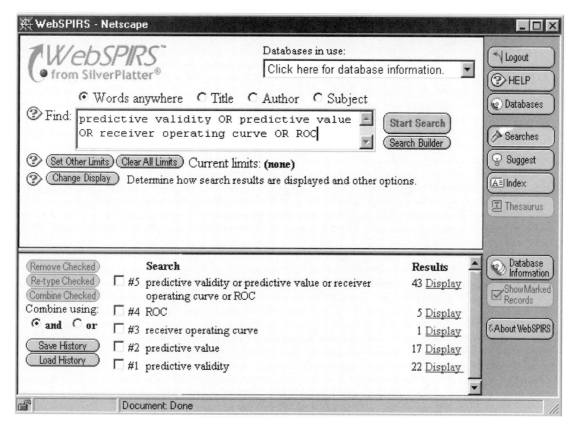

Figure 4.11

All four MOLES terms combined with OR. The MOLES including Set #1 OR Set #2 OR Set #3 OR Set #4 are combined into Set #5 with the OR command into a new set that contains 43 documents. Set #5 includes those documents that involve any one of these terms or documents that include more than one of these terms. Set #5 does not include the sum of the sets, because some documents contain more than one MOLES term. (All images from Silver Platter copyrighted in 2001, copied with permission.)

Number of Documents for Terms Combined Using OR

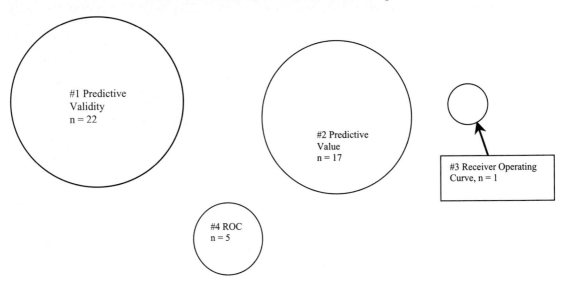

Number of Documents for Individual MOLES Terms

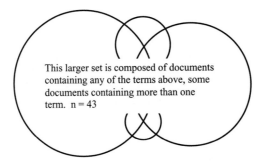

Figure 4.12

This diagram shows how the MOLES terms create a larger set when combined with OR.

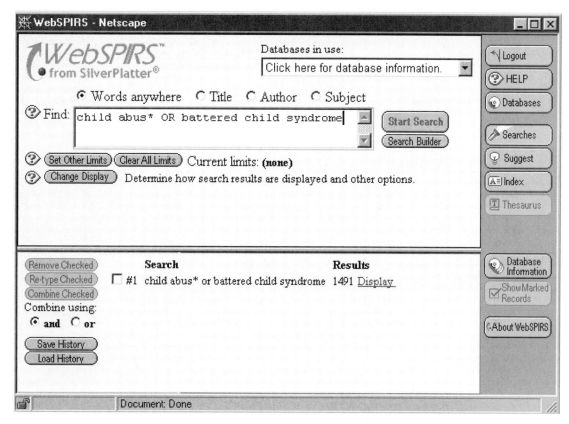

Figure 4.13

Child abuse terms combined with OR. This second set identifies Rune's topic. The set contains terms that concern child abuse OR battered child syndrome. It contains 1491 documents, far too many to view individually. Rune wants to construct another set regarding risk assessment that may help him to limit his search later. (All images from Silver Platter copyrighted in 2001, copied with permission.)

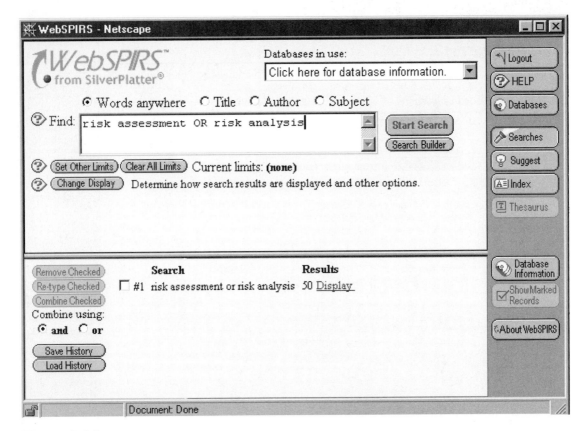

Figure 4.14

Risk-assessment terms combined with OR. This figure shows how an additional set contains 50 documents that concern risk assessment OR risk analysis. With these three sets (MOLES set, child abuse set, risk set), Rune will be able to limit his search to the intersect between the sets. (All images from Silver Platter copyrighted in 2001, copied with permission.)

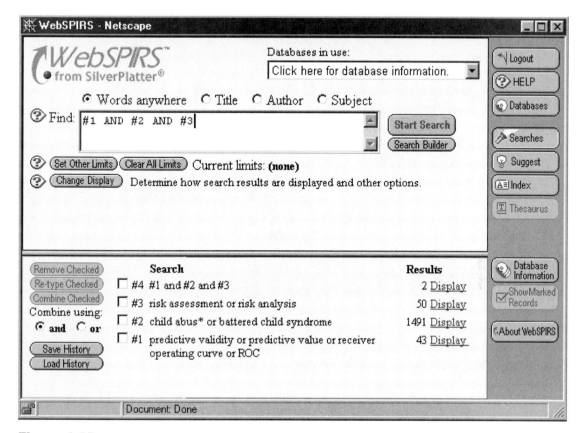

Figure 4.15

The AND command reduces the final set of documents to manageable size, just two documents. This final set, #4, consisting of sets joined by AND, contains only the *intersect* between the MOLES (Set #1) AND child abuse (Set #2) set AND risk assessment (Set #3). Thus, the AND command limits the search to a smaller number of documents that more finely represent the COPES question's subject. This intersect is shown graphically in the Venn diagram of Figure 4.16. (All images from Silver Platter copyrighted in 2001, copied with permission.)

Figure 4.16

Venn diagram
showing how AND
narrows the search.

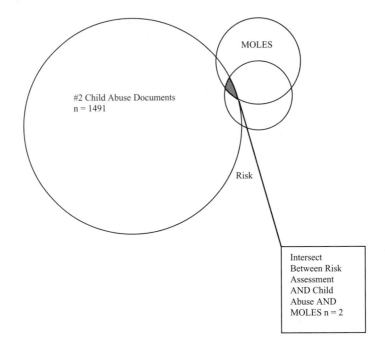

The two documents in Figure 4.17 are exactly on target with Rune's COPES question. The first one compares the predictive accuracy of the Washington and Illinois risk-assessment scales for estimating risk of child abuse. The second compares the inter-rater agreement of persons who independently rate child abuse risk. Rune got the original documents for these articles from the library to read their full text format. He also located an additional article that compared ten child abuse-risk assessment scales (Lyons, Doueck, & Wodarski, 1996). This review of risk-assessment scales was located, along with 15 other documents, at the intersect for the following terms:

(risk assessment OR risk analysis) AND (child abuse OR battered child syndrome)

Note that this mathematical expression's format, with terms connected by OR within parentheses, and parentheses connected by AND, will work in most databases. Several strings of parentheses can be connected in this way. Though this type of expression works fast, it denies the user an understanding of how elements in the expression come together, one by one. Consequently, if the expression finds no hits, the user does not know which terms were ineffective; so it is probably best to construct individual sets first before combining them.

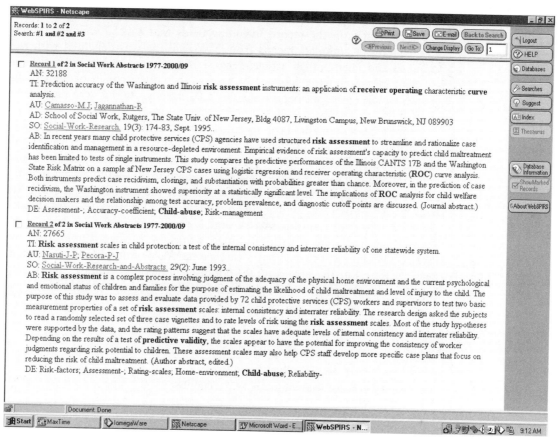

Figure 4.17

Text of two documents located at intersect between MOLES, child abuse terms, and risk-assessment terms. The search has narrowed to two documents that seem right on target regarding Rune's risk-assessment question. (All images from Social Work Abstracts copyrighted 2001, copied with permission from Freda Payne, Editor of *Social Work Abstracts*.)

When you retrieve golden evidence from a database, it is helpful to understand what is in the record including fields that can be searched. Figure 4.18 contains a complete record from SWAB. Rune was delighted with this Camasso and Jagannathan article, because it compared two popular risk-assessment measures. He telephoned Camasso to request copies of the risk-assessment scales for consideration at his CPS agency. At this writing, I don't know if he got a reply.

Rune's search might have specified which fields he wanted to search. Please note these fields in Figure 4.17. These fields are marked with the following symbols: AN—accession number, a number that identifies the record in the database; TI—title of the article; AU—author; AD—address for first author; SO—source for the publication, in this case the journal *Social Work Research*; AB—abstract giving an overview of the source; and finally DE—descriptors or terms that mark similar documents in the database.

If Rune had wanted to locate other works by Michael Camasso in the PsycINFO database, he could have searched the AU or Author field as shown in Figure 4.19. (Note the circle with the dot inside it next to "Author.") He would have found eight additional articles by that author, one about child abuse.

Figure 4.18

A closer look at components in record 1. Document number 1 was retrieved in Figure 4.17.

Record 1 of 2 in Social Work Abstracts 1977–2000/09
AN: 32188
TI: Prediction accuracy of the Washington and Illinois **risk assessment** instruments: an application of **receiver operating** characteristic **curve** analysis.
AU: Camasso-M.J. Jagannathan-R.
AD: School of Social Work, Rutgers, The State Univ. of New Jersey, Bldg 4087, Livingston Campus, New Brunswick, NJ 089903
SO: Social-Work-Research 19(3). 174–83, Sept. 1995.
AB: In recent years many child protective services (CPS) agencies have used structured **risk assessment** to streamline and rationalize case identification and management in a resource-depleted environment. Empirical evidence of risk assessment's capacity to predict child maltreatment has been limited to tests of single instruments. This study compares the predictive performance of the Illinois CANTS 17B and the Washington State Risk Matrix on a sample of New Jersey CPS cases using logistic regression and receiver operating characteristics (ROC) curve analysis. Both instruments predict case recidivism, closings, and substantiation with probabilities greater than chance. Moreover, in the prediction of case recidivism, the Washington instrument showed superiority at a statistically significant level. The implications of **ROC** analysis for child welfare decision makers and the relationship among test accuracy, problem prevalence, and diagnostic cut off points are discussed. (Journal abstract)
DE: Assessment; Accuracy-coefficient, **Child-abuse**, risk-management

(Copied with permission from Freda Payne, Editor of *Social Work Abstracts.*)

A Search Regarding an Assessment Question   This next search demonstrates an assessment question. It also demonstrates how to access the INFOTRAC (College) database through this book's evidence-based-practice Web site. But first, here is some background regarding the situation. Alyssa Perry works as a social worker at a 320-bed nursing home. Administrators at her facility are proud of how the facility places 70% of its residents back into the community. Alyssa works with a wide range of residents from their admission, through minimal care, all the way to the Alzheimer's unit. Alyssa had never seen an Alzheimer's client before she started working at the nursing home, and she told how moved she was to see clients who had deteriorated mentally.

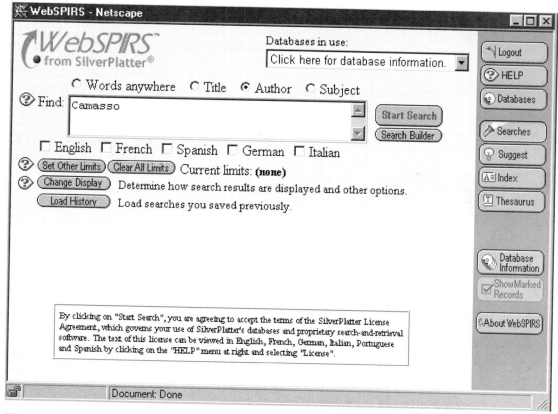

Figure 4.19

A search for Camasso in the Author field of the PsycINFO Database. (Note the • in the Author option.) (All images from Silver Platter copyrighted in 2001, copied with permission.)

Alyssa's concerns were particularly strong for family members who lost touch with their loved ones as their minds slipped away bit by bit. Consequently, Alyssa became concerned about a particular question while attending an Alzheimer's disease conference that included a session by Gail Pedersen titled: "Assessment Tools: Using the Clock Draw as a Dementia-Screening Tool." Alyssa was interested in the topic as it relates to decision making. Alyssa demonstrated her concern for better decision making in the following statement:

> A resident who is deemed incompetent due to the results of an assessment tool will most likely be assigned a guardian, or the individual's power of attorney for health care is activated. The resident's decision-making rights are taken away. If a measurement is not valid or reliable, then an individual's rights are taken away without just cause. (Perry, 2000, p. 2)

Other reasons for accurate and early identification of dementia concern the possibility that early treatment might slow dementia's progression or the client and family may benefit somehow by knowing of the problem early.

Here is Alyssa's COPES question:

> If nursing home residents at Lakeside Nursing and Rehabilitation in Chippewa Falls, Wisconsin, who are suspected of early Alzheimer's dementia, are administered the Clock-Drawing Test or a Mini-Mental State Exam, which measure will be the most reliable, valid, and most inexpensive, easy-to-administer screening test to determine early Alzheimer's dementia?

The bottom row of Alyssa's Search Planning Worksheet (Table 4.2) included search terms related to her assessment type of COPES question (Table 4.4). Though Alyssa's search included the MEDLINE, PsycINFO, Social Science Citation Index, and Science Citation Indexes, her search here will demonstrate how you could search her topic in this book's evidence-based-practice Web site and the INFOTRAC database (see Figure 4.20 through Figure 4.34).

Table 4.4   Bottom Row of Alyssa's Search Planning Sheet Regarding the Clock Draw Test

Client Type and Problem	What You Might Do	Alternate Course of Action	Intended Result	MOLES Appropriate to Assessment Question Type
Determine your question type, then insert elements of your question in spaces on right.	Alzheimer's OR dementia	Clock Draw* OR CLOX OR Clock Drawing Test	Mini-Mental State	Valid, reliable, fast, easy-to-administer screening test for dementia	(inter-rater OR inter-observer OR true positive OR sensitivity OR specificity OR false positive OR false negative

Figure 4.20

Logging onto the *Evidence-Based Practice for Social Workers and the Helping Professions* Web site. Log onto this book's EBP Web site at this address: www.evidence.brookscole.com. Note: Do follow along on your computer for best learning. (All images from University of Wisconsin–Eau Claire library pages copyrighted in 2001, copied with permission.)

Evidence-Based Practice for the Helping Professions

About EBP	COPES Questions	Plan a Search	Select a Database	Your Suggestions	References

About Evidence-Based Practice for the Helping Professions

The text contained in this website is copyrighted. It will appear in the following book:

Gibbs, L. (2002). *Evidence-Based Practice for the Helping Professions*. Brooks Cole Publishers.

Authors	Leonard Gibbs, Social Work Department, University of Wisconsin - Eau Claire; Eamon Armstrong, Family Medicine Clinic, Lehigh Community Hospital, Allentown, PA; & Josette Jones, School of Nursing, University of Wisconsin - Eau Claire

Figure 4.21

This book's Evidence-Based Practice Web site. The Web site will look different because of continuous revisions to keep it up-to-date and easy to use.

Evidence-Based Practice for the Helping Professions

| About EBP | COPES Questions | Plan a Search | Select a Database | Your Suggestions | References |

Planning a Search With the Help of MOLES
(Methodology Oriented Locaters for Evidence Searching)

| Planning Steps | Planning Sheet | MOLES | More Detailed Instructions |

Planning a search involves these steps:

1. In Row Two of the table below, insert the four elements of your question across.

Figure 4.22

Picking the "Plan a Search" option in this book's Web site. If you pick the "Plan a Search" option, you can scroll up and down to get help planning a search.

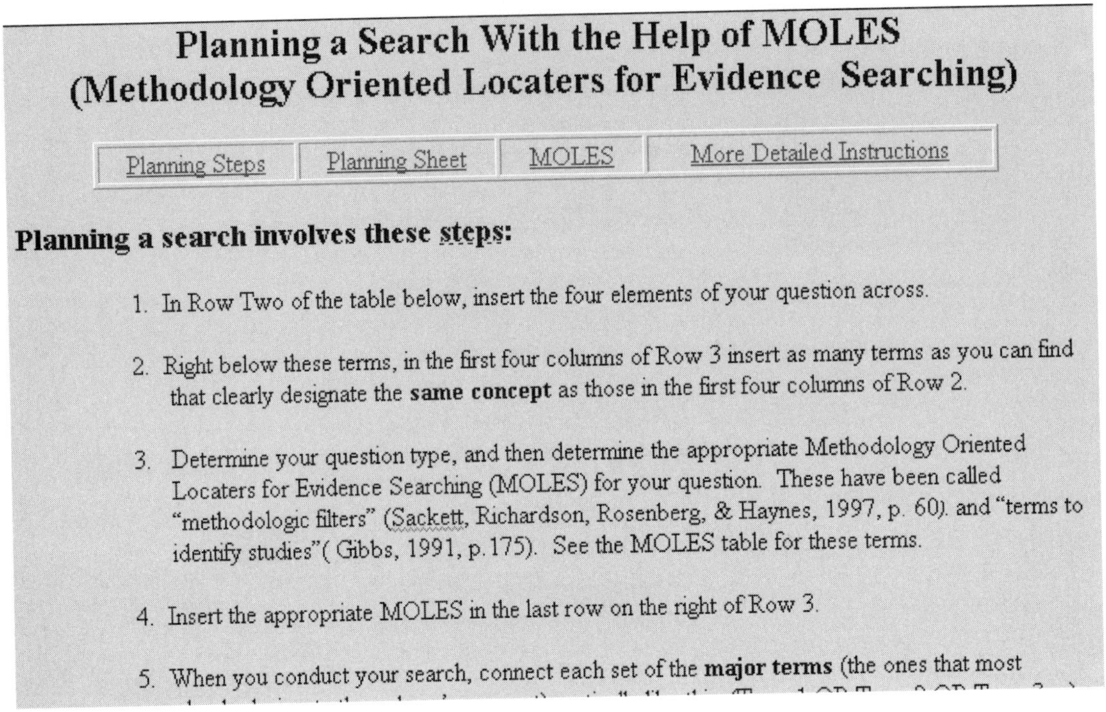

Figure 4.23

Using the worksheet in the "Plan a Search" option. On this screen you can click on the MOLES option to get ones specific to your question type.

MOLES for Each Question Type (You may mark MOLES and copy them right into the Planning Sheet above after opening the Planning Sheet.)

Effectiveness Questions	Prevention Questions	Risk/Prognosis Questions	Assessment Questions	Description Questions (With Qualitative Studies a Subset)	Syntheses of Studies (These work primarily with Effectiveness and Prevention Questions but may work with others.)
Random*	(Random*	(Risk Assessment	(inter-rater	(Random* Select*	meta-anal*
OR	OR	OR	OR	OR	OR
Controlled Clinical trial*	Controlled Clinical trial*	Predictive Validity	Inter-observer	Survey	meta anal*
		OR	OR	OR	OR
OR	OR	Predictive Value	True positive*	Representative	metaanal*

Figure 4.24

Locating Alyssa's appropriate MOLES for her assessment question. The MOLES can be highlighted, copied, cut, and pasted into the word document. The word document can be opened by clicking the mouse arrow on the document (Figure 4.25).

Search Planning Sheet (to add information to the search planning sheet and print it, open this Word document.) (Connect terms vertically with OR into sets, and combine sets with AND to limit your search. I find it useful to construct the MOLES set first, then dip into it with other sets using AND.)

	Column 1: Client Type and Problem	Column 2: What You Might Do	Column 3: Alternate Course of Action	Column 4: Intended Result	Column: MOLES Appropriate to Question Type (Effectiveness, Prevention, Risk Assessment, Description
Row 2: Determine Your Question Type, Then Insert Elements of Your Question in Spaces on Right					Leave Blank
Row 3: Insert Key Terms from Above, Synonyms, or Terms from Thesaurus or Controlled Language Vertically					In This box Insert appropriate MOLES for Your Question Type.

Figure 4.25

Alyssa can plan her assessment question on the Web site's Search Planning Sheet and print her plan for later reference. You can open the word document for a printable worksheet.

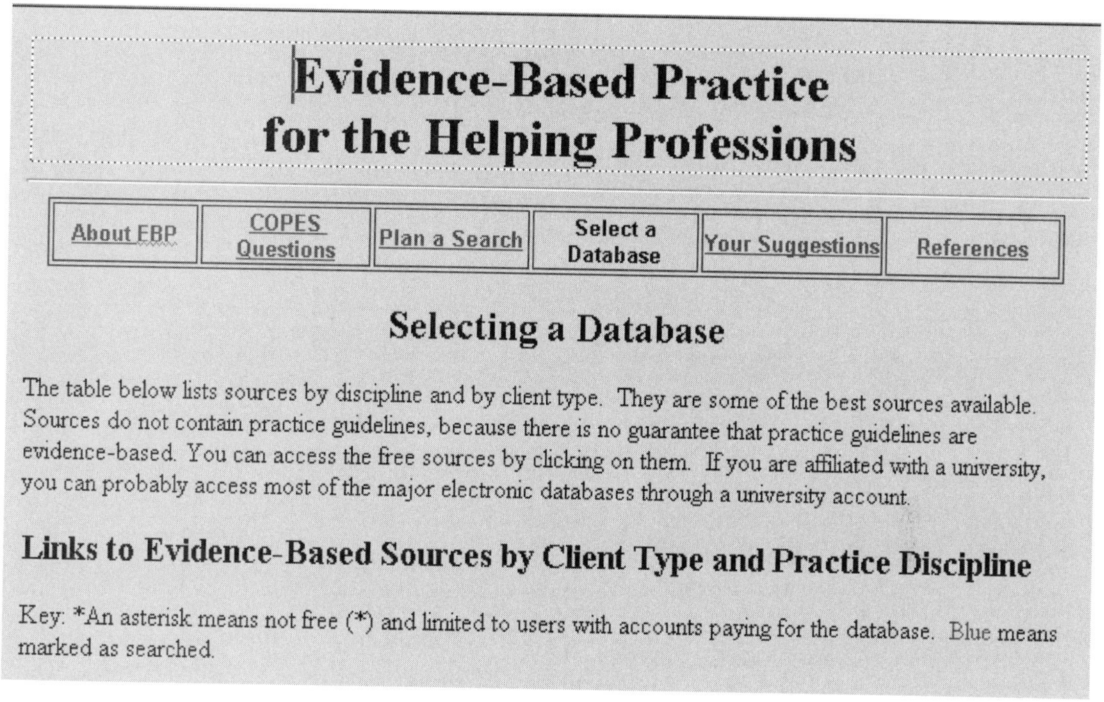

Evidence-Based Practice for the Helping Professions

| About EBP | COPES Questions | Plan a Search | Select a Database | Your Suggestions | References |

Selecting a Database

The table below lists sources by discipline and by client type. They are some of the best sources available. Sources do not contain practice guidelines, because there is no guarantee that practice guidelines are evidence-based. You can access the free sources by clicking on them. If you are affiliated with a university, you can probably access most of the major electronic databases through a university account.

Links to Evidence-Based Sources by Client Type and Practice Discipline

Key: *An asterisk means not free (*) and limited to users with accounts paying for the database. Blue means marked as searched.

Figure 4.26

Alyssa goes back to the "Select a Database" option on the book's EBP web site and selects an option.

Sources do not contain practice guidelines, because there is no guarantee that practice guidelines are evidence-based. You can access the free sources by clicking on them. If you are affiliated with a univers you can probably access most of the major electronic databases through a university account.

Links to Evidence-Based Sources by Client Type and Practice Disciplin

Key: *An asterisk means not free (*) and limited to users with accounts paying for the database. Blue m marked as searched.

Across: Discipline Down: Client Type	Social Work	Psychology	Nursing	Medicine
Teaching & Learning EBP	UK Social Services Research Group		Evidence-Based Health Care Centre for Evidence Based Nursing	Centre for Evidence-Based Medicine
All Clients	INFOTRAC (College)	INFOTRAC (College)	INFOTRAC (College)	*Cochrane Library (limited access) Cochrane Library

Figure 4.27

Alyssa then selects the "INFOTRAC (College)" option from the options listed. Your passcode for a free 4-month subscription to INFOTRAC (College) is on a card enclosed inside your book.

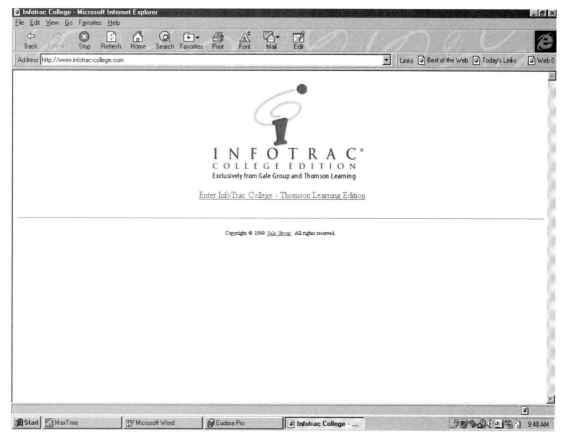

Figure 4.28

INFOTRAC home page. Now Alyssa has access to the source that this text used to provide documents for its exercises. (Images from INFOTRAC College Edition copyright 2001, reprinted with permission.)

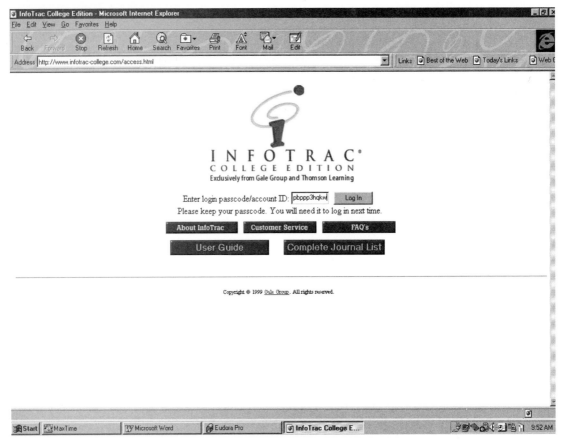

Figured 4.29

Alyssa identifies herself using this text's passcode. This passcode will be provided with your text on a card inserted into this text. (Images from INFOTRAC College Edition copyright 2001, reprinted with permission.)

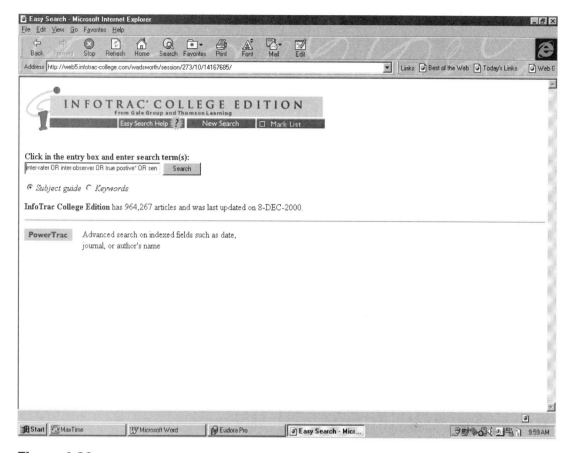

Figure 4.30

Alyssa then enters her MOLES for her assessment question connected by OR. (Images from INFOTRAC College Edition copyright 2001, reprinted with permission.)

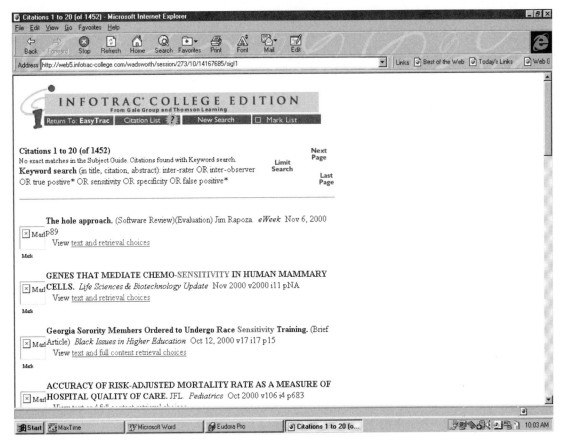

Figure 4.31

Her MOLES search nets 1452 documents in INFOTRAC. (Images from INFOTRAC College Edition copyright 2001, reprinted with permission.)

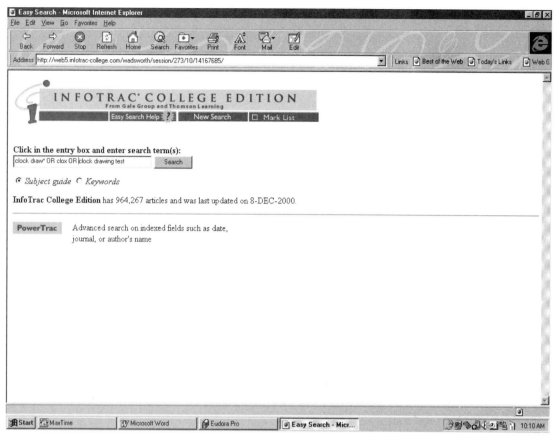

Figure 4.32

Alyssa enters her next most important terms concerning the clock test. (Images from INFOTRAC College Edition copyright 2001, reprinted with permission.)

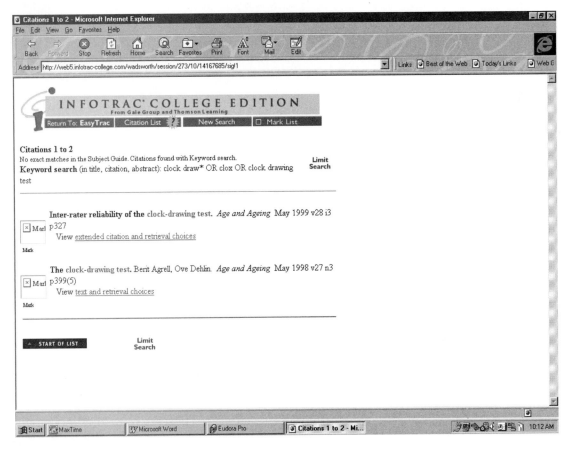

Figure 4.33

Alyssa finds only two documents regarding the clock test, so she doesn't need to apply her MOLES to limit her search to the best evidence. (Images from INFOTRAC College Edition copyright 2001, reprinted with permission.)

Step 5: Select the Most Appropriate Bibliographic Database

Anarchy reigns on the World Wide Web. The Web jungle can and does include any idea that anyone (and any nocturnal ring-tailed creature) can conceive. Journal editors and article reviewers do not screen sources on the Web. If you want to enter the Web jungle, go armed with MOLES. You might find sources more helpful whose addresses end with the following: .edu, .gov, .nhs.uk, or .ac.uk. Tread cautiously, and go armed with a guard dog virus protector around addresses containing .com—well, anywhere on the Web for that matter. Your dear aunts Edna and Myrtle can send you a virus with their Christmas greetings.

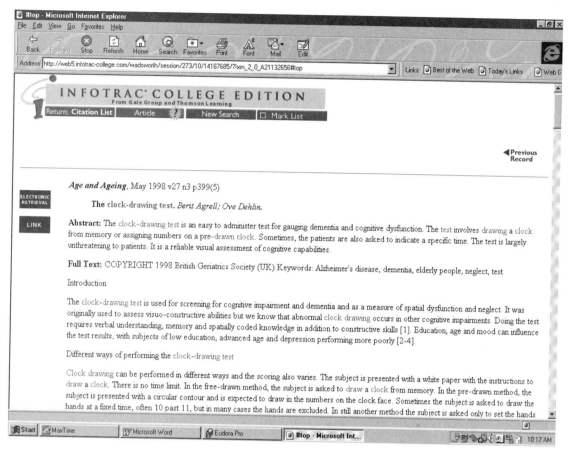

Figure 4.34

One of these documents includes a recent review regarding the clock-drawing test. (Images from INFOTRAC College Edition copyright 2001, reprinted with permission.)

Intended Use for This Book's Evidence-Based-Practice Web Site   This book's EBP Web site will help you to avoid the perils of the Web jungle. It intends to help you to locate reviews of studies and individual studies of value to practitioners that have been evaluated by reviewers and editors. This book's Web site will be useful to members of any helping profession and should save you time. By locating EBP sources in a single page, under the Select a Database option on this book's Web site, you can search for the current best evidence regarding a wide range of client types and settings.

The Evidence-Based-Practice Web Site's Organization   The matrix on the Web site's Selecting a Database page intends to make locating an appropriate database easier. Along the top, the columns include the following: Social

Work, Psychology, Nursing, and Medicine. On the vertical left in descending rows are the following: All Clients, Children Ages 0–12, Children Ages 13–19, Families and Groups, Aged, Physical Health, Mental Health, Corrections, Developmental Disabilities, Alcoholism and Other Drug Abuse, Income Maintenance, Information and Referral Including Laws and Legal.

Approximate Evidence-Based-Practie Web Site Contents (Web Site Under Constant Revision)   Not all sources on our Web site's "Selecting a Database" page are accessible. Go directly to sites without an asterisk (*) for free or consider subscribing to others. To help you remember which sites you have accessed, the ones you visit will turn color. Table 4.5 lists some of the more prominent free databases that can be accessed in this book's EBP Web site through its Selecting a Database page. Table 4.6 lists databases that appear on the same page that appropriately mark EBP Web sites, but these sites require access through a vendor. Most likely, text in Tables 4.5 and 4.6 will be somewhat dated, given my commitment to keeping the Web site current for users. You can help by entering suggestions by clicking on the *Your Suggestions* option on the site's home page.

Table 4.5	Free Databases in This Book's Evidence-Based-Practice Web Site	
Database	Contents	Source
ERIC	ERIC contains abstracts from educational research and technical reports. Selected full-text articles are available for thousands of ERIC digest records. The ERIC Document Collection is available in libraries on microfiche.	Use this address: www.infotrac-college.com and your passcode that accompanies this text.
INFOTRAC	The InfoTrac College Edition (ICE) combines hundreds of thousands of articles from major encyclopedias, reference books, magazines, pamphlets, and other sources in a single Web site. It was intended for students doing homework, making vacation plans, keeping up with current events, or researching any topic. It contained 965,150 articles when assessed in 2001.	
MEDLINE	For consumer health information, consider using MEDLINEplus. The National Library of Medicine (NLM) offers PubMed and Internet Grateful Med. MEDLINE contains 11 million references and abstracts. NLM has Medical Subject Headings for searching; and Loansome Doc for document delivery services (there may be local charges).	

Note. Parts from Index to Databases, University of Wisconsin MacIntyre Library, Eau Claire, Wisconsin. Reprinted by permission.

Table 4.6 | Databases Requiring Access Through a Vendor (Possibly Through a University's Subscriptions)

Database	Contents	Source
CINAHL	Provides access to English language nursing journals, publications of the American Nurses' Association, the National League for Nursing, and primary journals in other health disciplines (900 journals in all).	
Cochrane Library	The Cochrane Library, published quarterly, is an electronic publication designed to supply high-quality syntheses (meta-analyses) regarding health and psychiatric care. Presently there are approximately 1200 reviews of topics vital to practitioners. Systematic reviews include randomized controlled trials.	
Family Studies Database	This database combines Family Studies Database (FSD)(1970–present) and the Australian family & society abstracts (FAMILY)(1980–present). It provides over 198,000 abstracts and bibliographic records drawn from over a thousand professional journals, books, popular literature, conference papers, government reports, and other sources, regarding families, human development, and related topics.	Family Studies Database is produced and published by National Information Services Corporation (NISC), 3100 St. Paul Street, Baltimore, Maryland 21218 USA in association with the National Council on Family Relations (NFCR). Australian Family & Society Abstracts [FAMILY] is licensed from the Australian Institute of Family Studies.
Science Citation Index	The Science Citation Index is a multidisciplinary database, with an emphasis on the life and physical sciences. The searcher can identify related writings by indicating sources in which a known work by a given author has been cited. This index emphasizes scholarly research in 164 scientific disciplines.	
Social Sciences Citation Index	The Social Sciences Citation Index enables the searcher to locate sources that have been marked by a particular author or known work. Its indexes include 1725 journals spanning 50 disciplines including the social sciences, and related sources in the life sciences, chemistry, and physical sciences. This index emphasizes scholarly research in the social, behavioral, and related sciences.	

continued

Table 4.6 | Continued

Database	Contents	Source
Sociological Abstracts	Sociological Abstracts, published by Cambridge Scientific Abstracts, contains information from approximately 2500 journals. It covers sociology and related disciplines. It has an on-line thesaurus. Topics include: methodology & research technology, history & theory of sociology, social psychology, group interactions, culture & social structure, complex organization, social change & economic development, mass phenomena, political sociology & interactions.	
SWAB	Social Work Abstracts database, produced by the National Association of Social Workers, Inc., contains over 35,000 abstracts to articles, dissertations, and other materials from social work and related journals. Though the thesaurus is not available on-line, it is possible to search an index of the descriptors to find appropriate subject headings. Topics covered: social work (related fields) profession, theory & practice, areas of service, and social issues/social problems. Coverage: 1977–present .	

Note. Parts from Index to Databases copyright 2001 University of Wisconsin–Eau Claire MacIntyre Library, Eau Claire, Wisconsin. Reprinted by permission.

Applying MOLES to Rate Web Site Evidence Quality

Table 4.7 applies MOLES to rate some prominent Web sites listed in our book's evidence-based-practice Web site. The table lists the number and percent of records in each database retrieved by the MOLES for each of our five question types plus meta-analysis. Table 4.7 can provide an index of the methodological quality of a database. It lists the number of documents that would be retrieved by MOLES relative to the total number of records in the database. Comparing across will indicate which databases contain the best evidence relative to each question type. The *Average Percent* row of Table 4.7 shows that the evidence is of similar quality across Social Work (SWAB) psychology (PsycInfo) education (ERIC), nursing (CINAHL) and medicine (MEDLINE) that had, respectively, these average percentages of documents retrieved by the MOLES: 2.75%, 1.71%, 1.12%, 3.80%, and 2.03%. The INFOTRAC (College) database may contain documents retrievable by MOLES but to a lesser degree than the professional databases (*Average Percent* was .3% for INFOTRAC College Edition). The Cochrane Library contains only meta-analyses of randomized clinical trials; so its contents should include only documents retrieved by MOLES, or 100%.

Table 4.7 | Numbers and Percents of Records Retrieved by MOLES (Top Four Listed in Table 4.3) by Question Type in Six Databases

			Databases			
	SWAB	PsycINFO	ERIC	CINAHL	MEDLINE (PubMed)	INFOTRAC (College)
Effectiveness	1459 (4.17%)	53,784 (3.30%)	9042 (0.96%)	30,190 (6.70%)	301,421 (3.01%)	4432 (0.46%)
Prevention	1459 (4.17%)	53,784 (3.30%)	9042 (0.96%)	30,190 (6.70%)	301,421 (3.01%)	4432 (0.46%)
Risk	86 (0.25%)	5575 (0.34%)	1968 (0.21%)	4768 (1.06%)	64,090 (0.64%)	697 (0.07%)
Assessment	7 (0.00%)	541 (0.03%)	95 (0.01%)	540 (0.12%)	3,670 (0.04%)	383 (0.04%)
Description	2710 (7.74%)	49,329 (3.05%)	41,966 (4.56%)	29,702 (6.60%)	549,326 (5.49%)	7102 (0.74%)
Synthesis of Studies	69 (0.20%)	4029 (0.25%)	1440 (0.15%)	7270 (1.62%)	1085 (0.01%)	443 (0.05%)
Average Percent	2.75%	1.71%	1.12%	3.80%	2.03%	0.30%
Total Records in Database	35,000	1,620,000	942,000	450,000	10,000,000	965,150

Note. Searches done in December of 2000 in INFOTRAC and in February of 2001 for the rest. Search terms were as follows: effectiveness and prevention (random* OR controlled clinical trial OR control group*), risk/prognosis (risk assessment OR predictive validity OR predictive value), assessment (inter-rater OR inter-observer OR true positive*), descriptive (random* select* OR survey OR representative sample*), synthesis of studies (meta-anal* OR meta anal* OR metaanal*). In MEDLINE, the $ was substituted for *.

General Suggestions for Searching

Always remember that the point of a search is to get an accurate answer. You cannot get an accurate answer if you look only for evidence that confirms a given position. Resolve to look just as diligently for disconfirming evidence as for confirming evidence.

These suggestions may help you as you do the following exercises (Also see Table 4.8). As you examine what you have found, you may address the following questions:

- Did your search strategy convey the master concept and related concepts accurately? If not, revise your search terms.
- Did your search logic limit your search so severely that you netted few useful sources? If so, try searching each set of concepts before connecting them by AND.

Table 4.8 | Problems and Ways to Counter Them

Problem	Suggested Countermeasure
Too few references?	Select search terms that more accurately delineate the topic. Select a better database. Examine the search history to see that terms were not combined with AND too soon.
Too many references?	Combine the best search terms with AND. Apply MOLES combined with AND. Pick the one search term most specific to the topic. Use meta-analysis search terms.
Irrelevant references?	Select search terms that more accurately delineate the topic. Consult the database's thesaurus.
Not satisfied?	Consult a reference librarian who understands MOLES and evidence-based databases.
Still not satisfied?	State to yourself, to your colleagues, and to your clients that you do not have empirical evidence. Much of practice is so.

- Did your strategy miss a useful database? If this may be the case, try looking at this books Web site's database grid again, or try to gain access to databases that are not free on the Web site.
- Do records retrieved apply to your clients by client type, action you might take, alternate course of action, and intended result? If not, specify these variables more accurately.
- Have you addressed all of these questions and still found nothing of use to guide your practice? Then sufficient evidence may simply not exist to guide you at this time. State to yourself, to your colleagues, and to your clients that you are basing your actions on your own experience and speculation.
- Do you need to retrieve sources quickly? You can obtain full text of documents electronically in some cases or through a university's inter-library loan department, or through fax from some databases.

The exercises in this chapter are designed to give you experience conducting searches yourself. Though I have done the best I can to devise realistic and challenging exercises here, users will be using a wide variety of equipment, access to databases, and expertise. All will find MOLES useful. MOLES will dig regardless of the database. They will tell you quickly if evidence is weak. Once you have posed your question and isolated its best search terms, do remember to pick your MOLES most appropriate to your question type. The following cartoon appears here to remind you about your MOLES. Again, I often construct my MOLES set first. Then I find my MOLES set's intersect with terms that identify my topic using AND.

"We **MOLES** really dig for you!"

Exercise 4-1 Experience Conducting a Search Regarding a Treatment Program for Delinquency

Purpose

This exercise is designed to give you experience conducting a search and to provide an outline and worksheets for conducting any search.

Necessary Materials and Equipment

You will need:

* Equipment described in Table 4.1: Minimal Hardware Necessary to Conduct Electronic Searches
* Access to this book's Web site, Evidence-Based Practice for Social Workers at www.evidence.brookscole.com

- Worksheets included in this exercise (you might want to copy these worksheets for use in additional exercises and in later chapters before you write on them here).

Background

Heather Leeson (2000) works at Northwest Passage, a 3-month, adventure-based challenge program for delinquent boys in a wilderness area (www.nwpass.com). It is an Outward Bound type of program. Over the past year, Heather has worked with an average of nine male clients, average age 15 years, who have been convicted of a wide range of offenses that can include, for example, operating a motor vehicle without the owner's consent, battery, drug abuse, retail theft, burglary, criminal damage to property, sexual assault. The Northwest program seeks to rehabilitate the boys by exposing them to circumstances that require them to work together in challenging and often uncomfortable circumstances. The boys get regular group and individual counseling. The boys live with staff in a cabin on a remote lake surrounded by hardwood forests and muskeg swamps. In winter, the temperature can drop to −40° F. In summer, the mosquitoes can be so numerous that they sound like tires on a highway. The boys must perform chores together to maintain the cabin including cutting wood to heat the cabin. Periodically, staff members take the boys on 3-day canoe trips in summer and on winter camping trips. The boys also work on a ropes course high above the ground protected by a safety line. Heather thrives in this rugged environment. One of her ploys to establish dominance in the pecking order involves getting a boy to challenge her to a swimming race and beating him by a wide margin (she doesn't tell the boys that she was on a university swimming team).

Heather's COPES question arose out of her concern for the central mission of Northwest. She says, "I was personally curious if the program, which looks like it would help juveniles to not re-offend, really does help" (2000, p. 2). Here is Heather's COPES question:

> If adjudicated delinquent juvenile males complete a residential treatment program, will they have lower rates of recidivism after completing the program than juveniles who do not go through a program? (Leeson, 2000, p. 6)

Instructions

1. *Formulate your COPES question.* Please go to chapter 3 (Table 3.1) to determine the type of Heather's question. Determining her question type will help you to decide what MOLES to use.
2. *Clarify Your COPES question's terms to guide your electronic search.* Fill in the appropriate boxes in the following worksheet.

Blank Search Planning Worksheet

	Client Type and Characteristics	Course of Action	Alternate Course of Action	Intended Result	MOLES Relevant to Your Question Type (from Table 4.3)
Row 1 Terms from Your COPES Question					
Row 2 Synonyms That You Can Imagine					
Row 3 Controlled Language from a Thesaurus (Use first four columns immediately to the right only.)					
Row 4 Terms Chosen and Combined in the Search (First combine terms with OR vertically in each column; search each column; then combine these sets with AND horizontally.)					
Total Hits for Each Row Before Using AND to Combine Rows					

3. *Select the appropriate MOLES for your question type.* Be sure to include the appropriate MOLES (Table 4.3) for Heather's question type. Do also include search terms from the far right of Table 4.3 (regarding meta-analysis). These meta-analysis terms work best for effectiveness and prevention questions.

4. *Plan your search strategy.* Which terms do you suspect will mark your topic most effectively? Circle these terms in the Blank Search Planning Sheet. Which MOLES do you suspect will most effectively mark the best evidence regarding your question type? Circle these MOLES. Be sure to connect these major terms in sets in each column vertically with OR. Decide which of these sets you will search first. If the MOLES come up with nothing, what you will find in the other sets will most likely be weak, anecdotal, and essentially useless as evidence. Once you have searched the sets vertically individually, then combine sets with AND.

5. *Select the most appropriate bibliographic database.* Consult this book's Web site to locate databases. Some of these are described in Table 4.5 and Table 4.6.

6. *Conduct your search.* Recording your results in the following table will help you to avoid backtracking and missing key sources.

Search History Form

Database	Set No.	Search Terms	Number of Hits	Comments
	1			
	2			
	3			
	4			
	5			

Search History Form—Continued

Database	Set No.	Search Terms	Number of Hits	Comments
	6			
	7			
	8			
	9			
	10			
	11			
	12			
	12			
	13			
	14			

continued

Search History Form—Continued

Database	Set No.	Search Terms	Number of Hits	Comments
	15			
	16			
	17			
	18			
	19			
	20			

7. *Evaluate the results and revise the strategy if necessary.* If you are not satisfied with your search's results, the suggestions in Table 4.8 might help you.

Heather had a second COPES question that this exercise might have already helped to answer:

For boys adjudicated for delinquent behavior, what is the most effective treatment method or counseling method to reduce recidivism (new offenses posttreatment)?

You might try Sociological Abstracts with the meta-analysis term AND delinquency terms. Heather found evidence that she thought might help Northwest Passage to improve its methods using this approach. Did you find the article by Wilson and Lipsey (2000) regarding the effectiveness of wilderness challenge programs? She presented what she found to the board of Northwest Passage in hopes that it would guide their programming decisions.

Exercise 4-2 Practice Conducting a Search Regarding Client Satisfaction at a Women's Refuge House

Background

Jennifer Jensen (2000) works at Boulton Refuge House, which serves as a shelter for victims of domestic violence during a family crisis. Boulton is named after a police officer who was killed trying to help during a domestic violence situation. The house offers a variety of services including the following: a 24-hour telephone crisis line, a residence for victims that is staffed 24 hours a day, child care, advocacy in the courts, information and referral for basic needs, and counseling. Counseling can include support groups, individual counseling, and training in how to identify the signs of escalating violence and how to take action to avoid harm.

Jennifer and her colleagues want to know how effectively Boulton serves clients' needs as perceived by clients there. The agency has a client-satisfaction questionnaire, but Jennifer would like to locate a better client-satisfaction questionnaire that measures aspects of Boulton's program. Here is a COPES question relative to Jennifer's clients:

> If women in a residential shelter for abused women are polled regarding their satisfaction with their services at the shelter, with which elements in their care will they report being the most and least satisfied on a client-satisfaction measure?

Instructions

Please follow the steps in Exercise 4-1 to conduct this search. Documents regarding domestic violence and client satisfaction can be located in many databases. Ideally, try to locate a client-satisfaction instrument that has been applied to services for abused women. If this is too narrow, then try to locate client-satisfaction questionnaires that have been widely used and evaluated for their measurement qualities. Such instruments might serve Boulton's clients with some adaptation.

Exercise 4-3 Effectiveness of a Mentor

Background

Elizabeth Cotrone (2000) works intensively with nine middle school boys in a day-treatment program at Marriage and Family Health Services. The boys' behavior has caused such serious problems in school that they have been placed for a time with her program. The boys have been assessed to have ". . . Oppositional Defiant Disorder, AD/HD [Attention-Deficit/Hyperactivity Disorder], Depression, and other mental health issues" (p. 2). During her group and individual counseling with the boys, Liz has learned that many do not have a father living in the home with them to serve as a role model for them. She reasons that if the boys had a big-brother type of volunteer they could bond with another male who might model appropriate behavior and values. She is particularly concerned about one African American boy who lives in an almost completely white community.

Here is a question relative to Liz's thoughts about a mentor for her African American client:

> If gradeschool-age African American boys are mentored by an older male, as opposed to not having a mentor, will the mentored boys' behavioral problems be less frequent and severe and their school performance better?

Instructions

Please follow the steps in Exercise 4-1 to conduct this search. Be on the watch not only for the general effectiveness of mentoring programs but also for how the more effective programs are structured (assuming some are effective).

No conclusion is better than the method by which it was drawn. —**Professor Michael Hakeem,** *University of Wisconsin–Madison*

Treatment Effectiveness Research: Evaluate Study Quality and Apply Results to Practice

5

Overview

This first of four chapters concerning how to evaluate studies as guides to practice demonstrates how to evaluate studies that evaluate the effectiveness of treatment. The next three chapters concern how to evaluate systematic reviews or meta-analyses, how to evaluate assessment and risk/prognosis studies, and how to evaluate descriptive and qualitative studies. Each of these four chapters begins by describing the type of study conceptually and by example, then lists general criteria for evaluating studies that can be applied quickly, then provides a formal rating form, and, finally, provides an exercise that allows you to practice rating studies relative to their quality and implications for practice.

Suggestions for How to Read This Chapter

This chapter incorporates rating forms to assist those who want to weigh the quality and impact of studies that evaluate the effectiveness of treatment. Please use your own judgment in how much to rely on the forms. Initially, you may want to rate studies to gain practice in looking for key features of studies that make them more or less credible as evidence. Later, you may want to just be aware of these features as you do your reading. Do keep in mind that a study that has a high score for quality and impact of treatment may have a fatal error that eclipses all the other criteria on the rating form in its importance. For example, it might have been discovered that the author has fabricated some or all of the data or has some obvious bias. In such a case, use your judgment about how to weigh the study's findings.

An Example

This chapter begins with an example from practice. No universally applicable example is possible. Sometimes a search reveals absolutely nothing of value to your practice; so you must rely only on experience and client wishes, stating honestly why you do so. Sometimes the search reveals sound evidence, but dissimilarities between subjects in the study compared with your own clients may obscure whether the findings apply to your own; so you must decide how far you will push the generalization. Sometimes strong evidence applies directly to your COPES question, but even then there is the matter of application.

Can you, given practical and ethical limitations, actually apply the current best evidence to your actions? Box 5.1 demonstrates a critical appraisal of evidence relative to a vital life or death COPES question and a problem with application.

Box 5.1	An Example Regarding Evidence and an Alcoholic's Treatment

Jessie Davis (2000) did her field placement on a locked inpatient psychiatric unit that occupies one floor of a 200-bed hospital. One of her clients was a chronic alcoholic male in his mid 30s. He had been admitted to her ward 12 times in less than 2 months for alcohol detoxification, but he had refused treatment at each admission. Jessie was concerned that her client's alcohol addiction would kill him. She noted his yellowish skin, a symptom of liver damage, and other serious medical problems. Jessie worked closely with a psychiatrist who was also concerned about the grave nature of his health problems related to his addition. The psychiatrist told the client (quoting the client's internal medicine doctor), "If you leave this hospital and continue to drink, you will die." He replied, "I don't care. I still will not go into treatment."

Jessie told me that she sought the counsel of her wise and experienced field instructor about what to do. He lamented that, in the long run, about one-third of the ward's clients were admitted for alcohol and/or drug detoxification, but most got only detoxification and no treatment. He gave her a copy of Wisconsin Statutes, Chapter 51, containing an explanation for 72-hour commitment procedures and for longer involuntary commitment. Jessie wondered if it might be in her client's best interests to work with the client's family and the psychiatrist to try involuntary commitment for alcoholism treatment, but Jessie's field instructor explained that the funding agency that could help probably would not due to its policies about involuntary treatment.

Not convinced, Jessie called the funding agency to see if funding might be obtained. The agency's representative explained that, because alcoholics change their behavior only if they voluntarily seek help and take responsibility for their choices, the agency does not fund involuntary treatment. Jessie thanked the agency's representative and went to work. She posed the following COPES question:

> If chronic alcoholics are committed to treatment involuntarily, is it likely that their number of relapses will be lower than when an individual attends treatment voluntarily? (Davis, 2000, p. 3).

Jessie then followed procedures outlined in the previous chapter to locate evidence regarding differences in outcome for voluntary/involuntary treatment for alcoholics. Jessie looked for *disconfirming* evidence that refuted the state of affairs that she would like to have seen (i.e., that clients voluntarily participating in alcoholism treatment fared better than involuntary clients). She also searched also for *confirming* evidence that supported her position (i.e., that involuntarily treated alcoholics fared as well or better than voluntarily ones). The table below summarizes data related to Jessie's COPES question:

Evidence Regarding Outcomes for Alcoholics Entering Voluntary Versus Involuntary Treatment

Source (Disconfirming Evidence)	Study Description	Form for Rating Evidence Quality	Effect Size	Interpretation
O'Loughlin & Webb, 1996	A 1989–1992 comparison between 32 alcoholics who were involuntarily admitted for treatment at St. Patrick's Hospital in Dublin versus 32 voluntarily admitted. This was a quasi-experimental study comparing across the two groups.	The Quality of Study Rating Form (QSRF) score = 33 points. The QSRF score ranges from 0–100 with higher score meaning a better study. The QSRF will be explained later in this chapter.	Ten (31%) of voluntarily admitted and 12 (37.5%) of involuntarily admitted were readmitted to hospital; so absolute risk reduction *(ARR)** is 6.5% favoring voluntary treatment, and number needed to treat *(NNT)** is 15. These indices will be explained later.	Subjects were not randomly assigned to voluntary/involuntary treatment. This is a weak study because the involuntarily treated alcoholics were initially sicker with more physical symptoms (p for t-test <0.004) and older (p for t-test <.001) than the voluntarily treated; so post-treatment differences were likely due to pretreatment differences.
Walsh, Hingson, Merrigan, & Levenson, 1992	Workers in a large manufacturing plant in the NE of the U.S. who were assessed to have an alcohol abuse problem were randomly assigned to mandatory inpatient (MI) treatment (*n* = 63 followed up of 73 entering treatment), or to mandatory AA attendance (MAA) (64/71), or to a choice (64/71).	QSRF Score = 64	At 24 months follow-up, 36.5% of those in the mandatory inpatient group had no alcohol and the choice group had 17.2% *(ARR** = 19.3%, *NNT** = 5.18); mandatory AA had 16.4% no alcohol so absolute risk increase relative to choice was— 0.8%, *NNH** (to harm) = 125.	This randomized controlled trial provides strong evidence regarding effects of superiority of mandatory inpatient coercive treatment over giving the worker a choice of treatments. Results may apply to Jessie's client. Their average age was respectively for the MI, MAA, and choice groups: 33.1, 32.2, and 32.2 years respectively. On the other hand, Jessie's client was unemployed.

continued

Evidence Regarding Outcomes for Alcoholics Entering Voluntary Versus Involuntary Treatment—Continued

Source (Disconfirming Evidence)	Study Description	Form for Rating Evidence Quality	Effect Size	Interpretation
Miller & Flaherty (2000)	This narrative review of studies summarizes results of coerced or mandated addiction treatment (including alcoholism) for various populations including mandated treatment by courts, by employers, and by criminal justice and child welfare agencies. This review of studies includes a mixed bag of stronger and weaker studies.	Multiple Evaluations for Treatment Assessment (META) scores range from 0 to 100. META score = 9.5, a relatively weak review of studies. META will be explained later (in chapter 6).	None reported in any consistent format.	"The preponderance of the research literature confirmed the efficacy and consistent benefits from coerced addiction treatment or providing addiction treatment in lieu of alternative consequences. . . . The lack of research that showed coerced addiction treatment to be ineffective or adverse was striking" (p. 14).

*Absolute risk reduction means percent difference across treatment and control groups, and number needed to treat means number of similar clients needed to treat without benefit to benefit one.

These and other standards for rating evidence quality are explained later in this chapter.

Generally, the evidence in the accompanying table indicates that Jessie's client might benefit as well or better from involuntary inpatient treatment, compared with those participating voluntarily. Though O'Loughlin and Webb (1996) provide weak disconfirming evidence to this conclusion, O'Loughlin and Webb's findings were based on a small sample (i.e., 32 in each group). Their study showed that alcoholics treated involuntarily, who were statistically significantly older and sicker pretreatment, were readmitted to the hospital only 6.5% more frequently than those voluntarily admitted. This 6.5% difference could easily be due to initial pretreatment differences. Jessie's confirming evidence seems stronger. The randomized trail of coerced versus voluntary treatment by Walsh and her colleagues (1992) is the strongest. Their study scored 64 points on the QSRF (rating form to be explained later). Their study reported a 17.2% difference favoring those coerced into a 3-week inpatient treatment over those employees given a choice of which treatment or no treatment. Here the number needed to treat is 5.18, meaning that if Jessie's client is similar enough to those in the study, and assuming that findings based on coerced treatment would apply to those involuntarily committed to treatment, then about five would need to be coerced into inpatient treatment and not benefit to benefit one. The Miller and Flaherty (2000) review, though weak relative to the META rating form (i.e., 9.5 of a possible 100 points), does support the use of coercive treatment for addiction treatment, including alcohol addiction treatment as demonstrated within a variety of settings and addictions. Their conclusion appears in the table.

Jessie concluded from her assessment of the evidence, "Overall, my research findings state either that involuntary clients show they were more likely to successfully complete treatment, or there were no significant differences in success rates present when comparing to voluntary clients" (Davis, 2000, p. 7). Jessie advocated for her client's involuntary treatment without success, she fought the right battle but lost.

Deciding to Take Evidence-Based Action

Jessie's experience represents a common problem. Making the evidence-to-action leap has been my students' most formidable obstacle. If this experience can generalize more widely, I suspect that anyone who tries to implement evidence-based practice within the confines of any organization will likely bark their shins on obstacles. Here are some factors to consider when deciding whether you should try to take action based on evidence:

- Is the evidence of sufficient quality to warrant trusting its conclusions? Jessie's assessment of the randomized experiment and the Miller and Flaherty review over the weaker contrary evidence convinced her that the evidence favored trying involuntary treatment. (This and the next three chapters' rating forms will help you to weigh relative evidence quality.)
- Is the magnitude of the potential benefit (treatment effect, gain in accuracy of assessment, accuracy of description) sufficient to warrant action, considering the client's wishes, potential costs in time and effort, practitioner's training and ability, and other practical concerns? Jessie chose to try to overrule the client's wishes based partly on NNT = 5.18 (Walsh, Hingson, Merrigan, & Levenson, 1992). (Indices of treatment effect size and predictive validity in this chapter's rating forms will help you here.)
- Are clients, as described in the study, sufficiently like those in your own practice to warrant extrapolating the study's findings to the client(s) at hand? Jessie's client was a chronic alcoholic probably sicker than those in the trial, but the Miller and Flaherty (2000) review included court mandated treatment and criminal justice clients. (This concern will appear as a table at the end of each exercise in this chapter.)

Importance of Learning How to Critically Appraise Evidence

Because deciding what action to take guided by the current best evidence involves weighing the quality and applicability of evidence, these two steps (evaluating evidence and taking action) appear together in this and in the next three chapters. This chapter will be important to you professionally for several reasons:

- *First, practice guidelines are becoming a trend.* Influential members of the helping professions will publish practice guidelines and will argue that you consider these guidelines as guides to action (Howard & Jenson, 1999). Such guidelines can represent an advance or, possibly, a dogmatic step backward, depending on procedures used to develop them. Hopefully, practice guidelines will reflect thorough search procedures, a determined effort to present disconfirming and confirming evidence, objective standards for rating evidence quality, and easily interpreted indices to guide decision making. This chapter includes rating forms specific to these issues. Consequently, this chapter will help you to become a better-informed consumer of practice guidelines and standards.

• *Second, procedures for critically appraising evidence can help you to make better decisions.* This book's rating forms deal with topics that have often been omitted from the professional literature, including, for example, qualitative studies, risk assessment, number needed to treat, and inter-rater reliability to improve assessment criteria. The omission of risk assessment (chapter 7) serves as an excellent example. Though practitioners commonly weigh risk, a thorough treatment of risk assessment does not appear in any of social work's most prominent research methods texts relative to basic concepts that a practitioner can apply to evaluating a risk-assessment procedure (Bloom, Fischer, & Orme, 1999; Gambrill, 1997; Grinnell, 1997; Kirst-Ashman & Hull, 1999; Rubin & Babbie, 1997). Even in medicine, works regarding how to evaluate the predictive validity of medical tests have been relatively recent (Galen & Gambino, 1975). By including such content, this chapter's rating forms can help to address important issues of practical value.

• *Finally, this chapter holds practical promise for you because it will teach you to filter research, as opposed to trying to absorb it like a sponge.* The sponge approach to learning involves trying to absorb information uncritically by memory (Browne & Keeley, 1994). The inefficient sponge approach wastes time and puts clients at risk, because it mixes weak and strong evidence together to guide decision making. On the other hand, the filter approach involves letting most of the evidence pass through the filter to be discarded, leaving only the nuggets of best evidence. You have already started the filter approach by posing COPES questions and by learning to search efficiently using MOLES. This chapter's rating forms further augment the filter approach. Most of these rating forms have been pilot tested with students and have been revised accordingly. Each form constructs indices that can guide your decision making.

Organization for Chapters 5, 6, 7, and 8 in Table 5.1

Please see Table 5.1. If you study it carefully, you will note that it provides an outline for all that follows in this chapter and the next three. Note how Table 5.1 includes appropriate rating forms for each practice question type. These forms will help you to reduce some of the guesswork from evaluating and applying appropriate research to your practice. The rating forms can be applied formally, or they can at least provide an outline to keep in mind while reading what your literature search has found.

Please note that all of the exercises in chapters 5 through 8 rely on IN-FOTRAC (College) to locate articles for critique, not necessarily because IN-

Table 5.1 | Question Types Relative to Their Appropriate Best Evidence and Guides to Action

Question Type	Appropriate Rating for Evidence	Evidentiary Guides to Action
Effectiveness Questions: Chapter 5	Quality of Study Rating Form (QSRF)	Statistical significance, absolute risk reduction, number needed to treat, number needed to harm
Prevention Questions: Chapter 5	Quality of Study Rating Form-Prevention (QSRF-P)	Statistical significance, absolute risk reduction, number needed to treat, number needed to harm
Meta-Analysis (Primarily Effectiveness Questions): Chapter 6	Multiple Evaluations for Treatment Assessment (META)	Transformations to number needed to treat, combined number needed to treat
Assessment Questions and Risk-Assessment Questions: Chapter 7	Client Assessment and Risk Evaluation (CARE)	Inter-rater agreement, criterion-related validity, positive predictive value, negative predictive value
Description and Qualitative Questions: Chapter 8	Survey Rating Form (SRF) Qualitative Study Quality (QSQ)	Sample means and proportions, content ratings, frequencies

FOTRAC (College) provides the best evidence—it does not (see Table 4.7)—but because you can surely access the articles through INFOTRAC. This saves a lot of paper and cost.

The Need for Systematic Ways to Evaluate Evidence

Ideally, practitioners should be able to rely on reviewers to isolate the best evidence for them and to distill it for its essence to guide practice decision making. Unfortunately, conventional reviews have fallen far short of such expectations. Those who evaluate publications without reference to rating scales perform poorly at the task. Cooper (1984) reviewed research regarding judgments made by persons reviewing manuscripts to see if they were acceptable for publication in journals. Cooper included studies that evaluated levels of inter-observer correlation as well as agreement on the publish/don't-publish decision. He concluded: "In sum, the studies of evaluator agreement are somewhat disheartening" (p. 64).

More recently, Oxman and Guyatt (1993, pp. 126–127) reviewed ten studies evaluating (inter-judge agreement) across reviewers' ratings of journal articles. Reviewer agreement, as measured by correlation coefficient (a number ranging from –1 through 0 to +1 indicating respectively complete disagreement, no relationship at all, to perfect agreement) was 0.19 to 0.54. These values fall well below the .70 that often marks minimal inter-rater agreement.

Expertise does not seem to help raters. One would hope that content experts should be able to agree on the quality of evidence in their area of expertise better than those who lack such expertise. To test this idea, Oxman and Guyatt (1993) asked experts to review evidence in their area of expertise. Generally, such expert reviews have been narrative, meaning that the reviewer locates evidence, critiques it, and draws conclusions from it according to the expert's criteria. Oxman and Guyatt (pp. 128–130) compared ratings of 12 reviewers who rated the methodological rigor in 36 studies. Judges included content-area experts, research methodologists, clinicians with research training, and research assistants. The last three groups received training in how to apply ten criteria for evidence quality. The content-area experts received no training. On all ten criteria, the trained reviewers demonstrated greater agreement on their ratings of evidence quality than did the experts. Apparently, expertise does not ensure consistency in how experts rate evidence. Additionally, Oxman and Guyatt reported an inverse relationship between the reviewers' self-rated expertise and their consistency in rating evidence quality (i.e., the more they thought they knew, the less they in fact knew about how to consistently rate a study).

How Study Rating Forms Can Help Practitioners

If experts have not been able to rate evidence quality consistently, then how could their reviews be of any practical value? Such inconsistency among experts, coupled with increasing numbers of studies, could make it virtually impossible to make sense of the research evidence as a guide to practice.

There is hope. Scales to rate research quality and treatment impact have been devised to overcome raters' inconsistencies. Checklists for evaluating research have been available for a long time (Fischer, 1978, pp. 319–322), but recent instruments have scale qualities that go beyond checklists. Scales include specific instructions for rating their criteria; their criteria receive weights, and the scale yields a total score.

Most recent scales to rate research have been ones to rate *randomized controlled trials* (RCTs). At least 25 scales to rate RCTs have been developed since the first by Chalmers and others in 1981 (Moher, Jadad, et al., 1995, p. 63). Twelve of these twenty-five scales were evaluated by comparing raters against each other to see how well their study ratings agreed. These raters' reliability coefficients were greater than 0.70 in ten of the twelve studies (pp. 66–67). In another review of inter-rater agreement for scales to rate RCTs, interclass correlations exceeded 0.9 in 12 scales, were between 0.8 to 0.9 in 10 scales, and less than 0.8 in 3 scales (Juni, Witschi, Bloch, & Egger, 1999, p. 1056). Apparently, learning how to apply a study rating scale can foster consistency in ratings.

A Note Regarding Evaluation Forms and Exercises

The rest of this chapter presents two forms for rating evidence regarding effectiveness (the top two rows of Table 5.1, including effectiveness of a treatment and effectiveness of a prevention program). At least one exercise follows each form in this chapter through chapter 8. Each exercise begins with background from practice about a real issue, including a COPES question. Each exercise asks you to critically appraise an article that you can surely retrieve from INFOTRAC (College). All of these articles will remain in the INFOTRAC (College) database to support this text—a savings on costs and paper.

On the other hand, a price will be paid for using only INFOTRAC (College) articles. The INFOTRAC (College) articles do not contain enough information about the authors' locations to contact them personally regarding issues that might arise when deciding whether to apply their evidence to practice. For example, an exercise in a later chapter evaluates a language-development survey that has been designed to screen preschool children to see if they need special language training before they enter school. The original article identifies the authors' locations well enough that the reader could telephone them to request a copy of the language-development survey. Consequently, all exercises miss a chance to demonstrate a step in application. INFOTRAC (College) also limits the range of sources and examples.

Keep in mind also that any decision to apply evidence from research implies a judgment that subjects in the research are similar enough to your clients to justify inferring that the study's results would apply to your clients. Each exercise ends with a box that raises these issues, but the exercise cannot adequately address this similarity issue regarding unique situations with your own clients.

A Quick Overview of How to Rate Treatment Effectiveness and Prevention Articles

This section outlines the bare essentials for rating the quality of effectiveness and prevention studies for those who do not have the time and inclination to apply rating forms. This section has been only slightly altered from an outline suggested by Eamon Armstrong (2001), who graciously reviewed an earlier draft of this book. His excellent worksheet (see Box 5.2) captures the essence of issues involved in making a judgment and decision regarding the application of research that evaluates treatment and prevention programs. His worksheet expertly captures the essence of many sources (Slawson & Shaughnessy, 1997; Greenhalgh & Donald, 2000, p. 81; McKibbon, Eady, & Marks, 1999, pp. 40–43; Sackett, Richardson, Rosenberg, & Haynes, 1997, pp. 91–95, 106; Sackett, Straus, Richardson, Rosenberg, & Haynes, 2000, pp. 106–113, Card 4A-Therapy).

Box 5.2

A Worksheet for Critically Appraising Articles About Treatment

1. *Determine relevance* (based on conclusion of abstract): Is this article worth taking the time to read? (Section 1: A, B, C, D adapted with permission from Slawson & Shaughnessy, 1997.)

   A. Did the authors study an outcome that clients would care about?
      Yes (go on) No (stop)

   B. Is the problem studied one that is *common* to your practice? (Given your scant resources and time, your clients may get the greatest benefit if you research problems that occur most frequently.)
      Yes (go on) No (stop)

   C. Is the intervention feasible? (If you do not have the resources, time, training, or permission, why bother?)
      Yes (go on) No (stop)

   D. Will this information, if true, require you to *change* your current practice?
      Yes (go on) No (stop)

2. *Determine validity of a single study* (Sackett et al., 1997, pp. 91–96; Sackett et al., 2000, pp. 106–110): If the answers to all four of the preceding questions are "Yes," then continued assessment of the article is mandatory. Study design flaws are common; fatal flaws are arresting.

   A. Was the assignment of clients to treatment randomized? (Sackett, et al., 1997, p. 92)

   B. If random assignment was ensured, was the randomization list concealed from those assigning clients to treatment and from those evaluating outcome? (Sackett et al., 1997, p. 92)

   C. Were all subjects who entered treatment accounted for in its conclusion? (Sackett et al., 1997, p. 95) (Some may be lost to follow-up when outcome is measured, but this is not fatal if a sufficient number were accounted for.)

   D. Were subjects analyzed in the groups to which they were randomly assigned? (Sackett et al., 2000, p. 109)

   E. Were subjects and treatment personnel "blind" to which treatment was being received? (Sackett et al., 1997, p. 96)

   F. Aside from the experimental treatment, were the groups treated equally? (Sackett et al., p. 96)

   G. Were the groups similar at the start of the trial? (Sackett et al., 1997, p. 96)

3. *Determine the impact of the treatment to judge whether the treatment is worth the effort* (Greenhalgh & Donald, 2000, pp. 80–81):

		Outcome Event		Total	
		Yes	No		
Control (Not Treated or Got Alternate Treatment)		a	b	a + b	
Experimental Group (Got Treatment)		c	d	c + d	

Control event rate = risk of outcome event in control group = $CER = a/(a + b)$.

Experimental event rate = risk of outcome event in experimental group = $EER = c/(c + d)$

Relative risk reduction = $RRR = (CER - EER)/CER$

Absolute risk reduction = $ARR = CER - EER$

Number needed to treat = $NNT = 1 / ARR = 1/ (CER - EER)$ = number treated but not benefiting to benefit one (easily interpreted index of treatment impact).

95% Confidence interval for NNT (Sackett et al., 2000, Card 4A-Therapy) = estimated range of values for NNT with 95% chance that true value is within this range

$$= \pm 1.96 \sqrt{\frac{CER \times (1 - CER)}{\# \ of \ control \ subjects} + \frac{EER \times (1 - EER)}{\# \ of \ exper. \ subjects}}$$

4. *Should I apply these valid, important results to my client or clients?* (Sackett et al., 2000, p. 118)
    A. Do these results apply to my client(s)?
        (1) Is my client so different from those in the trial that the results do not apply? (Sackett et al., 2000, p. 118)
        (2) Is the benefit to my client(s) worth the cost, risk, and effort?
    B. Are my client(s)' values and preferences satisfied by the intervention offered? (Sackett et al., 2000, p. 123)
        (1) Do I have a clear assessment of the client(s)' values and preferences? (Sackett et al., 2000, p. 123)
        (2) Does this intervention and its potential consequences serve these values?

Note. From *Review of: Evidence-Based Practice for the Helping Professions: A Practical Guide with Integrated Multimedia,* by E. Armstrong, 2001, Allentown, PA: Lehigh Valley Family Practice Residence Program. Adapted with permission. This worksheet references its components from multiple sources.

You might want to just stop here, reading no further due to time pressures and limited resources. If so, you have an excellent worksheet to go on. The remainder of this chapter goes successively more deeply into how to rate studies that evaluate the effectiveness of treatment and prevention programs.

The Quality of Study Rating Form (QSRF) for Rating Evidence Regarding Effectiveness (Individual Studies)

Background

The Quality of Study Rating Form (QSRF) has been in development through successive iterations over a period of almost 20 years. It was developed initially to serve as an outcome measure for a randomized controlled trial that evaluated electronic versus manual search methods for answering evaluation questions that had been posed by social work students regarding their client(s) (Gibbs & Johnson, 1983). Successive versions of the form have incorporated changes that were suggested in a trial to evaluate the QSRF's measurement qualities (Gibbs, 1989). This trial compared ratings made by students in fall and spring 1986 fieldwork classes (respectively $n = 48, 40$) who rated three effectiveness studies. Their average rate of agreement was 81%, 95%, and 96% for total quality points among the three articles (p. 60). The proportions that calculated treatment effect size (standardized mean difference or $ES1$) accurately were 53%,

77%, and 94% (p. 60). The QSRF has been revised once since then (Gibbs & Gambrill, 1999, pp. 161–170) and still again for this text.

Please note that others have developed rating forms to rate effectiveness studies. You may want to take a look at an alternative one in the CONSORT system at this address: www.consort-statement.org. A look at the CONSORT form for rating a randomized controlled trial may help you to further understand the criteria on the QSRF. The CONSORT system's explanation covers more detail, but the QSRF has been checked for inter-rater agreement for those independently rating studies, something I did not see in the CONSORT discussion.

Takes Guesswork Out of Rating Effectiveness Studies

The QSRF will help you to rate studies relevant to answering effectiveness questions. The form was developed to answer the perennial question from students in training for practice whose assignment required them to locate and to evaluate research to guide their practice decision making: "Which of these studies is better?" "Which study shall I use?" "Which treatment has the greatest effect?" "Do these results apply to my clients?" The QSRF can be used to rate any effectiveness study, including single-subject ones, though it favors a randomized controlled trial. Studies that fall short of the ideal will get fewer quality points, because they support weaker inferences.

Designed So Best Effectiveness Studies Score Highest

The best yardstick for evidence regarding effectiveness is the randomized controlled trial (RCT). RCTs sometimes provide counterintuitive evidence that refutes practice wisdom. For example, delinquency-prevention programs were heralded as a panacea that would literally scare the delinquency out of youths by exposing them temporarily to prison life. Such programs proliferated until a randomized controlled trial done by James Finckenauer (1982) demonstrated that controls not participating in the program were involved in fewer acts of delinquency at 6 months follow-up than those treated by a margin of 29.9%. Here the number needed to harm was 3.34 (i.e., the number participating in treatment not harmed to harm one within a given outcome interval). In another context, the occasionally counterintuitive quality of RCTs has saved many from a harmful and expensive surgery called extracranial-intracranial bypass that was intended to prevent stroke. This surgery was performed to prevent stroke by delicately attaching an artery from outside the head to increase blood flow into the brain. Surgeons who had been performing the surgery were astonished to learn that the surgery made patients worse off than those in a control group. Instead of helping, the surgery *increased* the probability of stroke by 14% (Vertosick, 1998, p. 108). The number needed to harm, that is, the number needed to participate in treatment not having a stroke to cause one stroke, was 7.14 (i.e., $100/14 = 7.14$).

The QSRF gives more points to studies that follow criteria for a well-conducted RCT for these reasons: (a) RCTs help to avoid harming clients, because RCTs sometimes provide counterintuitive results; (b) RCTs are ethically defensible, because preliminary evidence indicates that those treated as part of an RCT do better than those treated outside one (possibly due to closer monitoring) (Devereaux, 2000, p. 4); and (c) RCTs help you to best know the truth about what helps clients, because they rule out factors other than treatment more effectively than other designs do (Gibbs, 1991, pp. 71–100).

Includes Indices of Study Quality and Treatment Impact

The QSRF includes two types of indices. The QSRF's total quality points provide an index of confidence in the study's validity, because it include characteristics of studies that more effectively control for bias. The QSRF also includes indices that may be compared across studies to estimate the relative magnitude of a treatment's effect, including standardized mean difference (*ES1*), absolute risk reduction (*ARR* or *ES2*), and number needed to treat (*NNT* or *ES3*). These three indices of a treatment's effect size can be used to make comparisons across studies. The last two are the easiest to understand and to interpret. And finally, the QSRF and all of the critical appraisal forms in this chapter end with a section that concerns whether the study's findings apply to one's own clients.

Instructions for Scoring

Please spend a few minutes previewing the QSRF (Table 5.2). Note that it contains three parts. The first includes background information regarding the client type, intervention method, outcome measures used to compute indices of treatment effect size (explained in the Explanation of Criteria section), and the source of the study. The second section includes Items 1 through 18 to assess quality. These 18 are all summed in Item 19. Item 19 ranges from 0 to 100; the closer to 100, the more confidence the rater can place in the study's findings. Items 20, 21, and 22 are three indices of treatment effect size. These indices summarize the impact of treatment in standardized units. Explanations for each of these three indices of effect size appear in the Explanation of Criteria section, which follows. These three indices, particularly number needed to treat, can aid decision making about whether to take action based on the study's findings.

Explanation of Criteria Regarding Study Quality

The first section of the QSRF states the identifying information regarding the client type (e.g., depressed, middle-aged men); intervention method (e.g., aerobic exercise four or more times a week); and the outcome measure(s)—preferably ones that can be used to calculate treatment effect size (e.g., score on Beck Depression Inventory).

Experience with the QSRF's reliability indicates that reliability will be highest for all-or-nothing points for each item; so give either zero points or the particular point value indicated if the study meets the criterion, as numbered on the form and described in the following list:

1. *Who:* The author describes who is treated by stating the subject(s)' average age *and* standard deviation of age, *and* sex or proportion of males and females, *and* clearly defines clients' presenting problem(s).
2. *What:* The authors tell what the treatment involves so specifically that you could apply the treatment with nothing more to go on than their description, *or* they refer you to a book, videotape, CD-ROM, article, or Web address that describes the treatment method.
3. *Where:* Authors state where the treatment occurred so specifically that you could contact people at that facility by phone, letter, or E-mail address.
4. *When:* Authors tell the *when* of treatment by stating how long subjects participated in the treatment in days, weeks, or months *or* tell how many treatment sessions were attended by subjects.
5. *Why:* Authors either discuss a specific theory that describes why they used one or more treatment methods, *or* they cite literature that supports the use of the treatment method.
6. *Subjects randomly assigned to treatment or control:* The author states specifically that subjects were *randomly assigned* to treatment groups or refers to the assignment of subjects on the basis of a table of random numbers, computer algorithm, or accepted randomization procedure. This means that the procedure resulted in each subject having an equal chance of being assigned to treatment or control groups. Random assignment ensures better than any other procedure that control or treatment groups are initially similar before treatment begins, so posttreatment differences can be attributed to treatment effects. Random assignment concerns the internal validity of a study. If the author says subjects were randomly assigned but assigns subjects to treatments by assigning every other one or by allowing subjects or others to choose the treatment groups somehow other than by random procedure, then subjects are *not* randomly assigned.
7. *Analysis shows equal treatment and control groups before treatment:* Even though subjects have been randomly assigned, unequal treatment and control groups can occur by chance; so, to guard against this, the authors need to make comparisons across treatment and control groups on key client characteristics to see that they are similar prior to treatment (e.g., sex, race, age, economic status, condition, strengths).
8. *Subjects blind to being in treatment or control group:* Subjects who know they are in a control group can experience effects of being there including demoralization or competition with experimentals (Cook & Campbell, 1979, p. 55). Subjects who know they are in a treatment group can experience powerful healing effects because they expect them (Brown, 1998). Give points for subjects blinded if two or more groups get some kind of treatment, if controls get some form of sham treatment that is not

expected to have an effect but gives assurance to subjects that something is being done, if subjects serve in a delayed treatment control group where they serve as controls but get treatment later, or if subjects truly do not know whether they are in a treatment or control group.

9. *Subjects randomly selected for inclusion in study:* Selection of subjects is different from *random assignment. Random selection* means that subjects are taken from some potential pool of subjects for inclusion in the study by using a table of random numbers or other statistically random procedures. For example, if subjects are chosen randomly from among all residents on a psychiatric ward, the results of the study can be generalized more confidently to all residents of that ward. Random selection concerns generalizing results of the study to others outside the study, or external validity.

10. *Control (nontreated) group used:* Members of a *nontreated control group* do not receive a different kind of treatment; they receive *no* treatment. An example of a nontreated control group would be a group of subjects who are denied group counseling while others are given group counseling. Subjects in the nontreated control group may receive treatment at a later date but do not receive treatment while experimental group subjects are receiving their treatment.

11. *Number of subjects in smallest treatment group exceeds 20:* Those in the treatment group or groups are those who receive some kind of special care intended to help them. It is this treatment that is being evaluated by those doing the study. The results of the study will state how effective the treatment or treatment groups have been when compared with each other or with a nontreated control group. In order to meet Criterion 11, *the number of subjects in the smallest treatment group must be at least 21.* (Not everyone will agree with this number. Apply a statistical power analysis if possible.) Here, *number of subjects* means total number of individuals, not number of couples or number of groups.

12. *Outcome measure has face validity:* Face validity is present if the outcome measure used to determine the effectiveness of treatment makes sense to you. A good criterion for the sense of an outcome measure is whether the measure evaluates something that should logically be affected by the treatment. For example, drinking behavior has face validity as an outcome measure for treating alcoholism. An intelligence quotient may not have face validity as an indicator for alcoholism treatment.

13. *Treatment outcome measure was checked for reliability:* For this criterion to be met, to merely say that the outcome of treatment was measured in some way is not enough. The outcome measure itself must be evaluated to check its reliability. *Reliability*—the consistency of measurement—is frequently measured in an outcome evaluation study by comparing the findings of investigators who independently rate the performance of individuals in treatment or control groups. Another less frequently used way to measure reliability of outcome measures is to have the same individual rate the performance of subjects, then re-rate their performance. In

single-subject studies, two raters may rate the subject's behavior independently for cross-rater comparison.

The reliability criterion is satisfied here only if the author of the study affirms that *evaluations were made of the outcome measure's reliability (for example, inter-rater agreement), and the author lists a numerical value of some kind for this measure of reliability.* Where multiple outcome criteria are used, reliability checks of any one of the major outcome criteria satisfy Criterion 13.

14. *Reliability measure has value greater than .70 or percent of rater agreement greater than 70%:* The reliability coefficient in Criterion 13 is .70 or greater (70% or better). Reliability coefficients typically range from −1 (perfect disagreement), through 0 (no pattern of agreement or disagreement), to 1 (perfect agreement).

15. *Those rating outcome rated it blind:* This criterion concerns the way bias can enter into measurement if the person measuring outcome knows whether the subject being measured is from a treatment or control group, or, worse, the person measuring outcome is in a position to determine the outcome measure. As an example for the latter, a large study had as an outcome whether persons with chronic mental illness treated in the community were readmitted to a hospital. Those administering the special treatment were in a position to decide whether the clients would be readmitted, which was an outcome criterion in the study (Test & Stein, 1977, pp. 14–15; Gomory, 1999, pp. 154–155). *Give the points for this criterion only if the person conducting the outcome measuring did not know which subjects were in treatment or control groups.*

16. *Outcome of treatment was measured after treatment was completed:* At least one outcome measure was obtained after *treatment was completed.* After release from the hospital, after drug therapy was completed, after subjects quit attending inpatient group therapy—all are posttreatment measures. For example, if subjects were released from the mental hospital on November 10, and some measure of success was obtained on November 11, then the study meets Criterion 16. Outcome measured both during treatment and after treatment is sufficient to meet this criterion.

17. *Test of statistical significance was made and* p < .05: Tests of statistical significance are generally referred to by phrases such as "differences between treatment groups were significant at the .05 level" or "results show statistical significance for. . . ." *Statistical significance* refers to the probability of obtaining an observed difference between treatment or control groups as great as or greater than by chance alone. Give credit for meeting this criterion only if the author refers to a test of statistical significance for a major outcome variable naming the statistical procedure (e.g., analysis of variance, chi square, *t* test) *and* gives a *p* value, for example $p < .05$, *and* the *p* value is equal to or smaller than .05. (With small samples in exploratory studies, .10 may be better to reduce the chance that one will miss a real difference, but generally .05 is the convention.)

18. *Follow-up was greater than 75%:* The proportion of subjects successfully followed up refers to the number contacted to measure outcome compared with the number who began the study. Ideally, the two should be the same (100% followed up). To compare the proportion followed up for each group studied (i.e., treatment group(s), control group), determine the number of subjects who initially entered the study in the group and determine the number successfully followed up. (If there is more than one follow-up period, use the longest one.) Then, for each group, divide the number successfully followed up by the number who began in each group and multiply each quotient by 100. For example, if 20 entered a treatment group, but 15 were followed up in that group, the result would be: $(15/20)100 = 75\%$. Compute the proportion followed up for all groups involved in the experiment. If the *smallest* of these percentages exceeds 75%, the study meets this criterion.

19. *Total quality points* (TQP) *(add 1–18):* Simply add the point values for Criteria 1–18 and record this value in Box 19. This value will range between 0 and 100.

20. *Effect size (ES1) or standardized mean difference* (magnitude of difference between groups in standard deviation units) calculated by the following:

$$ES1 = \frac{\bar{x}_t - \bar{x}_c}{S_c}$$

= (mean of treatment – mean of control or alternate treatment)/standard deviation of control or alternate treatment

This formula is for computing *ES1* (standardized mean difference or difference in standard deviation units) when outcome means of treatment and control groups are given (Cohen, 1988, p. 20; Hedges, 1984, p. 31). To compute an effect size from information presented in a study's report, select two means to compare; for example, outcome might be a mean of a treatment group compared with a mean of a nontreated control group. Subtract the mean of the second group from the mean of the first group and divide this difference by the standard deviation of the second group. (Standard deviations are indicated by various symbols, including *s.d.*, S, *s*, SD, or σ.) *ES1* may be a negative number or positive number. If the outcome measure's score gets greater as client outcome improves and *ES1* is positive, then the treatment has had a positive effect, proportionate to the size of *ES1*. In this case, if *ES1* is negative, then the treatment harms.

21. *Effect size (ES2) or absolute risk reduction:*

$ES2 = p_t - p_c = $ ((number improved in treatment/total number in treatment group) × 100) – ((number improved in alternate treatment or control/total number in alternate treatment or control) × 100)

Absolute risk reduction (*ES2*) refers to the event rate in treatment relative to the event rate in the control group (Greenhalgh & Donald,

2000, pp. 157–159). Assume that you are comparing the proportion in a treatment group who are improved against the proportion in a control group who are improved. Say that 70% of those in the treatment group are improved and 50% of those in the control group are also improved for a particular outcome measure at follow-up (usually the longest follow-up contact). *ES2* (absolute risk reduction) then equals 70% minus 50%, or 20%. Thus, the proportion of improvement attributable to the treatment may be 20% (depending on your level of confidence in the experiment's design and execution).

22. *Effect size (ES3) or number needed to treat:*

$$NNT = \frac{100}{ES2}$$

"*NNT (ES3)* is the number of [clients] that a clinician must treat with the experimental treatment in order to create a good outcome or to prevent one bad outcome in comparison to the control treatment" (Furukawa, 1999, p. 1). For example, if *ES2* (absolute risk reduction) is 20%, then *NNT* is 100/20, or 5. *This means that five persons would need to be exposed to the treatment and not benefit to benefit one.* This assumes, of course, that the study effectively rules out extraneous factors and bias, as reflected in Criterion 19 of the QSRF. If controls do better, then this number is the number needed to harm

Taking Action Based on the QSRF

This section includes an assortment of topics related to the QSRF's content. Some parts of this section are more technical than many would like, but I have included discussion in this section because it provides a deeper understanding than one gets by just filling out the QSRF. You may read this section in more depth later if you like when, for example, you want a step-by-step procedure for computing number needed to treat, or you may want to estimate *NNT (ES3)* from absolute risk reduction (*ES2*) or from standardized mean difference (*ES1*).

Weighing Study Quality   The first 19 criteria on the QSRF concerned the confidence that you can have in an inference that the treatment caused a change—the greater the total quality points *(TQP)*, the more confidence. The *TQP* score is just a guide. A higher *TQP* score merely implies greater confidence in a study's causal inference. The *TQP* score is only an ordinal scale, that is, a study with 80 points is higher than one with 40 points but not necessarily twice as credible. Twelve years of experience with at least 800 students using successive versions of the QSRF have demonstrated that the best study that each student can locate regarding a particular COPES question averages about 60 points. A *TQP* score of 80 and above marks an unusually strong study regarding effectiveness questions. Because the *TQP* score reflects confidence in the study's methodology, the *TQP* score has implications for action with clients: *Where several studies exist regarding the same COPES question, pick the study that*

Table 5.2 | Quality of Study Rating Form (QSRF)

Client type(s) _____

Intervention method(s) _____

Outcome measure to compute *ES1* _____

Outcome measure to compute *ES2* _____

Outcome measure to compute *ES3* _____

Source in APA format _____

Criteria for Rating Study

Clear Definition of Treatment					6. Subjects randomly assigned to treatment or control. (10 pts.)	7. Analysis shows equal treatment and control groups before treatment. (5 pts.)	8. Subjects blind to being in treatment or control group. (5 pts.)
1. Who (4 pts.)	2. What (4 pts.)	3. Where (4 pts.)	4. When (4 pts.)	5. Why (4 pts.)			

Criteria for Rating Study (cont.)

9. Subjects randomly selected for inclusion in study. (4 pts.)	10. Control (nontreated) group used. (4 pts.)	11. Number of subjects in smallest treatment group exceeds 20. (4 pts.)	12. Outcome measure has face validity. (4 pts.)	13. Treatment outcome measure was checked for reliability. (5 pts.)	14. Reliability measure has value greater than .70 or percent of rater agreement greater than 70%. (5 pts.)

Criteria for Rating Study (cont.)   **Criteria for Rating Effect Size**

15. Those rating outcome rated it blind. (10 pts.)	16. Outcome of treatment was measured after treatment was completed. (4 pts.)	17. Test of statistical significance was made and $p < .05$. (10 pts.)	18. Follow-up was greater than 75%. (10 pts.)	19. Total quality points (add 1–18).	20. Effect size = ($ES1$) = SD units = (mean of treatment—mean of control or alternate treatment) ÷ (standard deviation of control or alternate treatment)

Criteria for Rating Effect Size

21. Effect size ($ES2$) = Absolute risk reduction = (Percent improved in treatment) – (percent improved in control)	22. Effect size ($ES3$) = Number needed to treat = 100 ÷ $ES2$

Note. From Quality of Study Rating Form (QSRF) by L. Gibbs and E. Gambrill, *Critical Thinking for Social Workers: Exercises for the Helping Professions,* Thousand Oaks, CA: Pine Forge Press, 1996, 1999, by Pine Forge Press: adapted with permission; "Quality of Study Rating Form: An Instrument for Synthesizing Evaluation Studies" by L. E. Gibbs, 1989, *Journal of Social Work Education, 25*(1), p. 67. Copyright 1989 by the Council on Social Work Education: adapted with permission; and from L. E. Gibbs, *Scientific Reasoning for Social Workers,* pp. 193–197, Copyright owned by L. E. Gibbs.

has the better quality. Keep in mind that a study may have a fatal error that transcends the QRSF Score (e.g., researcher compromised the randomization).

Estimating the Magnitude of a Treatment's Impact on Clients   Effect size can be weighted by study quality according to various complex procedures (Detsky, Naylor, O'Rourke, McGeer, & L'Abbé, 1992, p. 261). *ES2* (absolute risk reduction) and *ES3* (number needed to treat) can be weighted roughly to reflect study quality as follows:

$$ES2 \text{ weighted by study quality} = (TQP/100) \times ES2$$

$$ES3 \text{ weighted by study quality} = (TQP/100) \times ES3$$

The total quality points *(TQP)* score does not tell much about the impact of treatment. You need to know how much of a difference you might expect if your clients are exposed to the same treatment—this assumes that your clients are similar enough to those in a study to have the study's results generalize to your own. All three indices of treatment effect size on the QSRF can help you to estimate the magnitude of a treatment's effect, but number needed to treat seems the most understandable and interpretable to clients; therefore, the following discussion concerns *NNT.*

Statistical Significance Versus Clinical Significance and Number Needed to Treat   As practitioners learn to search efficiently for the best evidence related to their COPES questions, they will increasingly confront a common problem: How can studies be applied to taking action? Practitioners will need some index of expected benefit to clients. If an expected benefit is trivial, then practitioners want to save valuable time and resources. If an expected benefit is substantial, then practioners will want to take action based on the evidence.

An appropriate statistical test's statistical significance level provides one index for treatment impact. *Statistical significance* is the probability that the observed difference between treatment groups or control can be explained by chance variation. A $p < .05$ means that, given the observed difference and error variance, about 1 in 20 experiments would arrive at the observed difference due to chance alone. The smaller the p level, the greater the confidence you can have that the difference observed is not due to error in measurement.

Statistical significance provides a clue to taking action, because practitioners need to know how likely an observed difference between treatment groups and control may merely reflect chance; but a study may find statistical significance regarding what practitioners would consider a trivial difference in outcome between treatment and control groups, depending on sample size and other variables. Therefore, in addition to statistical inference, practitioners need some standard of comparison to judge the magnitude of a treatment's effect. "If a treatment is to be useful to practitioners, it is not enough for treatment effects to be statistically significant; they also need to be clinically meaningful" (Chambless & Hollon, 1998, p. 11). *Clinical significance* (practical significance) means that the treatment produces a great enough effect to warrant the risks, inconvenience, and costs of an intervention. Here is a formal definition for clinical significance:

> Clinical significance is the perception of an important change in an attribute or behavior in oneself or another as a result of treatment. (Jayaratne, 1990)

The *number needed to treat* provides the decision maker with an easily computed and easily interpreted index to estimate practical or clinical significance. The following composite definition for *NNT* reflects key features from several definitions: *With reference to a randomized controlled trial that yields binary results (nominal either-or),* NNT *refers to the number of persons who must participate in an experimental treatment who will not benefit to create one good outcome, or to prevent one bad outcome, in comparison to the control treatment within a given interval of time* (Cordell, 1999, p. 434; Furukawa, 1999, p. 1; Moriarty, 1998, p. 505). If those in the *control group* do better than those in the treatment group, then the index becomes the *number needed to harm (NNH)* (Cordell, 1999, p. 436). *NNT* can be computed for quasi-experimental studies that do not include random assignment but must be interpreted there with less confidence.

A Simplified Procedure for Computing Number Needed to Treat in Binary Data   The worksheet in Figure 5.1 comes from Bandolier and can be downloaded directly from their Web site: www.jr2.ox.ac.uk/bandolier/index.html (just enter number needed to treat calculator in the search option on the home page). Their worksheet will guide you to compute *NNT*. The L'Abbé plot can summarize percentages for several outcomes from one study or can summarize outcomes from several studies. If the points plotted are to the right of the diagonal line in the L'Abbé plot, then the treatment has a harmful effect. Greater distances above and below the diagonal mark stronger *NNT*s or *NNH*s, respectively.

Transformations Among Indices of Treatment Effect Size   Sometimes you will encounter articles that give you a standardized mean difference (*ES1*) but not the more easily interpreted absolute risk reduction (*ES2*) and number needed to treat (*ES3*). Beyond interpreting *ES1* values of .2, .5, and .8 as being "small," "medium," and "large," respectively (Cohen, 1977), and looking at distributions of standardized mean difference values found in meta-analyses (Glass & Kliegel, 1983, p. 31), *ES1* is difficult to interpret as a guide to decision making in practice. As one solution, you may use computer programs to work an approximate transformation from standardized mean difference to absolute risk reduction (Schwarzer, n.d.), or you can use a formula (see Formula 5.1 and Formula 5.2). The following section comes from a fuller discussion in my earlier text (Gibbs, 1991, pp. 206–212).

If insufficient information is given to compute *ES2*, it can sometimes be approximated. If you can assume that groups to be compared have characteristics that are normally distributed, are of approximately equal variance, and

Figure 5.1 | Number Needed to Treat *(NNT)* Calculator

First fill in the answers to the questions, where appropriate, graph the data on the L'Abbé plot, and finally do the *NNT* calculation.

	Question/Action	Answer
A	What is the intervention (i.e., drug dose or frequency)?	
B	What is the intervention for?	
C	What is the successful outcome (and when or over what time did it occur)?	
D	How many had the intervention?	
E	How many had successful outcome with the intervention?	
F	Express this as a percentage ($100 \times E/D$) and as a proportion (E/D).	
G	What is the control or comparison group?	
H	How many people had the control?	
I	How many had successful outcome with the control?	
J	Express this as a percentage ($100 \times I/H$) and as a proportion (I/H).	

Now graph the percentages of the trial on the graph from the percentages from F and J. This can be done for different outcomes of a trial or individual trials in a systematic review or meta-analysis.

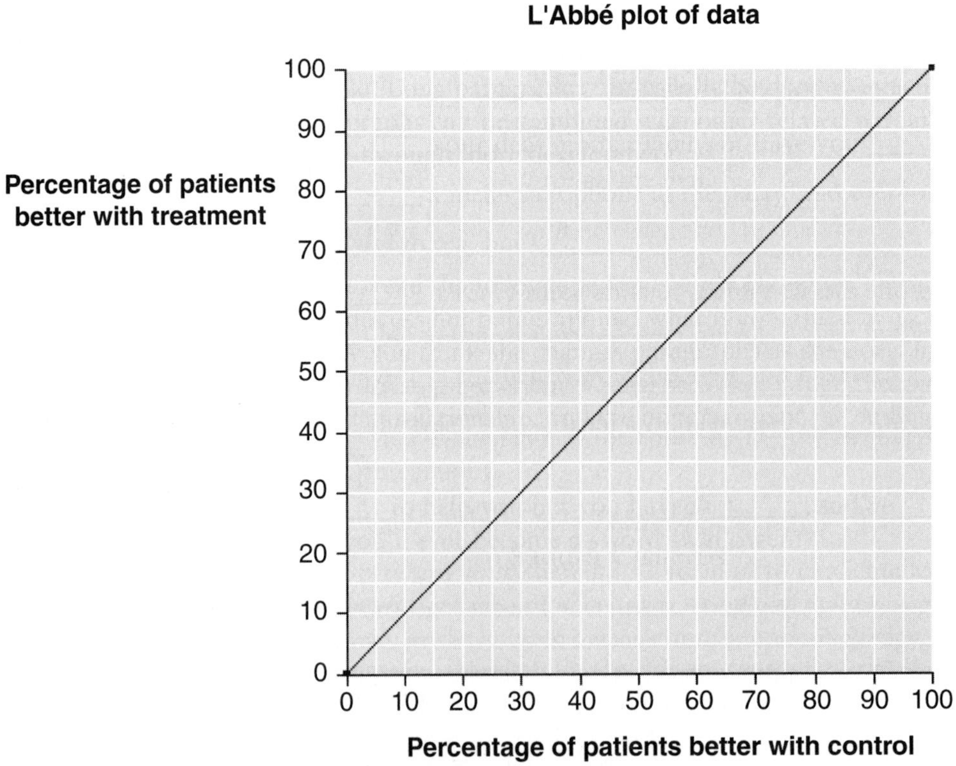

L'Abbé plot of data

Percentage of patients better with treatment *(y-axis)*

Percentage of patients better with control *(x-axis)*

Figure 5.1 | Continued

Now calculate the *NNT* using the proportions from F and J.

$$\text{NNT} = \frac{1}{\boxed{\text{F}} - \boxed{\text{J}}} = \frac{1}{\boxed{} - \boxed{}}$$

$$\text{NNT} = \frac{1}{\boxed{}} = \boxed{}$$

Note. From "Number needed to treat *(NNT)* calculator," Bandolier [January 1999]. Retrieved March 4, 2002, from the World Wide Web: www.jr2.ox.ac.uk/bandolier/index.html Copyright by Bandolier. Adapted by permission.

are of approximately equal size and that individuals change in equal amounts, then there are ways to approximate *ES2* given *ES1* or from common tests of statistical significance (Rosenthal, 1984, p. 25; Rosenthal & Rubin, 1982, p. 167).

Assuming such conditions, to approximate *ES2* from *ES1*, apply this formula: Where *ES1* is a medium-size .53:

Formula 5.1: Transformation from Standardized Mean Difference to Approximate Absolute Risk Reduction

$$ES2 = \frac{ES1}{\sqrt{(ES1)^2 + 4}}$$

$$ES2 = \frac{.53}{\sqrt{(.53)^2 + 4}}$$

$$ES2 = .26 \text{ or about 26\% difference.}$$

Where you have a *t* test of statistical significance with value 1.688 and 38 degrees of freedom:

Formula 5.2: Transformation from *t*-Test Result to Approximate Absolute Risk Reduction

$$ES2 = \sqrt{\frac{t^2}{t^2 + df}}$$

$$ES2 = \sqrt{\frac{1.688^2}{1.688^2 + 38}}$$

$$ES2 = .26$$

Exercise 5-1 Effectiveness of a Program to Reduce Alzheimer's Disease Caregiver's Depression and Burden

Purpose

This exercise is designed to demonstrate how the QSRF may be applied to an article that evaluates the effectiveness of a program. It is also designed to provide experience deciding whether to apply an evaluation study's findings as a guide for action.

Background

You may want to review Susan Montgomery's story at the beginning of chapter 1 to get background for this exercise. One fact about nursing homes may surprise you. Many nursing homes frequently care for clients during a crisis and then place the family member back into the home. One nursing home in the Eau Claire, Wisconsin, area places at least 70% back into their homes (Howe, L., personal communication, Lakeside Nursing and Rehabilitation, June 5, 2001); so nursing home staff members try to help families with their caregiver burdens and depression. The following article concerns an important problem for nursing home social workers. Here is Susan's question:

> Regarding family caregivers helping demented aged persons, which method of support for caregivers will result in the best quality of life for the caregivers?

Instructions

Please go to INFOTRAC (College) through this address on the World Wide Web: www.infotrac-college.com/access.html. Enter your passcode. This book provides one. Then enter Newcomer and Yordi and DuNah and Fox and Wilkinson, and then click on Enter. These are the authors for the following article: Newcomer, R., Yordi, C., DuNah, R., Fox, P., & Wilkinson, A. (1999). Effects of the Medicare Alzheimer's Disease Demonstration on caregiver burden and depression. *Health Services Research, 34*(3), pp. 669–689. This is INFOTRAC Article A55610150.

Discussion

I have asked you to use INFOTRAC (College) for all of the exercises in this chapter, not because INFOTRAC provides the best evidence (see Table 4.7), but because you can surely get access to the articles through INFOTRAC. I could have used sources from large free databases (e.g., MEDLINE and ERIC), but I could not count on these massive databases to keep sources for these exercises.

Please note that to fill out the QSRF you will need information from Table 1 in the article, but Table 1 has been omitted here. For the sake of brevity here, please note that Table 1 lists the mean and standard deviations for the treatment and control groups respectively as: 78 years, s.d. 8.06 years and 78 years and s.d. 8.35 years. Table 1 also lists the percentage male as 28% and 26%, respectively. Table 1 also lists comparisons showing the T and C groups as very similar on client stressors, married, caregiver stressors, and income.

Your instructor has answers to the following questions. Please note that his exercise realistically reflects a common problem for evidence-based practitioners: you do not always find positive results. A finding of "no difference" *is* a finding. You can learn as much from such a finding as you can from a positive finding. Integrity in evidence-based practice implies that you let the evidence guide you, because you care about knowing what is best for clients.

Questions

1. Why is this question of particular importance to answering Susan's question?

_____

_____

2. Please fill out the Quality of Study Rating Form for the preceding article. How many points did you give it under total quality points? $TQP =$

_____

3. What were the strong and weak points of this study?

_____

_____

_____

4. Please examine Table 2 from the article (found following Question 7 at the end of this exercise). What was the ES1 for caregiver burden for 36-month follow-up? → *is 20 (Effect size)* →

5. Please examine Table 2 from the article. What was the ES1 for caregiver depression at 36-month follow-up?

6. Are clients, as described in the study, sufficiently like those in your own practice to warrant extrapolating the study's findings to the client(s) at hand? Use the following table for comparison. [These are the kinds of questions Susan would have to address before applying findings to her clients.]

Area for Comparison	Your Clients	Study Clients
Client Problem		
Client Strengths		
Age		
Sex		
Race		
Ethnic Background		

continued

Area for Comparison	Your Clients	Study Clients
Your Resources Versus Study Resources for Implementing Treatment or Assessment Procedure		
Other Concerns		

7. Based on this article, would you recommend that the case management procedure—the article gives reference to reports that describe it in more detail—be implemented?

Table 2 from Newcomer, Yordi, DuNah, Fox, & Wilkinson (1999)

Outcome Measure	Treatment Group			Control Group		
	N	Mean	s.d.	N	Mean	s.d.
Caregiver BurdenΨ						
Baseline	2728	14.3	7.09	2576	14.3	7.17
6 Months	2268	14.4	7.91	2138	14.9*	8.17
12 Months	1702	14.1	8.07	1597	14.4	8.62
18 Months	1437	13.7	8.20	1283	14.3	8.62
24 Months	1528	13.8	8.20	1354	14.2	8.60
36 Months	986	13.7	8.49	920	14.2	8.73
Caregiver Depressionθ						
Baseline	2731	4.24	3.29	2576	4.21	3.28
6 Months	2269	4.29	3.42	2139	4.48	3.52
12 Months	1705	4.28	3.40	1597	4.42	3.68
18 Months	1439	4.17	3.55	1288	4.53*	3.80
24 Months	1531	4.06	3.51	1356	4.36*	3.65
36 Months	988	4.20	3.52	922	4.49	3.61

Note: Mean scores are unadjusted.

*$p < .05$; **$p < .01$; ***$p < .001$ difference between the treatment and control group. t-tests were used to determine significant differences between the two groups.

ΨScores can range from 0 to 32. Higher scores indicate greater caregiver burden (Zarit, Reever, & Bach-Peterson, 1980).

θScores can range form 0 to 15. Higher scores indicate greater caregiver depression (Yesavage et al. 1983).

Note: From Newcomer, R., Yordi, C., DuNah, R., Fox, P., Wilkinson, A. (1999). Effects of the medicare Alzheimer's disease demonstration on caregiver burden and depression. *HSR: Health Services Research*, *34*(3), 678. Copyright 1999 by Health Services Research. Copied with permission.

Exercise 5-2 Effectiveness of Cognitive-Behavioral Training in Job-Finding for Long-Term Unemployed People

Purpose

This exercise is designed to demonstrate how the QSRF may be applied to an article that evaluates the effectiveness of a program. It is also designed to provide experience deciding whether to apply an evaluation study's findings as a guide for action.

Background

The former governor of Wisconsin, Tommy Thompson, at this moment heads the Department of Health and Human Services in Washington. He is famous for his initiatives on welfare-to-work programs. Many will be forced off income-maintenance programs if his initiatives continue; so it may be beneficial to know which types of program are effective for helping those so affected.

Instructions

Please go to INFOTRAC through this WWW address: www.infotrac-college.com/access.html Enter your passcode. Then enter the names of the authors for this article connected by AND. Proudfoot, J., Guest, D., Carson, J., Dunn, G., & Gray, J. (1997). Effect of cognitive behavioral training on job-finding among long-term unemployed people. *The Lancet, 350*(9071), pp. 96–100. This is INFOTRAC Article A19638029.

Discussion

Your instructor has answers to the following questions. Please note that this exercise *does* find positive results. I have included it here particularly because its abstract contains information that allows you to compute number needed to treat directly without resorting to a transformation from standardized mean difference.

Questions

1. Would this article be of particular importance for welfare-to-work clients?

   _____

   _____

2. Please fill out the Quality of Study Rating Form for the preceding article. How many points did you give it under total quality points? $TQP =$

   _____

3. Please calculate your $ES2$, or absolute risk reduction (all you need is in the abstract). What is $ARR?$ _____

   _____

4. Please calculate number needed to treat. What is *NNT* here? _____ .
   If you compare two treatments, and find *NNT* smaller in one treatment compared with the other, and assuming approximately the same *TQP* values and follow-up intervals for both studies, which treatment would you favor, the one with the *smaller NNT* or the one with the *larger NNT*? Why?

   _____

   _____

   _____

5. Are clients, as described in the study, sufficiently like those in your own practice to warrant extrapolating the study's findings to the client(s) at hand? Use the following table for comparison.

Area for Comparison	Your Clients	Study Clients
Client Problem		
Client Strengths		
Age		
Sex		
Race		
Ethnic Background		
Your Resources Versus Study Resources for Implementing Treatment or Assessment Procedure		
Other Concerns		

6. Based on this article, would you recommend cognitive-behavioral training if your clients resemble those in the study sufficiently to apply to your own clients? Why, or why not?

   _____

   _____

   _____

   _____

   _____

The Quality of Study Rating Form for Rating a Prevention Study (QSRF-P)

Background

Most interventions focus on what to do once a problem has happened. Doing so is analogous to waiting to close the door until after the cat has made its escape. A primary prevention study evaluates the effectiveness of an effort to prevent the *initial occurrence* of a problem. Prevention concerns a vital issue because prevention can cost far less than intervening after the fact (e.g., preventing teenage pregnancy and related events that may follow including poor prenatal care, unstable home environment for the child, inadequate parenting skills).

Purpose

The QSRF-P will help you to compute a single index of study quality ranging from 0 to 100 that reflects confidence in the prevention study's causal inference (Criterion 20, total quality points). It will also help you to get experience deciding whether to act on a prevention study's findings. You will be shown how to compute three indices of treatment effect size that express expected treatment impact in units that workers and clients can understand (particularly Criteria 22 and 23, absolute risk reduction and number needed to treat).

Instructions

Please spend a few minutes previewing the QSRF-P (Table 5.3). Note that it contains three parts. The first includes background information regarding the client type, intervention method, outcome measures used to compute indices of treatment effect size (explained in the Explanation of Criteria section) and the source of the study. The second section includes Criteria 1 through 19 to assess quality. These 19 are all summed in Criterion 20. Criterion 20 ranges from 0 to 100; the closer to 100, the more confidence that the rater can place in the study's findings. Criteria 21, 22, and 23 are three indices of treatment effect size. These indices summarize the impact of treatment in standardized units. Explanations for each of these three indices of effect size appear in the Explanation of Criteria section. These three indices, particularly number needed to treat (number needed to participate in a prevention program and not to benefit to prevent one instance), can aid decision making about whether to take action based on the study's findings.

Explanation of Criteria on QSRF-P Regarding Study Quality

In the first section, state identifying information regarding the client type (e.g., sexually active boys and girls ages 12 through 18). State the intervention method (e.g., peer-led pregnancy prevention program). State the outcome measure(s) used to calculate treatment effect size (e.g., number of pregnancies, number who report using condoms at every intercourse). Give no partial points. Give either 0 points or the particular point value indicated if the study meets the criterion, as numbered and described here:

1. *Who:* The author describes who is treated by stating the subject(s)' average age *and* standard deviation of age, *and* sex or proportion of males and females, *and* clearly defines the behavior(s) to be prevented.

2. *What:* The authors describe the prevention program so specifically that you could apply the program with nothing more to go on than their description *or* they refer you to a book, videotape, CD-ROM, article, or Web address that describes the program.

3. *Where:* Authors state where the program occurred so specifically that you could contact people who conducted the prevention program by phone, letter, or E-mail address.

4. *When:* Authors tell the when of the prevention program by stating how long subjects participated in it in days, weeks, or months *or* tell how many treatment sessions were attended by subjects.

5. *Why:* Authors either discuss a specific theory that describes why the prevention program should work, *or* they cite literature that demonstrates the prevention program's effectiveness in a previous trial.

6. *Subjects randomly assigned to prevention program or control:* The author states specifically that subjects were *randomly assigned* to the prevention program groups or refers to the assignment of subjects on the basis of a table of random numbers, computer algorithm, or accepted randomization procedure. This means that the procedure resulted in each subject having an equal chance of being assigned to the prevention program or control groups. Random assignment ensures better than any other procedure that control or program groups are initially similar before treatment begins, so posttreatment differences can be attributed to effects of the program. Random assignment concerns the internal validity of a study. If the author says subjects were randomly assigned but assigns subjects by assigning every other one from a list or by allowing subjects or others to choose the treatment groups somehow other than by random procedure, then subjects are not randomly assigned.

7. *Analysis shows equal program and control groups before treatment:* Even though subjects have been randomly assigned, unequal prevention group and control groups can occur by chance. To guard against initial dissimilarity, the authors need to make comparisons across the program group and control groups on key client characteristics to see that they are similar prior to treatment (e.g., risk factors related to the behavior to be prevented).

8. *Subjects blind to being in prevention or control group:* Subjects who know they are in a control group can experience effects of being there including demoralization or competition with experimentals (Cook & Campbell, 1979, p. 55). Subjects who know they are in a prevention group can experience positive effects because they expect them (Brown, 1998). Give

points for subjects blinded if two or more groups get some kind of pre-vention program, if controls get some form of sham program that is not expected to have an effect but gives assurance that something is being done, or if subjects serve in a delayed treatment control group where they serve as controls but get the prevention program later, or if subjects truly do not know whether they are in a prevention group or control group.

9. *Subjects randomly selected for inclusion in study: Selection* of subjects is different from *random assignment.* Random selection means subjects are taken from some potential pool of subjects for inclusion in the study by using a table of random numbers or other statistically random procedures. For example, if subjects are chosen randomly from among all high-risk teenagers in a school, the results of the study can be generalized more con-fidently to all such students in that school. Random selection concerns generalizing results of the study to others, or external validity.

10. *Control (nontreated) group used:* Members of a *nontreated control group* do not receive a different kind of prevention program; they receive *no* treatment. An example of a nontreated control group would be a group of teenage girls at high risk for pregnancy who do not get into a pregnancy-prevention program, while others are given an explicit pregnancy-prevention program. Subjects in the nontreated control group might receive the pro-gram at a later date but do not receive it while program group subjects are receiving their prevention program.

11. *Number of subjects in smallest treatment group exceeds 20:* Those in the treatment group or groups are those who receive some kind of special care intended to help them. It is this treatment (prevention program) that is being evaluated by those doing the study. The results of the study will state how effective the prevention or prevention programs have been when compared with each other or with a nontreated control group. In order to meet Criterion 11, *the number of subjects in the smallest prevention (treatment) group must be at least 21.* (Not everyone will agree with this number. Apply a statistical power analysis if possible.) Here, *number of subjects* means total number of individuals, not number of couples or number of groups.

12. *Outcome measure has face validity:* Face validity is present if the outcome measure used to determine the effectiveness of treatment makes sense to you. Regarding prevention programs, such outcomes should truly reflect what the prevention program intends to accomplish. A good criterion for the sense of an outcome measure is whether the measure evaluates some-thing that should logically be affected by the program. For example, a school violence-prevention program should reduce the number of reported incidents of physical fights among students. This would be more valid as an outcome than the number of violence-prevention meetings attended.

13. *Treatment outcome measure was checked for reliability:* For this criterion to be met, it is not enough to merely say that the outcome of the preven-tion program was measured in some way. The outcome measure itself must be evaluated to check its reliability. *Reliability*—the consistency of

measurement—is frequently measured in an outcome evaluation study by comparing the findings of investigators who independently rate the performance of individuals in treatment or control groups. Another less frequently used way to measure reliability of outcome measures is to have the same individual rate the performance of subjects, then re-rate their performance. In single-subject studies, two raters may rate the subject's behavior independently for cross-rater comparison.

The reliability criterion is satisfied only if the author of the study affirms that evaluations were made of the outcome measure's reliability (for example, inter-rater agreement), and *the author lists a numerical value of some kind for this measure of reliability.* Where multiple outcome criteria are used, reliability checks of any one of the major outcome criteria satisfy Criterion 14.

14. *Reliability measure has value greater than .70 or percent of rater agreement greater than 70%:* The reliability coefficient in Criterion 13 is .70 or greater (70% or better).

15. *Those rating outcome rated it blind:* This criterion concerns the way bias can enter into measurement if the person measuring outcome knows whether the subject being measured is from a treatment or control group, or, worse, the person measuring outcome is in a position to determine the outcome measure. As an example for the latter, a large study had as an outcome whether chronically mentally ill persons treated in the community were readmitted to a hospital. Those administering the special treatment were in a position to decide whether the clients would be readmitted, which was an outcome criterion in the study (Test & Stein, 1977, pp. 14–15; Gomory, 1999, pp. 154–155). *Give the points for this criterion only if the person conducting the outcome measuring did not know which subjects were in treatment or control groups.*

16. *Outcome of the prevention program was measured after the program was completed:* At least one outcome measure was obtained after *the prevention program was completed.* Ideally, a prevention program's effects should not decay to produce no effect after the program ends. Its effects should continue for some interval after the program ends. For example, if high risk for pregnancy teenagers receive a prevention program that ends at the end of the school year in 9th grade, then its effects should be observed in the grades to follow. If outcome is measured both during and after the prevention program, it also meets this criterion.

17. *Test of statistical significance was made and* $p < .05$: Tests of statistical significance are generally referred to by phrases such as "differences between treatment groups were significant at the .05 level" or "results show statistical significance for. . . ." Give credit for meeting this criterion only if the author refers to a test of statistical significance for a major outcome variable stating the name of the statistical test (e.g., analysis of variance, chi square, *t* test) *and* gives a *p* value, for example $p < .05$, *and* the *p* value is equal to or smaller than .05. (With small samples in exploratory studies, .10 may be better to reduce the chance that one will miss a real difference, but generally .05 is the convention).

18. *Follow-up was greater than 75%:* The proportion of subjects successfully followed up refers to the number contacted to measure outcome compared with the number who began the study. Ideally, the two should be the same. To compare the proportion followed up for each group studied (i.e., prevention group(s), control group), determine the number of subjects who initially entered the groups and determine the number successfully followed up. (If there is more than one follow-up period, use the longest one.) Then, for each group, divide the number successfully followed up by the number who began in each group and multiply each quotient by 100. For example, if 20 entered a prevention group but 15 were followed up in that group, the result would be: (15/20)100 = 75%. Compute the proportion followed up for all groups involved in the experiment. If the *smallest* of these percentages exceeds 75%, the study meets this criterion.

19. *Base rate comparison* has particular importance as a standard for judging prevention programs. Ideally, careful records within the agency will show the prior rate of the behavior before the prevention program began. This base rate experience can provide a benchmark to judge the effects of the program. For example, the rate of pregnancy for the high-school juniors and seniors 2 years prior to the program can be compared with the rate for juniors and seniors during the 2 years after the program. *Give points for this criterion only if records have been kept for a specific interval (e.g., two years) regarding the rate of the behavior among high-risk persons prior to the prevention program and also during the same interval of time after the prevention program, and the behavior changes substantially— you decide what* substantially *means.*

20. *Total quality points* (TQP) *(add 1–19):* Simply add the point values for Criteria 1–19 and record this value in Box 20. This value will range between 0 and 100.

21. *Effect size (ES1)* (magnitude of difference between groups in standard deviation units) calculated by the following:

$$ES1 = \frac{\overline{x}_t - \overline{x}_c}{S_c}$$

$$= \frac{\text{(mean of prevention group)} - \text{mean of control or alternate treatment}}{\text{standard deviation of control or alternate treatment group}}$$

This formula is for computing *ES1* (difference in standard deviation units) when outcome means of treatment and control groups are given (Cohen, 1988, p. 20; Hedges, 1984, p. 31). To compute an effect size from information presented in a study's report, select two means to compare; for example, outcome might be a mean of a prevention group compared with a mean of a nontreated control group. Subtract the mean of the second group from the mean of the first group, and divide this difference by the standard deviation of the second group. (Standard deviations are indicated by various symbols, including *s.d.*, S, *s*, SD, or σ.) *ES1* may be a negative number or positive number. If the outcome measure's score gets greater as client outcome improves and *ES1* is positive, then the prevention program has had a positive effect, proportionate to the size of *ES1*. If *ES1* is negative, then the prevention program has a harmful effect.

22. *Effect Size (ES2) or absolute Risk Reduction:*

$ES2 = p_t - p_c =$ ((number improved in treatment/total number in treatment group) $\times$ 100) – ((number improved in alternate treatment or control/total number in alternate treatment or control) $\times$ 100)

Absolute risk reduction refers to the event rate in the prevention program relative to the event rate in the control group (Greenhalgh & Donald, 2000, pp. 157–159). Assume that you are comparing the proportion in a prevention group against the proportion in a control group regarding a given event (suicide, divorce, first offense, pregnancy). Say that 70% of those in the prevention program experienced the event and 50% of those in the control group did. *ES2* (absolute risk reduction) then equals 70% minus 50%, or 20%. Thus, the proportion of improvement attributable to the prevention program may be 20%.

23. *Effect size (ES3) or number needed to treat:*

$$NNT = \frac{100}{ES2}$$

"*NNT* is the number of [clients] that a clinician must treat with the experimental treatment in order to create a good outcome or to prevent one bad outcome in comparison to the control treatment" (Furukawa, 1999, p. 1). For example, if *ES2* (absolute risk reduction) is 20%, then *NNT* is 100/20, or 5. *This means that five persons would need to be exposed to the prevention program and not benefit to prevent one event.* This assumes, of course, that the study effectively rules out extraneous factors and bias, as reflected in Criterion 20 of the QSRF.

Exercise 5-3 Effectiveness of a Program to Prevent HIV Infection for African American Adolescents

Purpose

This exercise is designed to demonstrate how the QSRF-P may be applied to an article that evaluates a prevention program and to apply its findings as a guide for action.

Background

Shannon Ransom (personal communication, May 29, 2001) works as a case manager for 80 clients in the Milwaukee office of the AIDS Resource Center of Wisconsin. She works primarily with children infected with the human

Table 5.3 | Quality of Study Rating Form (QSRF-P)

Client type(s) _____

Intervention method(s) _____

Outcome measure to compute *ES1* _____

Outcome measure to compute *ES2* _____

Outcome measure to compute *ES3* _____

Source in APA format _____

Criteria for Rating Study

Clear Definition of Treatment					6. Subjects randomly assigned to treatment or control groups. (10 pts.)	7. Analysis shows equal prevention and control groups before treatment. (5 pts.)	8. Subjects blind to being in prevention or control groups. (5 pts.)
1. Who (4 pts.)	2. What (4 pts.)	3. Where (4 pts.)	4. When (4 pts.)	5. Why (4 pts.)			

Criteria for Rating Study (cont.)

9. Subjects randomly selected for inclusion in study. (4 pts.)	10. Control (nontreated) group used. (4 pts.)	11. Number of subjects in smallest group (prevention or control) exceeds 20. (4 pts.)	12. Outcome measure has face validity. (4 pts.)	13. Outcome measure was checked for reliability. (5 pts.)	14. Reliability measure has value greater than .70 or percent of rater agreement greater than 70%. (5 pts.)

Criteria for Rating Study (cont.)

15. Those rating outcome rated it blind. (5 pts.)	16. Outcome of treatment was measured after prevention program was completed. (4 pts.)	17. Test of statistical significance was made and across prevention and comparison or control groups $p < .05$. (5 pts.)	18. Follow-up was greater than 75%. (5 pts.)	19. Substantial improvement in the prevention program group over base rate of the problem prior to the program. (15 pts.)	20. Total quality points (add 1–19).

Criteria for Rating Effect Size

21. Effect size (*ES1*) in SD units = (mean of prevention program − mean of control) ÷ (standard deviation of control)	22. Effect size (*ES2*) or absolute risk reduction = (percent improved in prevention program) − (percent improved in control)	23. Effect size (*ES3*) or number needed to treat = 100 ÷ *ES2*

Note. From Quality of Study Rating Form (QSRF) by L. Gibbs and E. Gambrill, *Critical Thinking for Social Workers: Exercises for the Helping Professions,* Thousand Oaks, CA: Pine Forge Press, 1996, 1999, by Pine Forge Press: Adapted with permission; "Quality of Study Rating Form: An Instrument for Synthesizing Evaluation Studies" by L. E. Gibbs, 1989, *Journal of Social Work Education, 25*(1), p. 67. Copyright 1989 by the Council on Social Work Education: adapted with permission; and from L. E. Gibbs, *Scientific Reasoning for Social Workers,* pp. 193–197, Copyright owned by L. E. Gibbs.

immunodeficiency virus (HIV) and those sick with effects of the virus, acquired immunodeficiency syndrome (AIDS). In addition to children and adolescents, Shannon's clients include pregnant women who are HIV positive, women with AIDS who have HIV-positive children, and HIV-infected teenagers.

Shannon follows babies born to HIV-infected women for 18 months to be ready to help if their newborns become positive for the virus. Of 12 newborns that she followed last year, one baby became positive. To prevent such tragic cases, Shannon and other professionals on her interdisciplinary team make every effort to see that infected expectant mothers take their medications (Zidovudine and Nevirapine) to avoid transmitting the virus to their newborns. Her efforts are well-founded in evidence. A trial that randomly assigned HIV-infected mothers to Zidovudine or to placebo reported 8.3% (SE 4.5%) and 25.5% (SE 7.2%) newborn HIV infection rates respectively at 39 weeks follow-up (Reduction of HIV Transmission from Mother to Infant, 1994, p. 584). Here, the absolute risk reduction is 17.2% (i.e., 25.5% − 8.3% = 17.2%) and number needed to treat is 5.8 (i.e., 100/17.7 = 5.8); so all Shannon and her colleagues need to do to prevent one infant infection over 39 weeks is to see that 6 HIV-infected mothers take their medications faithfully.

Shannon says, "I make sure my clients get medical care; I work with multiple problems related to poverty and related to their illness. I help them to get food stamps and income maintenance programs to pay for insurance and housing. I help them to maneuver through the health care system, and I teach them about HIV and its risk to an uninformed sex partner. I counsel regarding mental health and alcohol and other drug problems" (S. Ransom, personal communication, May 29, 2001).

Of her adjustment to stresses in her work, Shannon says:

> I'm OK now. I had my field placement with primarily gay men before I came to Milwaukee. When I started working with the women they said, "What's a little white woman going to do to help me?" And I said, you'll see. . . . Many of the children have not seen a white woman, and they touch my hair and my face. . . . I don't take it home with me. It's hard, but I am making a difference. I helped a boy who was not attending school and was not taking his medications. His mom was really sick. When kids are born and not HIV positive in 18 months, that's a victory.

Though Shannon works primarily with mothers and children, the AIDS Resource Center has a prevention office too. She reasons that if she can help high-risk adolescents to avoid infection she can save lives. One of Shannon's COPES questions is as follows:

> For African American adolescents, is there an effective HIV-prevention program that will reduce high-risk sexual behaviors and increase the use of condoms?

Instructions

Please go to INFOTRAC through this book's Web site: www.infotrac-college.com/access.html Enter your passcode. Then enter Jemmott AND Jemmott AND Fong AND McCaffree. These are the authors for: Jemmott, J. B., Jemmott, L. S., Fong, G. T., & McCaffree, K. (1999). Reducing HIV risk-associated sexual behavior among African American adolescents: Testing the generality of intervention effects. *American Journal of Community Psychology (Special Issue: Adolescent Risk Behavior)*, 27(2), pp. 161–187. This is INFO-TRAC Article A55438333.

Discussion

Try to place yourself in Shannon's shoes. She often helps her agency's prevention efforts to reach high-risk adolescents, and she wants her interdisciplinary team to base its efforts on potentially the most effective prevention efforts.

Questions

1. Is this study related directly to Shannon's important COPES question?

   _____

   _____

   _____

2. Please fill out the QSRF-P for the preceding article. How many points did you give it under total quality points? $TQP = $ _____

   _____

3. What were the prevention study's strong and weak points?

   _____

   _____

   _____

   _____

4. What is the standardized mean difference for unprotected coitus at 6 months follow-up? Can you estimate *ES2* (absolute risk reduction) and *ES3* (number needed to treat) based on the section labeled Transformations Among Indices of Treatment Effect Size? Here's what you will need: Table 1 in the article shows that, for a 6 months follow-up, the 269 HIV prevention program participants' mean frequency of unprotected coitus was .474, *SD* = 1.48, and for the 227 health program participants it was .704, *SD* = .157.

5. Are clients, as described in the study, sufficiently like those in your own practice to warrant extrapolating the study's findings to the client(s) at hand? Use the following table for comparison. Please do the best you can from the brief description of Shannon's location and clients.

Area for Comparison	Your Clients	Study Clients
Client Problem		
Client Strengths		
Age		
Sex		
Race		
Ethnic Background		
Your Resources Versus Study Resources for Implementing Treatment or Assessment Procedure		
Other Concerns		

6. How would you become informed about how to replicate the HIV-prevention program described in this article using culture-sensitive risk reduction based on social cognitive theory, reasoned action, and theory of planned behavior?

Note. Figure 2 of the article shows that at 6-month follow-up, the HIV-prevention group scored about a minus 1.7 on the Risky Sexual Behavior Index while the health control group scored about a plus 1.7 on the index. The article's text indicates that this difference favors the HIV-prevention group with statistical significance ($p < .007$).

Meta-Analysis: Evaluating Review Quality and Applying Findings to Practice

6

Meta-Analysis: A Tool for Synthesizing Effectiveness Studies

The QSRF and the QSRF-P have provided building blocks for a meta-analysis. These two forms were designed to rate a single effectiveness study. The unit of analysis for these two forms was data from individual subjects participating in each study, one form for each study. In a meta-analysis, the unit of analysis becomes the study; so, if the meta-analysis includes ten studies, the number for the meta-analysis is ten. Meta-analyses are studies of studies. A meta-analysis is a synthesis of studies that is done in a systematic way according to indices of study quality and treatment effect size. "This involves all of the analysis methods used to interpret and to perform a structured synthesis of data collected from several unrelated [treatment effectiveness studies] (Nony, Cucherat, Haugh, & Boissel, 1997, p. 487). Ideally, a meta-analysis will weight studies of higher quality more heavily, or will allow the reader to make comparisons across studies based on some index of study quality, and will also include a summary of treatment effect size. One of the earliest meta-analyses was done by G. V. Glass, a social scientist who synthesized 475 studies comparing 18 forms of psychotherapy (Glass & Kliegel, 1983).

The features that follow identify a meta-analysis (Cook, Mulrow, & Haynes, 1997, p. 378):

- Focused on answering a practice question (e.g., a COPES question)
- Based on a comprehensive search for studies following an explicit search strategy
- Studies included based on specific criteria uniformly applied

- Rigorous critical appraisal of evidence
- Findings stated in quantitative terms for index of study quality (e.g., QSRF) and treatment effect size (e.g. standardized mean difference, number needed to treat)

Why Meta-Analyses?

Meta-analyses can save time by synthesizing evidence specific to a particular practice question. Busy practitioners simply do not have the time and, often, the expertise to synthesize literature to guide their practice. Literature grows at an incredible rate. One estimate states that the health sciences literature for just 1992 would include 2 million articles, enough to fill a book shelf 1640 feet long (Mulrow, 1994, p. 597). Of course, you do not have to scan through this much material mechanically, given your skills for posing COPES questions and for searching electronically, but searching may locate too much to synthesize.

In addition to saving time, *a competent meta-analysis can help to avoid bias.* Good meta-analyses include an extremely thorough search for published research as well as unpublished research (e.g., reports to funding agencies, proceedings of conferences, and internal reports). By including a wider sample of high-quality literature, meta-analyses help to avoid biases that can accompany publication. Additionally, meta-analyses follow specific criteria like those defined in the META form shown later in Table 6.1. Because they follow such criteria, meta-analyses can more objectively summarize research findings; therefore, meta-analyses can help to avoid relying on experts' opinions that sometimes do not reflect an accurate reading of the current best evidence (Antman, Lau, Kupelnick, Mosteller, & Chalmers, 1992).

Meta-analyses can lead to changes in treatment procedures in time to avoid harm and to adopt effective methods. One interesting comparison between cumulative meta-analyses (performing a new analysis each time a new study has been added) versus opinions of experts showed that experts continued to recommend ineffective and even harmful treatments well after the meta-analysis had demonstrated otherwise (Antman et al., 1992). Meta-analyses can demonstrate trends in literature regarding effectiveness before they are evident to nonsystematic reviewers, as applied to psychotherapy, delinquency prevention, school funding, job training, and reducing anxiety to surgical patients (Mann, 1994, table on p. 960).

Potential Drawbacks to Meta-Analysis

As with any aid to practice decision making, meta-analysis must be used with caution. Early criticisms of meta-analysis cautioned against analyses that disregarded bias in the selection of studies for inclusion in the analysis and also cautioned against giving equal weight to strong and weak studies (Wilson & Rachman, 1983). The META form addresses these issues. Other criticisms are less easily addressed. One particularly troublesome problem concerns potential disagreement between meta-analyses that combine many smaller studies compared with one single large study regarding the same treatment. Large trials (over 1000 subjects) disagreed with meta-analyses 10% to 23% of the time (Ioannidis, Cappelleri & Lau, 1998, p. 1089). This figure was based on a comparison of four large trials and their corresponding meta-analyses. Ioannidis and his colleagues think the inconsistencies might be due to differences across the study populations (e.g., severity of problem, age) and also due to the way outcome was measured (length of follow-up interval, definition of outcome). This inconsistency points out an important implication for using individual studies and meta-analyses to guide action in one's practice: Always examine the study to see whether its subjects resemble your client(s) closely enough to warrant generalizing the meta-analysis's findings to your clients. If their subjects are dissimilar to your clients, use caution when generalizing to your clients.

Another potential problem with meta-analysis concerns aggregated number needed to treat from many studies. Please note that there is controversy regarding computing *NNT* from composite values in a meta-analysis. Some are concerned that composite values may be based on different lengths of follow-up; so longer follow-up studies with a greater chance for failure over the longer interval would probably reflect a larger number needed to treat. In such instances, it may be unwise to uncritically combine *NNT* across studies with varying follow-up intervals (Charlton, Hopayian, D'Amico, Deeks, & Moore, 1999).

Multiple Evaluations for Treatment Assessment Form

Background

An earlier version of the multiple evaluations for treatment assessment (META) form has been class tested in a research methods class. It was developed in response to research methods students and fieldwork students whose assignments required that they locate and evaluate research literature to guide their practice. Students have increasingly discovered meta-analyses related to their COPES questions.

The META form's criteria for rating a meta-analysis come from multiple sources. These sources concern general criteria for rating the quality of a meta-analysis (Buckingham, Fishor, & Saunders, 2000; Dunkin, 1996; Ioannidis & Lau, 1998; Moher & Olkin, 1995; Nony, Cucherat, Haugh, & Boissel, 1997; Wilson & Henry, 1992); techniques for combining indices of treatment effect size (Lau, Ioannidis, & Schmid, 1997); and techniques for combining indices of study quality (Tritchler, 1999).

Purpose

The META form is designed to compute a single index of the quality of a meta-analysis. Higher scores indicate a stronger analysis. The META form provides a rating of what to look for in a meta-analysis. The form can also help you to gain experience applying a meta-analysis to a practice problem.

Instructions

Please read the Explanation column (Table 6.1) for each criterion on the META form with an eye to applying the criteria to what you read. The form is intended to rate the quality of a meta-analysis, which is sometimes called a systematic review, a synthesis of studies, or a study synthesis. Give one point for each check mark. Scores can range from 0 to 100. This is only an ordinal scale, meaning that a score of 20 is higher than a score of 10 but not necessarily twice as high. No norms exist for the META yet.

Table 6.1 | Multiple Evaluations for Treatment Assessment (META)

Source in APA Format (American Psychological Association, 2001)

Criterion	Points (One Point for Each Criterion Checked)	Explanation
Research Question		
1. Search question used to guide search for literature stated and filed in advance.		*Give points only if the authors state that they formulated their search question and filed it* before *starting to collect studies for review.* Before the search for studies begins, the authors should pose a COPES question or similarly specific question and file it for record keeping by some disinterested person outside the study. Filing this specific question will help to ensure that the meta-analysis was not a fishing expedition. Fishing expeditions fall prey to the tendency for patterns to exist even in random data.
2. Search question states who.		The authors' COPES question describes who is treated (e.g., acceptable ages, gender) *and* clearly defines clients' reason for being studied.
3. Search question states intervention (treatment).		The authors' COPES question names the intervention or treatment program being evaluated in studies to be included in the meta-analysis.
4. Search question states that an alternate intervention or control was used.		The authors refer to an alternate treatment by name, if studies are to be included that pit one treatment against another, or states that comparison of treatment will be made against a control group.

Table 6.1 | Continued

Criterion	Points (One Point for Each Criterion Checked)	Explanation
5. Search question states intended outcome.		The authors state specifically which outcome(s) will be compared across studies in the study analysis.

Initial Identification and Collection of Reports for Research*

Criterion	Points (One Point for Each Criterion Checked)	Explanation
6. All sources for studies searched listed.		Give point only if the authors state that they have listed in their report all of the *bibliographic sources* they searched to locate studies for inclusion in their meta-analysis. Sources may name the following, for example: hard cover abstracts, electronic bibliographic databases, conference presentations, government sources, and research grant reports. Someone evaluating the meta-analysis for possible selection bias will need to know the titles of such sources to see which, if any, might have been left out.
7. Search terms listed.		For electronic searches in bibliographic databases, the author's list their search terms used to locate studies. For example, they may list MOLES including the following: random* OR control group OR clinical trial.*
8. States interval of publication dates for studies included.		Give points only if the authors state *both* the beginning and ending dates for publication for studies included in the meta-analysis or state how far back from the time of the search the search went.
9. Criteria for including/excluding individual studies.		*If the authors list criteria that they applied to sift through studies to decide which ones to include in their analysis, then give the point here.* For example, authors might include only girls age 12–14 from low socioeconomic status enrolled in schools in their pregnancy-prevention study's meta-analysis.
10. List of studies included.		The authors give a total number of studies included in their meta-analysis, *and* they list these studies in sufficient detail in a bibliography so that you could get your hands on reports for these included studies.
11. List of studies excluded.		The authors give a total number of studies excluded from their meta-analysis, *and* they list these studies in sufficient detail in a bibliography so that you could get your hands on reports for these excluded studies.

continued

Table 6.1 | Continued

Criterion	Points (One Point for Each Criterion Checked)	Explanation
Analysis of Documents*		
12. Index of study quality computed.		The authors apply some index of study quality—like the QSRF or the QSRF-P—that provides a numerical value to rate the quality of studies included in the meta-analysis. The system for rating study quality only needs a numerical value; it need not be as elaborate as the QSRF.
13. Index of study quality rated blind.		If reviewers rated study quality on some numerical index, those reviewers were *masked* as to the name of each study's author(s). Reviewers blind to the author's name will be less influenced by that author's status or affiliations.
14. Reliability for index of study quality.		If reviewers rated study quality on some numerical index, then those reviewers' ratings can be compared to see if they agree. Give the points for this criterion only if *two or more raters' ratings for study quality were compared and the authors state that these ratings were done independently* (blind to the other raters' rating).
15. Satisfactory reliability for index of study quality.		For Item 14, if the raters' reliability was compared using a reliability coefficient, then give the points if this reliability coefficient for independent ratings of study quality equals or *exceeds .70.*
Reaching Generalizations About the Whole Body of Research*		
16. Index of treatment effect size calculated.		The QSRF and the QSRF-P included three indices of treatment effect size, including: standardized mean difference (*ES1*), absolute risk reduction (*ES2*), and number needed to treat (*ES3*). There are many other such indices (e.g., odds ratio). This criterion is met if the authors utilize *any treatment effect size index.*
17. Inter-rater reliability for coding effect size ratings.		This criterion is met if the authors state specifically that *independent raters* calculated an index of treatment effect size *and* these calculations were checked for reliability *and* the reliability value for these ratings equals or exceeds .70. Give points only for analyses that state all three.

Table 6.1 | Continued

Criterion	Points (One Point for Each Criterion Checked)	Explanation
18. Justification for particular index of treatment effect size.		Whole books summarize ways to calculate, synthesize, and interpret indices of treatment effect size (Hedges & Olkin, 1985). Give the point for this criterion if the authors *cite literature* that justifies using their particular index of treatment effect size.
19. Plot individual effect sizes.		Plots of effect sizes can give a wonderfully specific picture at a glance. For example, the L'Abbé plot (See Figure 5-1) shows percentage improved in treatment versus percentage improved in control group. From this plot, you can tell at a glance whether those in treatment fared better than controls and by how much. Give points for this criterion if the authors include *any plot of effect sizes*. Other types of plots include stem and leaf plots and means and confidence intervals around a grand mean.
20. Report summary statistic for treatment effect size.		Give the points for this criterion if the authors *combine the individual treatment effect sizes into some summary statistic and they give a reference* that tells you how this summary statistic is calculated.
21. Relationship between study quality and treatment effect size evaluated for correlation		A relationship may or may not exist between the rigor of study quality and the tendency to find negative or positive results. Still, this possibility needs to be investigated. *Give points for this criterion only if the authors describe some form of data analysis to look at the relationship between study quality–and study findings.* This analysis may plot study quality against positive or negative results. The plot may be a funnel plot or may merely involve dividing the studies into strong and weak ones and seeing if effects of treatment are higher in the weaker or stronger studies.
	Total number checked (21 possible) ———— Score = (number checked/21) × 100 ————	

Table 6.1 │ Continued

ES1 Standardized mean difference (weighted average across studies, may include several outcome types, e.g. risk score, condom use, knowledge of sexually transmitted disease in studies of effect of HIV Prevention Programs)? _____

ES2 Absolute risk reduction (weighted average across studies)? _____

ES3 Number needed to treat (weighted average across studies)? _____

---

*Three divisions on this form follow dimensions from Dunkin (1996). Revised after suggestions from Fall 2000 Methods of Social Work Practice at University of Wisconsin—Eau Claire.

Exercise 6-1 Primary Prevention Mental Health Programs for Children and Adolescents: A Meta-Analytic Review

Purpose

This exercise is designed to demonstrate how the META form may be applied to a meta-analysis to rate its overall quality and to isolate indices of treatment impact (effect size). The exercise is also designed to help practitioners to draw practice implications from a meta-analysis as a guide for action (or no action).

Background

Roger Hodgson specializes in mental health work with children and adolescents in an outpatient clinic. His clients, in descending order of their frequency, include: ". . . depression, learning disorders (e.g., attention deficit disorder), conduct disorders including oppositional kids, and kids dealing with transition including divorce" (R. Hodgson, personal communication, May 27, 2001). His widely respected knowledge, quick wit, and sense of fun gain the trust of those who know him, including his clients. Typically, Roger counsels his clients and their family members regarding problems after they have arisen, but he reflects about prevention. Roger says, "I think of it [preventing mental health problems] all the time, but that is not in the context of my work. . . . The real prevention stuff has to come from the community, from the schools and the courts. . . . I suspect that mediation skills, how to avoid violence, how to talk instead of lashing out, and programs that include a cognitive behavior component with peer modeling in them might be most effective. . . . I go to the schools and talk to teachers. . . . I go to M-Teams in the schools. . . . I would like to know what to suggest to them for prevention."

Here is Roger's COPES question:

What are the most effective primary prevention programs for preventing mental health problems among adolescents and children?

Instructions

Please go to INFOTRAC (College) through this book's Web site at: www. infotrac-college.com/access.html Enter your passcode. Then enter: Durlak AND Wells. These are the authors for the following article: Durlak, J. A., & Wells, A. M. (1997). Primary prevention mental health programs for children and adolescents: A meta-analytic review. *American Journal of Community Psychology (Special Issue: Meta-analysis of primary prevention programs)*, 25(2), 115–152. This is INFOTRAC Article A19793489.

Discussion

As you read the Durlak and Wells meta-analysis, imagine how much work it would be for a single practitioner to locate and to review all of the same literature. The effort would be a full-time job going far beyond the resources and patience of any practitioner, regardless of how determined, to know the answer to the COPES question given. Consequently, as you read the Durlak and Wells meta-analysis, take the time to read it slowly and carefully to apply the META form's criteria. It is worth the time. Not all meta-analyses are this well done.

Questions

1. Does this meta-analysis relate directly to Roger's question about how to prevent mental health problems among adolescents and children? Why, or why not?

   _____

   _____

2. Please fill out the META form for the article. What was its Score?

   85.7%. (11 ÷ 12)X 1 0 0)

3. What were the meta-analysis's strengths and weaknesses?

   _____

   _____

   _____

   _____

4. The article refers to several indices of the magnitude of a primary prevention program's effects on indices of adolescents' and children's mental health. The abstract speaks of mean effect (standardized mean effect size, *ES1*), and it also refers to differences in success rates (absolute risk

reduction, *ES2*). Perhaps the easiest index to interpret is *ES3*, or number needed to treat. *NNT* can be computed from the approximations in the article's Table VI: Binomial Effect Size Display of Success Rates for Different Prevention Programs, which appears on pages 15 and 16.

   a. Using the figures in Table VI, please calculate the absolute risk reduction for each of the 13 types of program (i.e., *ARR* = success rate for intervention minus success rate for controls).

   b. For each of these 13 *ARR* values, calculate the corresponding number needed to treat $(NNT = \dfrac{100}{ARR})$.

5. Would you recommend that primary prevention be school-based or parent training? Why?

_____

_____

_____

6. Which transition program might give the greatest benefit? Why?

_____

_____

_____

7. Which age group might benefit most from affective education? Why?

_____

_____

_____

8. Which age group might benefit most from interpersonal problem solving? Why?

_____

_____

_____

9. What might Roger tell community officials about the relative impact of primary prevention programs based on behavioral versus nonbehavioral methods?

_____

_____

_____

10. The Durlak and Wells (1997) meta-analysis has undergone some criticism that should also come up along with their article. These articles should appear along with the Durlak and Wells article when you search their names. Please take a look at these critical articles and the rejoinder from Durlak

and Wells to get a better understanding for issues in their analysis. What are some of these issues?

_____

_____

_____

_____

11. Are clients, as described in the study, sufficiently like those in your own practice to warrant extrapolating the study's findings to the client(s) at hand? Not much is known about Roger's specific clients other than their general types. Use the following table for your assessment.

Area for Comparison	Your Clients	Study Clients
Client Problem		
Client Strengths		
Age		
Sex		
Race		
Ethnic Background		
Your Resources Versus Study Resources for Implementing Treatment or Assessment Procedure		
Other Concerns		

7 | Assessment and Risk Studies: Evaluating Study Quality and Applying Results to Practice

Overview

Assessment refers to the process of evaluating clients (individuals, groups, communities) to determine their strengths and problems so as to make better judgments and decisions to help them. Practice can involve a wide range of client types, settings, and interventions that require assessment. For example, child welfare workers assess homes whose applicants want to adopt a child. This assessment and consequent decision will profoundly affect a child's life and that of its parents. Also in child welfare, protective service workers assess homes where children have been abused and removed from the home to see if the child can safely return home. In corrections, assessments concern important issues. (The CITTT describes a contested sex offender sentencing hearing that involved conflicting assessment for risk by a probation officer, a psychologist, and a social worker.) In schools, assessments determine whether children will receive special services due to learning disabilities or emotional disabilities. (The MITTT demonstrates such assessment in a school.) Mental health workers assess mental health problems and decide which interventions will be most appropriate. Professionals in mental health regularly assess potential for violence and for suicide. Assessment is an integral part of decision making in practice. Box 7.1 underscores the importance of assessment.

Methodological Concerns Regarding Assessment

Though good assessment applies principles of measurement, assessment in practice often violates elemental measurement principles. Some assessment

Box 7.1	**Selecting a Sex Offender Risk-Assessment Scale**

Melissa Candell (2001) works as a probation and parole agent with sex offenders, serving her clients in the community. Her agency's mission places the welfare of the community first, but its agents also try the best they can to serve the needs of clients to rehabilitate them. Melissa sees her clients regularly on report days, but she also tries to help clients on other occasions by counseling them individually or in groups, by helping them to get specialized treatment, and by helping them to arrange for training in job skills or education. She also has also been involved in writing presentence reports that synthesize gathering information to be presented to a judge. Judges rely heavily on presentence reports; so what they contain can have a profound impact on the course of a life.

The judge makes the final determination regarding whether a convicted offender will be placed on probation (a suspended sentence served in the community) or will be incarcerated, and for how long.

Here's Melissa's COPES question:

> If convicted sex offenders on probation or parole are administered the Rapid Risk Assessment of Sex Offender Recidivism (RRASOR) or the Minnesota Sex Offender Screening Tool (Mn-SOT), which would be the most accurate in predicting the rate at which a sexual offender could reoffend?

Melissa applied the Client Assessment Risk Evaluation (CARE) form that follows in this chapter to rate the quality of these two instruments. She found that the RRASOR and the Mn-SOT scored 11 and 3 points, respectively, favoring the former. She applied the forms to six of her clients to gain experience with them and presented her findings to other probation and parole agents in her agency.

---

measures in wide use by psychologists have been criticized as being essentially useless against standards for good measurement. For example, Lilienfeld, Wood, and Garb (2001) reviewed evidence regarding the reliability and predictive accuracy of three projective tests. These tools ". . . often serve, for instance, as aids in diagnosing mental illness, in predicting whether convicts are likely to become violent after being paroled, in evaluating mental stability of parents engaged in custody battles, and in discerning whether children have been sexually molested" (p. 82). These three projective tests include the Rorschach Ink Blot Test, the Thematic Apperception Test, and the Draw-a-Person Test. Lilienfeld and his coauthors interpreted the literature to raise serious doubts regarding the reliability and validity of all three. They concluded, "We find it troubling that psychologists commonly administer projective instruments in situations for which their value has not been well established by multiple studies. . . ." (p. 87).

Stanley Witkin (2001), editor of the journal *Social Work,* also has concerns over how assessment often violates basic measurement principles:

> The problem is that social work education is woefully inadequate when it comes to teaching students about measurement. Sure, we encourage the proper reverence for this form of scientific expression. And the mandatory research courses provide basic information about questionnaire construction, reliability, and validity in the context of conducting or interpreting research. But the context in which most social workers confront measurement issues is not formal research, but practice: How to evaluate the labels, predictions, and judgments generated by measurement instruments such as those that "reveal" that a person is "clinically depressed," a good or bad candidate for a program, or of "average" intelligence. How are social workers to assess this information? (p. 102).

Witkin (2001) raised issues regarding assessment measures used in practice including their *validity* (whether the measure accurately measures what it is intended to measure) and their *reliability* (whether the measure yields consistent results without excessive variability). Also, assessment procedures must be simple and quick to use, or they will not have widespread use in practice.

The worksheet in Box 7.2 can provide a quick way to evaluate an assessment/risk evaluation instrument relative to Witkin's issues. The worksheet presents a quick guide to evaluating an assessment/risk instrument. It may be sufficient in itself for busy practitioners, but if you want greater depth you can read the rest of this chapter. This worksheet also follows ideas from Eamon Armstrong (2001) and ideas documented elsewhere (Sackett et al., 2000, pp. 67–103, Card 2A; Gibbs, 1991, chapter 10).

Box 7.2

A Worksheet for Critically Appraising Articles About Assessment and Risk

1. *Determine relevance* (based on conclusion of abstract). Is this article worth taking the time to read? (Section 1: A, B, C, D adapted with permission from Shaughnessy & Slawson, 1997)
   A. Did the authors study an assessment/risk instrument that would matter to service to your clients?
      Yes (go on) No (stop)
   B. Is the assessment/risk issue studied *common* to your practice?
      Yes (go on) No (stop)
   C. Is it feasible that you might apply their assessment/risk instrument?
      Yes (go on) No (stop)
   D. If you knew results from this assessment/ risk instrument, would it *change* the way you serve your clients?
      Yes (go on) No (stop)

2. *Determine the reliability of the assessment/risk instrument.*
   A. Have *independent* raters checked the assessment/risk instrument's inter-rater agreement?
   B. Is the coefficient for rater's inter-rater reliability sufficiently high (e.g., above .70)?

3. *Determine the ease of use for the instrument.*
   A. Does the assessment/risk instrument take too long to administer?
   B. Does the assessment/risk instrument take too long to score?

4. *Determine the validity for the assessment/risk instrument.*

Sensitivity = $a/(a + c)$

Specificity = $d/(b + d)$

Pretest probability (prevalence) = $(a + c)/(a + b + c + d)$

Positive predictive value = for a given critical value or cutoff score on the instrument, this is the probability that, if a client is positive on the test, then the client will be positive relative to the gold standard = $a/(a + b)$.

Negative predictive value = for a given critical value or cutoff score on the instrument, this is the

Later Actual Behavior or Another Valid Measure
(Gold Standard)

	Present	Absent	Totals
Positive on test	a	b	$a + b$
Negative on test	c	d	$c + d$
Totals	$a + c$	$b + d$	$a + b + c + d$

Assessment or Risk Test Results

probability that, if a client is negative on the test, then the client will be negative relative to the gold standard $= d/(c + d)$

A. Was the instrument compared against the gold standard in a blind and independent test?

B. Was the instrument tested against the gold standard in a second location other than where it was developed?

C. Is *PPV* sufficiently high to warrant the instrument's use?

D. Is *NPV* sufficiently high to warrant the instrument's use?

E. Is the gain in accuracy in predicting a positive event against the gold standard sufficient to warrant the instrument's use ($PPV - $ pretest probability) = gain in predictive accuracy for positive).

5. *Should I apply these valid, reliable, easily applied results to my clients?* (Sackett, Straus, Richardson, Rosenberg & Haynes, 2000, p. 118)

A. Do these results apply to my clients?
   1. Are my clients so different from those in the study that the results do not apply?
   2. Is the benefit to my clients by using the instrument worth the cost, risk, and effort?

B. Are my client(s) values and preferences satisfied by the assessment/risk instrument offered? (Sackett, Richardson, Rosenberg & Haynes, 2000, p. 123)
   1. Do I clearly understand my clients' values and preferences?
   2. Does the assessment/risk instrument serve these values?

Client Assessment and Risk Evaluation Form

The Client Assessment and Risk Evaluation (CARE) form more thoroughly addresses assessment and risk estimation. The CARE form can apply to both assessment and risk evaluation because any assessment should ideally carry with it some indication of client risk (the probability of a future undesirable event). All assessments need to be tested against a gold standard of some sort.

Background

Assessment concerns one of the most vital tasks in practice. Assessment lies beneath decisions about whom to assist, what form of intervention will best serve whom, and which individuals present the greatest risk. The CARE form was developed to assist practitioners in weighting the quality of assessment procedures. I like the acronym, CARE, because it catches the essence of why you would turn to measures: because you CARE enough about clients to make your assessments as carefully as you can.

Purpose

The CARE form is designed to compute a single index of the quality of a client assessment procedure that reflects the assessment's ease of use, reliability (particularly inter-rater), and predictive validity. With respect to predictive validity, the CARE form heavily weights the assessment's ability to estimate risk (the probability of an undesirable event). Higher scores indicate a stronger analysis. The CARE form provides an index of what to look for in a practical, useful, assessment procedure.

Instructions

Please read the Explanation for each criterion on the CARE form with an eye to applying the criterion to any assessment procedure. The form was intended to rate the quality of any assessment procedure, regardless of whether the procedure follows a published measure, an interview guide, agency procedure, or common practice. Give one point for each check mark. The form is based on the assumption that any assessment procedure ought to be simple to apply, reliably scored, and of predictive value regarding what clients will do in the future or against a more valid measure. Scores can range from 0 to 100. This is only an ordinal scale, meaning that a score of 20 is higher than a score of 10 but not necessarily twice as high. No norms exist for the CARE form.

The CARE form assumes background that does not appear in most practice and research texts. If items on the CARE form appear unfamiliar to you, please read the Detailed Explanation for CARE Criteria that appears following this form. Criteria can be rated on the CARE form from documentation that accompanies assessment procedures without understanding specifics in the Detailed Explanation. Standards for risk assessment and for judging the validity of an assessment against a more valid assessment procedure follow the same pattern here, but discussion concerns risk for consistency.

Table 7.1 | Client Assessment and Risk Evaluation (CARE)

Source in APA Format (American Psychological Association, 2001)

Criterion	Points (One Point for Each Criterion Checked)	Explanation
Utility of Assessment Procedure for Practice		
1. Assessment procedure easy to learn.	/	Physically examine the assessment's procedure and its scoring procedures to rate this. Estimate whether you and your coworkers could do an assessment and score it without confusion simply by following the procedure's instructions.
2. Assessment in less than 10 minutes.	0	The assessment's administration would take *less than 10 minutes* of additional time above what the client contact would generally take. To estimate time, do a trial with a few actual cases or with a role-played interview to actually time how long the assessment requires, or rely on published reports.
3. Assessment's scoring less than five minutes.	/	Try scoring a few assessments to see how long the scoring takes. Allow for experience as a way to shorten scoring time. Scoring should take *less than 5 minutes*. You may rely on published reports of time required to score.
Reliability (i.e., Consistent with Each Administration Over Time, Across Raters, or Internally Across the Instrument's Items)		
4. Assessment procedure was checked for inter-rater reliability.		This means that two or more raters arrived at their assessments without conferring at all with the other raters. Give no points unless the authors state explicitly that assessments were done *independently*. Inter-observer, cross-observer, across-raters mean inter-rater.
5. Some (any) inter-rater reliability coefficient computed.		Any inter-rater coefficient will do here so long as the *assessments were made independently and any coefficient of agreement was computed.*

page 778 Left upper — handwritten note

continued

Table 7.1 | Continued

Criterion	Points (One Point for Each Criterion Checked)	Explanation
6. Kappa coefficient of inter-rater reliability for assessment exceeds 0.70.		The authors must both compute a *Kappa to rate the agreement of assessments by independent workers, and the Kappa must exceed 0.70.* Since decisions in practice are binary (act/do not act), inter-rater reliability and its most appropriate statistic (Kappa) are criteria here. See Figure 7.1
7. Assessment procedure checked for form of reliability other than inter-rater reliability (e.g., test-retest, split half, internal consistency).		This criterion is met if the authors check for reliability using any procedure other than inter-rater reliability.
8. Reliability coefficient computed other than Kappa above .70 or 70%.		Give the points here if the authors compute a coefficient of reliability other than Kappa (e.g., Pearson *r*, Cronbach's *alpha*, Kuder-Richardson *formula 20*) *and* value above .70.

Predictive Validity (The client's assessment demonstrates that it can actually predict how the client will perform in the future. The following discussion refers to risk, which is the probability of an undesirable behavior, but the same principles for this discussion can apply to other standards for judging accuracy against a more valid criterion.)

9. Those who developed the assessment procedure did a systematic review of studies to isolate indicators that might have predictive value to estimate risk.		Look here for *a tabular literature review that lists studies and which indicators were of predictive value in each study.* Give no points if you cannot find such a table in the report.
10. The authors clearly describe criteria for including clients of a particular type in their risk-assessment study.		Merely stating the client type (e.g., suicidal or depressed persons) is not enough. Authors *must state the specific criterion or measure* (e.g., specifically defined prior suicidal behaviors, Zung Self-Rating Depression Scale) for including subjects in the study. Knowing inclusion criteria allows practitioners to judge whether study findings apply to their clients.
11. The risk-assessment study's results were collected prospectively.		This means that *indicators of risk were collected; then clients were followed to see what they would do,* and then the indicators were evaluated for predictive efficiency against what the clients actually did or against another gold standard.

Table 7.1 | Continued

Criterion	Points (One Point for Each Criterion Checked)	Explanation
12. The risk-assessment study was done prospectively *and* the study resulted in greater than 80% being contacted at follow-up.		Divide the number who were contacted at the end of the study regarding their actual behavior by the number who took the risk-assessment measure at the beginning of the study, and multiply by 100.
13. During the data analysis, those who recorded the subject's actual behavior were blind to what each subject's risk-assessment score had been.		This analysis will compare the risk assessment's earlier results against what actually happened later to judge whether the assessment was accurate. Give a point only if *the authors state that those who recorded the predicted behavior were blind to what the prediction had been.*
14. The risk-assessment measure's predictive accuracy was checked in at least one validation study.		Risk scales may predict well where they were developed but sometimes do not elsewhere. To meet this criterion, *the measure's accuracy needs to be tested on a sample other than where it was developed.*
15. The risk-assessment scale's positive predictive value *(PPV)* was higher than the prevalence rate (base rate, prior probability) by at least 10%.		Applying a risk-assessment procedure that will not predict better than chance (prevalence rate) makes no sense. (See Figure 7.2.)
16. *PPV* is greater than .80.		The study computed positive predictive value, or gives sufficient data to do so, and *PPV* is greater than .80. If more than one computation of *PPV*, then the average *PPV* is greater than .80.
17. *NPV* is greater than .80.		The study computed negative predictive value, or gives sufficient data to do so, and *NPV* is greater than .80. If more than one computation of *NPV*, then the average *NPV* is greater than .80.
18. Using the same subjects, the authors compared positive predictive value *(PPV)* for practitioners' predictions against *PPV* for the risk-assessment scale's predictions, and the latter is higher.*		This kind of study pits the predictive accuracy of practitioners' assessments against a risk-assessment scale. This kind of evaluation assumes that the practitioners do not know the risk-assessment scale's score when they make their judgment. (See Figure 7.2.)

*Some studies report only sensitivity, specificity, and prevalence. You can still compute *PPV* with Bayes's Theorem as follows:

$$\frac{(\text{prevalence})\,(\text{sensitivity})}{(\text{prevalence})\,(\text{sensitivity}) + (1 - \text{prevalence})\,(1 - \text{specificity})}$$

continued

Table 7.1 | Continued

Criterion	Points (One Point for Each Criterion Checked)	Explanation
19. The authors state specifically that they have used a receiver operating curve (ROC) analysis to establish the risk assessment's cutoff or division criteria (e.g., dividing point between high/low risk categories).		Any risk-assessment scale involves a trade-off. If you want to maximize your instrument's sensitivity to detect true positives, you will also increase our number of false positives. ROC analysis allows practitioners to make an informed judgment about where best to set the scale's division point(s). For a detailed description, consult MedCalc at www.medcalc.be/roccman.html
	Total number checked (19 possible) ———— Score = (number checked/19) × 100 ————	

Summary Statistics for Assessment Procedure

Inter-rater reliability Kappa for assessment procedure

Positive predictive value for assessment procedure

Negative predictive value

Note. Adapted with permission from "Form for Rating a Risk-Assessment Measure (Considerations Before Adopting a Risk-Assessment Measure in Your Practice)," by L. Gibbs , 2002. In A. Roberts & J. Greene (Eds.), *Social Worker's Desk Reference,* New York: Oxford University Press.

Detailed Explanation for CARE Criteria

CARE Criteria for Ease of Use (Items 1 Through 3)

Items 1 through 3 on the CARE form rate ease of use for an assessment procedure. They need no explanation.

CARE Criteria Regarding Reliability (Items 4 Through 8)

Items 4 through 8 on the CARE form concern inter-rater reliability, the form of reliability that seems most vital to practice decision making, for two reasons. First, at the very least, out of fairness to clients, a client who gets an assessment from one worker should expect to have the same assessment from another worker. Such inter-rater agreement ensures some degree of consistency and fairness in the ways clients are treated. For example, assume that two community corrections workers apply the Sex Offenders Risk Assessment Guide (SORAG) approach to risk assessment (Quinsey, Harris, Rice, & Cormier, 1998). Those who developed the SORAG systematically reviewed sex offender literature to isolate personal characteristics of offenders associated with reoffense. The SORAG's 5-page rating scale is based on offender characteristics, including, for example, the following: Childhood (e.g., did not live with biological parents until age 16), Adult Adjustment (e.g., failure on conditional release prior to sex offense), Offense Variables (e.g., under age 26 at first offense), and Diagnostic Information (e.g., antisocial personality disorder diagnosis).

See Figure 7.1 for an example of inter-rater agreement, where Worker 1 assesses clients using the SORAG and Worker 2 independently does the same assessment. Note how instances of agreement across the raters would appear in the upper left and lower right diagonals.

Secondly, inter-rater agreement lends itself particularly well to an analysis that closely reflects real practice decision making in terms of binary judgments. Decisions in practice tend to be binary—either act or do not act—types of decisions. For example, in the SORAG risk-assessment example in Figure 7.2, conservative action, possibly a recommendation for incarceration, might accompany a high SORAG assessment. Likewise, for high risk-cases, child protective service workers might recommend that high risk for reabuse cases get conservative action, possibly recommending that the child not be placed back in its home. Practice decisions are often classical nominal types of binary—either act or do not act—ones.

Item 6 on the CARE form lists Kappa as a measure of nominal inter-rater reliability. Figure 7.1 gives the formula for computing Kappa relative to the SORAG example.

CARE Criteria for Predictive Validity (Items 9 Through 17)

The CARE form's final items concern an assessment's predictive validity, arguably the most important type of validity by far for an assessment. The following discussion

Figure 7.1

Example of Inter-Rater Agreement Between Two Workers Regarding Potential for Violence Using the SORAG (How to Compute a Kappa Inter-Rater Reliability Coefficient Regarding SORAG).

Rater 1 Estimation
of Risk on SORAG

	High	Low	Row Totals (across)
Rater 2 Estimation of Risk on SORAG — High	50 — Expected frequency = 37.8 — Cell n_{11}	4 — Cell n_{12}	54 — $n_{1\bullet}$
Low	6 — Cell n_{21}	20 — Expected frequency = 7.8 — Cell n_{22}	26 — $n_{2\bullet}$
Column Totals (down)	56 — Cell $n_{\bullet 1}$	24 — Cell $n_{\bullet 2}$	$n = 80$

f_o = Frequency of observed agreement
= Total for cells having the same row and column numbers
= 50 + 20
= 70

P_o = Proportion of observed agreement

$$= \frac{f_o}{n}$$

$$= \frac{70}{80}$$

$$= .88$$

f_e = Frequency of expected agreement

$$= \frac{\sum_{i=1}^{T} n_i \cdot n_i \cdot}{n}$$

= Multiply the Row 1 total by the Column 1 total and divide by n; multiply the Row 2 total by the Column 2 total and divide by n; sum these values.

$$= \frac{54 \times 56}{80} + \frac{26 \times 24}{80}$$

$$= 37.8 + 7.8$$

$$= 45.6$$

$$P_e = \frac{f_e}{n}$$

$$= \frac{45.6}{80}$$

$$= .57$$

$$= kappa = \frac{P_o - P_e}{1 - P_e} = \frac{.88 - .57}{1 - .57} = .72$$

concerns risk assessment, but its principles can apply to any test of an assessment's ability to stand up to scrutiny relative to some gold standard for performance. In risk assessment, that gold standard will be whether the risk assessment predicted later actual behavior. The gold standard may also be a more credible, but perhaps more costly and time-consuming, assessment by another means.

Much of this section was taken from the *Social Worker's Desk Reference* (reprinted with permission from Gibbs, L. (2002). Assessing Risk in Social Work Practice: Essential Elements. In A. Roberts & J. Greene (Eds.), *Social Worker's Desk Reference,* New York: Oxford University Press.

Obviously, with so much at stake in practice [major concerns in my practice were potential for violence and for suicide], risk assessment warrants careful consideration. The concepts in this section will help to define basic issues essential to evaluating a risk-assessment procedure.

- *Clinical versus statistical approaches to estimating risk:* In contrast to a clinical experience, also called an intuitive approach to estimating risk, the Sex Offenders Risk Assessment Guide (SORAG) provides one example of a statistical or actuarial approach to risk assessment (Quinsey et al., 1998). Those who developed the SORAG systematically reviewed sex offender literature to isolate personal characteristics of offenders associated with re-offense, developed a risk-assessment measure incorporating the kinds of items listed earlier, and tested its predictive accuracy to see if the SORAG predicted later offenses. Such explicit statistically based methods as the SORAG almost always outperform clinical experience methods (impressions based on practice experience) in their predictive accuracy. Grove and Meehl (1996) reviewed 136 studies comparing these two methods. They concluded that the ". . . mechanical [statistical, actuarial] method is almost invariably equal to or superior to the clinical method" (p. 293). Other reviewers have discovered the same (Baird & Wagner, 2000; Dawes, Faust, & Meehl, 1989). You can find examples for risk-assessment measures in child welfare (Lyons et al., 1996); corrections (Hanson, 1998); and mental health (Klassen & O'Connor, 1989; Lidz, Mulvey, & Gardner, 1993).

- *Communicating about risk:* Regardless of whether you apply statistical or clinical means to assess risk, you can go a long way toward understanding risk better if you can be more explicit when stating risk. Practitioners may be more or less sure about what a client may do. To communicate about risk, practitioners often use vague quantifying adjectives in their case notes, including, for example, the following: . . .*probably, most likely, certainly, possibly.* These vague quantifying adjectives are so inexact that they mislead. These four adjectives conveyed the following range of probabilities, respectively, when 18 social workers were asked to estimate what these words implied in terms of times among 100 events: 50%–90% (sd =12), 51%–95% (sd = 10), 75%–100% (sd = 8), and 25%–85% (sd = 13) (Gibbs, 1991, p. 138). Such wide ranges of meanings for vague adjectives convey almost no meaning in a case record. Stating risk in terms of probabilities conveys much more meaning. Probabilities are numbers ranging from 0 to 100, or 0 to 1, that refer to the likelihood of an event. A probability of 1 means that an event is absolutely certain to happen; .5 means the event is exactly as likely as not to happen; 0 means absolutely no chance to happen, and all values between. The following discussion includes how to evaluate any risk-assessment effort in terms of such specific probabilities.

- The binary (either action or do not act) nature of decision making in practice: As stated earlier, decisions tend to be binary in practice. Assessment indicates that, relative to some cutoff or critical value as threshold, you either take action or you do not. You recommend parole from prison for a criminal offender on indeterminate sentence, or you do not. You judge that the hospital patient abuses alcohol and recommend AODA treatment, or you do not. A binary assessment relative to a binary outcome lends itself to the format for understanding assessment as described here.

- Evaluating any risk-assessment effort's predictive accuracy: Clinical and statistical means for assessing risk can be held to the same standard—do they accurately predict in advance what will happen? This refers to what researchers call *predictive validity*, meaning that, relative to the classical binary risk-assessment situation, those judged high risk shall later exhibit the risk behavior; those judged low risk shall not (Swets, Dawes, & Monahan 2000). Figure 7.2 summarizes an efficient way to display elements for judging a risk assessment's predictive validity that has been a part of the research literature for some time (Galen & Gambino, 1975; Gibbs, 1991, 217–237).

Please look first at the vertical left of Figure 7.2. It conveys results of a hypothetical child abuse Risk-Assessment Effort (either clinical or statistical). Then look across the top of Figure 7.2 to the Later Actual Behavior or Another More Valid Measure (gold standard of actual later behavior to evaluate risk assessment's accuracy). This binary standard across the top represents what actually happened later to the cases. The binary standard across the top for an assessment instrument can also be another assessment made by a more credible standard (e.g., psychiatrist's assessment based on structured interview as a standard for judging the accuracy of a test to screen for depression). Ideally, this diagram implies a prospective study where predictions are made, records kept, and predictions judged against actual later behaviors. Understanding what constitutes a prospective study will aid in rating studies on this chapter's rating form.

The worker can estimate risk accurately in two ways. If the worker classified a case as positive (abuse predicted) and the standard of Later Actual Behavior confirms this, then the estimate is a true positive (*TP*). If the worker classified a case as negative (no abuse predicted) and the Later Actual Behavior confirms this, then the estimate is a true negative (*TN*). There are also two types of error. False positives (*FP*) occur when the worker predicts an abuse,

Figure 7.2 | Judging a Child Abuse Risk Assessment's Predictive Value

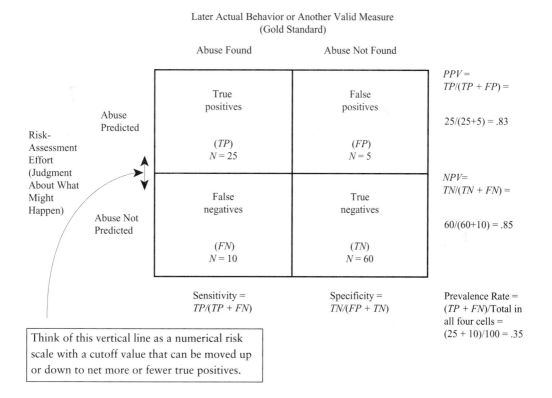

Later Actual Behavior or Another Valid Measure
(Gold Standard)

but the behavioral standard does not find abuse later. False negatives (*FN*) occur when the worker predicts no abuse, but the behavioral standard finds a later abuse. False negatives (awful stories of children returned to their homes and killed) carry the most visible consequences for worker and client. False positives are bad, too, because they mean that the child may be unnecessarily removed from the home and valuable limited resources wasted. These two errors imply a trade-off. Any risk-assessment scale can be adjusted by moving the cutoff value up or down (see Figure 7.2), but doing so will minimize one type of error by increasing the other, likewise involving a trade-off between true positives and true negatives.

So what is the bottom line in risk assessment? Regarding the issue of accuracy, *positive predictive value* (*PPV*) refers to the proportion of cases predicted to abuse who in fact do abuse later. In Figure 7.2, *PPV* is .83, meaning that if the estimate is positive based on the risk-assessment scale, in the long run in 83% of cases, those with a positive risk assessment will exhibit the predicted behavior. The *PPV* tells the most about practitioners' accuracy, because it implies that the worker has made a judgment to be evaluated later against the Later Actual Behavior standard. Positive predictive value reflects the classical practice situation: the worker goes by imperfect information regarding a mixed group of clients to estimate what will happen to them later.

In contrast, *sensitivity* refers to the proportion of known abuse cases who were positive on the risk-assessment test. Sensitivity refers to a retrospective look at risk assessment, not the real prospective problem of prediction. Do not confuse *PPV* and sensitivity.

Specificity refers to the proportion of known abuse cases who were negative on the risk-assessment test. *Negative predictive value* (NPV) refers to the proportion of cases predicted not to abuse who in fact do not later abuse (in Figure 7.2, this is .85 or 85%). *NPV* is a close second to *PPV* in its importance for practice.

Exercise 7-1: Screening for Depression Among Acutely Ill Geriatric Inpatients with a Short Geriatric Depression Scale

Purpose

This exercise is designed to help you to gain experience applying the CARE to evaluate an assessment instrument.

It is also designed to help you to gain experience deciding whether to take action based on your evaluation of an assessment instrument.

Background

You may recall Alyssa Perry's story from chapter 4. You may recall that she was concerned about the need to identify signs of early dementia among her nursing home's residents. She sought a quick assessment measure so she could identify dementia in time to help as much as possible and to avoid community placement for those affected by dementia. She also wanted to identify dementia as opposed to depression. Her literature search located a narrative review regarding the Clock-Drawing Test as a screening test for dementia and cognitive depression.

Unfortunately, INFOTRAC does not have an original study of the Clock-Drawing Test, but it does have a study of the Geriatric Depression Scale (GDS) that can be used for practice here. Here is a related COPES question:

> For elderly residents of a nursing home who may be suffering from depression, will the Geriatric Depression Scale (GDS), compared with the Brief Assessment Scale (gold standard), result in GDS having sufficient predictive validity and ease of use?

Instructions

Please go to INFOTRAC, www.infotrac-college.com/access.html Enter your passcode, and enter: Shah AND Herbert AND Lewis. You should retrieve the following article: Shah, A., Herbert, R., Lewis, S., Mahendran, R., Platt, J., &

Bhattacharyya, B. (1997). Screening for depression among acutely ill geriatric inpatients with a short geriatric depression scale. *Age and Aging, 26(3),* 217–223. This is INFOTRAC Article number A19616097. This study compared a psychiatrist's rating for depression among elderly persons on the Brief Assessment Schedule (gold standard) against the GDS10 and GDS4 depression screening tests.

Questions

1. Why would it be vital to the welfare of residents of a nursing home to be able to identify those suffering from depression?

   Improve strategies for improving treatment can only be implemented after recognition of the depression

2. What is the CARE score for this assessment article?

3. What are the major strengths and weaknesses of this study relative to the CARE criteria?

   Strengths: easy to learn assessment procedure, it takes less than 10 min in assessment, and less than 5 min in scoring

4. Was there any test of inter-rater agreement across independent raters (as a check for reliability)?

   No.

   01 = .72 / .72

   0.81 = 1 - 90 (=0.89)

5. For Table 1, in the article what were the average positive predictive values and the average negative predictive values for the GDS4 for the three cut-off scores? Average *PPV* _____ *0.86* _____

   Average *NPV* _____ *0.72* _____

6. Please interpret in your own words what the *PPV* and *NPV* mean in terms of prediction accuracy for GDS4.

   PPV ask questions positively to find out depression level

   NPV ask questions negatively

7. For Table 1, what were the average positive predictive values and the average negative predictive values for the GDS10 for the three cutoff scores?

   Average *PPV* _____ *0.72* _____

   Average *NPV* _____ *0.85* _____

8. Are clients, as described in the study, sufficiently like those in your own practice to warrant extrapolating the study's findings to the client(s) at hand? Use the following table for your assessment.

   assess sensitivity and specificity level

   I do not have any clients yet.

Area for Comparison	Your Clients	Study Clients
Client Problem		
Client Strengths		
Age		
Sex		
Race		
Ethnic Background		
Your Resources Versus Study Resources for Implementing Treatment or Assessment Procedure		
Other		

Exercise 7-2 Assessing Risk of Falls Among Elderly Persons

Purpose

This exercise is designed to help you to gain experience applying the CARE to evaluate a risk-assessment instrument.

It will also help you to gain experience deciding whether to take action based on your evaluation of a risk-assessment instrument.

Background

An elderly person's fall can begin a cascade of negative events that can lead to an early and painful death. The person falls and breaks a bone. Then, to heal the fracture, convalescence immobilizes the person who cannot exercise to maintain flexibility, strength, and cardiovascular fitness. The person loses strength; becomes bedridden; and can die of stroke, pneumonia, or other problems.

Consequently, it makes sense to identify aged persons who are at risk for falling and then to take corrective action through exercises that may make the persons more stable, less prone to falling. A COPES question regarding such risk follows:

For aged persons living in a nursing home who may be at risk for falling, will the Timed Up & Go Test or the STRATIFY test best predict which elderly persons will fall?

Instructions

Please go to INFOTRAC, www.infotrac-college.com/access.html Enter your passcode, and locate two articles. The first can be found by searching Oliver AND Britton AND Seed AND Martin AND Hopper. This article is: Oliver, D., Britton, M., Seed, P., Martin, F. C., Hopper, A. H. (1997). Development and evaluation of evidence based risk assessment tool (STRATIFY) to predict which elderly inpatients will fall: Case-controlled and cohort studies. *British Medical Journal, 315*(7115), 1049–1054. This is INFOTRAC Article Number A19992159. The second can be found by searching similarly the names of its authors as follows: Shumway-Cook, A., Brauer, S., & Woollacott, M. (2000). Predicting the probability for falls in community-dwelling older adults using the Timed Up & Go Test, *Physical Therapy, 80*(9), 896–903. This is INFO-TRAC Article Number A65571172.

Questions

1. What is the total CARE score for the Oliver et al. (1997) article regarding the STRATIFY risk of falls assessment?

   _____

2. What are the major strengths and weaknesses of this risk-assessment study relative to the CARE criteria?

   _____

   _____

   _____

   _____

3. What is the positive predictive value for the STRATIFY?

   _____

4. What does *PPV* refer to as an indicator of predictive validity?

   _____

5. What is the total CARE score for the Shumway-Cook et al. (2000) article regarding the Timed Up & Go Test?

   _____

6. What are the major strengths and weaknesses of this risk-assessment study relative to the CARE criteria?

   _____

   _____

   _____

   _____

7. What is the positive predictive value for the Timed Up & Go Test?

_____

8. Based on the evidence regarding the Timed Up & Go Test and the STRAT-IFY, which measure would you consider the strongest? (You might look at the CARE scores and the *PPV* for each. If you are in practice, you might also consider your reflections on Question 9, which follows.

9. Are clients, as described in the study, sufficiently like those in your own practice to warrant extrapolating the study's findings to the client(s) at hand? Use the following table for your assessment.

Area for Comparison	Your Clients	Study Clients
Client Problem		
Client Strengths		
Age		
Sex		
Race		
Ethnic Background		
Your Resources Versus Study Resources for Implementing Treatment or Assessment Procedure		
Other		

10. Please reread the COPES question given earlier. Which article relates most directly to the COPES question?

_____

11. Given the relative merits of the Timed Up & Go and the STRATIFY risk-assessment scales, which would you use? Why?

_____

_____

_____

_____

Exercise 7-3 Improving the Positive Predictive Value of Screening for Developmental Language Disorder

Purpose

This exercise is designed for you to gain experience applying the CARE to evaluate an early assessment instrument.

It will also help you to gain experience deciding whether to take action based on your evaluation of an assessment instrument.

Background

Betsy McDougall Gibbs works as the coordinator for the Early Childhood and Special Needs Program for the Eau Claire Public Schools in Eau Claire, Wisconsin. Eau Claire, a community of about 50,000, is predominantly white with Hmong its largest minority. The Eau Claire area's primary industries are computer technology and service for the wider region, much of it farming, which includes a high proportion of dairy farms.

Betsy helps preschoolers to get a running start so their little feet can best keep up with their classmates when they get to school. She and her staff try to identify speech and language problems early so they can enroll children in special programs to meet their needs. Indicators for problems include delays in using phrases and sentences, difficulty following directions, seeming to not hear, and seeming to have problems processing information. Referrals for potential speech and language problems frequently come from pediatricians, nurses, social workers, parents, and day-care providers. Referrals need to be evaluated. Betsy and her team are always on the lookout for methods that will help them to distinguish between kids who do and do not need services so they can expend precious resources more efficiently.

Betsy's COPES question follows:

> For preschool children in a medium-size community, will a parent-report language screening questionnaire effectively distinguish between children who need preschool language services and those who will not?

Instructions

Please go to INFOTRAC: www.infotrac-college.com/access.html Enter your passcode, and search for the following article: Klee, T., Pearce, K., & Carson, K. (2000). Improving the positive predictive value of screening for developmental language disorder. *Journal of Speech, Language, and Hearing Research, 43*(4), 821–833. This is INFOTRAC Article A64189663.

Keep in mind that any assessment measure needs to be checked against a gold standard of some kind. As you read this article, make a mental note of what that standard is and its credibility. Also, make note of any discussion of the Language Development Survey's reliability.

Questions

1. What makes this question of vital concern to those who work with early education special needs children?

2. What is the total CARE score for this article?

3. What are the major strengths and weaknesses of this assessment study relative to the CARE criteria?

4. What is the positive predictive value for the revised Language Development Survey?

5. What does *PPV* refer to as an indicator of predictive validity?

6. What is the negative predictive value for the revised Language Development Survey?

7. What does *NPV* refer to as an indicator of predictive validity?

8. Is there a check of reliability for the revised Language Development Survey?

9. Are clients, as described in the study, sufficiently like those in your own practice to warrant extrapolating the study's findings to the client(s) at hand? Use the following table for your assessment.

Area for Comparison	Your Clients	Study Clients
Client Problem		
Client Strengths		
Age		
Sex		
Race		
Ethnic Background		
Your Resources Versus Study Resources for Implementing Treatment or Assessment Procedure		
Other		

8

Descriptive and Qualitative Studies: Evaluating Study Quality and Applying Results to Practice

Descriptive Studies: Tools for Generalizing About Client Needs and Perceptions of Services

Descriptive studies typically harness survey technology to answer questions regarding client needs and perceptions. Descriptive studies typically require the following: (a) a clear conception of the research question, (b) questions clearly posed on questionnaires or interview guides, (c) a clear delineation of a population, (d) samples representatively chosen from that population, (e) careful data collection to avoid biasing respondents and to avoid error in recording responses, and (f) an appropriate statistical analysis. Surveys of client needs assessment and satisfaction with their services typify descriptive studies.

For another example, Acosta and Toro (2000) cited literature that documents how homeless persons rarely rely on services that can help them, but few needs assessments have been done to determine what homeless persons list as being their most pressing needs. Acosta and Toro used a probability sampling technique to select 301 homeless adults in Buffalo, New York. They developed a Needs Assessment Questionnaire (NAQ) based on literature and also asked a group of 25 randomly chosen homeless persons from three agencies serving homeless to react to the questionnaire; they did not do a qualitative study, which might have strengthened their survey. They revised the NAQ based on their pretest and trained eight interviewers over several weeks to administer the interview to avoid biasing their respondents. They also checked interviewer inter-rater agreement on 31 of the 301 interviews for an agreement

| Box 8.1 | **Determining Preferences for Selecting a Nursing Home** |

Jacqueline Helland (2001) works as a hospital social worker on a medical/surgical unit. Her clients typically include patients there for hip replacements, fractures, or knee replacements. Many of her clients are elderly. One of Jacque's most frequent tasks is to arrange for a client's discharge to a nursing home. This arrangement can take into account the preference of the client, the client's family members, the doctor, and social services workers. Jacque says, "This question is important to the client because it is important that professionals involved in this vital decision, including doctors, discharge planners, and certain nursing home employees, should be aware of what this client group is looking for and what influ-

ences them when making such a decision" (p. 3). Jacque posed this COPES question:

> If patients who have received nursing home orders from their doctors take a survey regarding their preferences in selecting a nursing home, what would the patients list as the most influential factors?

Her best source, a survey of doctors and caregivers (Jarboe & McDaniel, 1985) discovered that the most common reason listed for a selection was the nursing home's location. That survey helped Jacque to design and conduct a survey of a convenience sample of 36 of her own clients regarding their preferences at their discharge. These clients listed Location of the Home (44.4%), Previous Residence in Nursing Home (33.3%), Location of Family (25%), Bed Availability (17%), Reputation of Facility (3%), and Services Offered at Facility (3%) as their preferences (Helland, 2001, Appendix H in Jacque's paper).

of 85% to 100%. Their findings might surprise you. The homeless respondents rated a need for safety, further education, and transportation above affordable housing! "In addition, medical/dental treatment, need for health care information, job placement, and job training were ranked about as high as their housing needs" (p. 7 in Acosta & Toro, 2000, INFOTRAC Article Number A65378034).

Why Descriptive Studies?

Accurate estimates based on survey technology make surveys one of the shining examples of applied social science technology. For example, carefully stratified random samples of approximately 1500 can provide a fairly accurate picture of alcohol use practices nationally (www.drugabusestatistics.samhsa.gov). Surveys regularly predict the outcome of elections, unless they are extremely close.

Survey Rating Form

Background

Survey technology has been one of the earliest and most trusted advances in applied social science. The survey rating form (SRF) is based on principles of survey research (Babbie, 1973; Bainbridge, 1989; Czaja & Blair, 1996; Maisel & Persell, 1996).

Purpose

The SRF is designed to compute a single index of the quality of any type client survey (including needs assessment and client satisfaction). Higher scores indicate a stronger survey study that may range from 0 through 100. This section is designed to provide you with practice with SRF to determine whether to apply survey results to your own practice.

Instructions

Please read the Explanation for each criterion on the SRF form with the intent of applying the criteria to what you read. Give one point for each check mark. Scores can range from 0 to 100. This is only an ordinal scale, meaning that a score of 10 is higher than a score of 5 but not necessarily twice as high a score. No norms exist for SRF, nor data for its validity (other than the literature cited here), nor reliability checks for independent ratings using the form.

Table 8.1 | Survey Rating Form (SRF)

Source in APA Format (American Psychological Association, 2001)

Criterion	Points (One Point for Each Criterion Checked)	Explanation
Clear About What the Author(s) Wanted to Know		
1. Importance of the study		The authors (a) cite literature that states specifically why the survey is worth doing, *and* (b) the literature supports the need for the survey, *and* (c) the authors address how the survey fills a gap or need.
2. Authors stated hypothesis before study began		The authors stated in writing, before gathering data, their reasons for selecting particular variables for study or stated their hypothesis. Give the point for this one for any evidence that they did so with another person (e.g., research proposal) before collecting any data. This keeps the research from becoming a fishing expedition where even random data appear to contain some structure.

Table 8.1 | Continued

Criterion	Points (One Point for Each Criterion Checked)	Explanation
3. Pretested the Questionnaire or interview guide		The authors state specifically that they pretested their questionnaire or interview guide on persons similar to those whom they would eventually survey.

Clear Question Wording. Examine the three principal questions (most important to your potential use for the study's results) on the questionnaire or interview guide (if at least three are not given in the article, then give no points for question wording on items 4 through 8).

Criterion	Points	Explanation
4. No double-barreled questions (i.e., multiple-headed, two questions posed as one, multiple questions)		Give one point if you cannot find a double-barreled question among the survey's questions (i.e., two questions posed as one, usually connected by *and* or *or.*
5. No leading or loaded questions		Give one point if you cannot find a leading or loaded question. Such questions tell the respondent, often in a subtle way, what the researcher expects for an answer. Here are examples: "Please list your reasons for being satisfied with your services here on the Neurosciences Ward." (This could be converted to a nonleading format by asking two questions as follows: "Have you been satisfied with your services on the Neurosciences ward? Yes [ ] No [ ] Both Yes and No [ ]." Then ask for explanations for each.
6. No questions that go beyond the expected vocabulary of respondents		Give one point if you cannot find a single word in a question on the survey that might confuse respondents because it goes beyond their level of education, cultural background, or life experience.
7. No vague questions		Give one point if you cannot find a question that seems unclear to you.
8. No extremely long or complex questions		Give one point if you cannot find a single question that you could word more clearly or more briefly but say the same thing.
9. Subjects assured anonymity or confidentiality		Those who did the study state that they gave respondents assurance that their responses would be kept anonymous (i.e., their names would not appear in any way on their responses) or that they would be kept confidential (no one but the researcher would know who gave what response).

continued

Table 8.1 | Continued

Criterion	Points (One Point for Each Criterion Checked)	Explanation
Sampling Procedures		
10. Population stated		The authors state specifically the population from which they drew their sample (e.g., the population for a study of client satisfaction might be every family that adopts a child from the Friends Agency from June 1, 2002, to December 1, 2002). If you are clear about exactly who qualifies for membership in the population, then give this point.
11. Random or stratified random sampling procedure		The authors state that they have selected the sample to take the questionnaire or to be interviewed according to a random or stratified random procedure *and* they describe precisely how they did their selection (table of random numbers, specific computer algorithm).
12. Survey instrument checked for reliability		The authors state that their questionnaire was checked in some way for reliability *and* at least one of the reliability coefficients is above .70 or 70% agreement.
13. At least 80% of those selected for inclusion in sample included in study		Divide the number who actually completed their interviews or questionnaires by the number of subjects selected for study, and multiply this quotient by 100 to get the percent studied.
Analysis		
14. Analysis done by disinterested worker		The authors state that workers who did the analysis had no stake in the study's outcome. Ideally, those doing the analysis should be independent of the agency to prevent intentional bias.
15. Data checking applied		It is amazing how often errors can creep into data collection, coding, and analysis. If the authors refer to any data-checking procedure (e.g., plotting data, checking for illogical values, checking for outliers), then give one point here.

Table 8.1 | Continued

Criterion	Points (One Point for Each Criterion Checked)	Explanation
16. Sample size determined statistically		The authors state specifically what statistical procedure was applied (based on confidence interval, p value, and variance) to determine how many subjects they needed to study.

Study Findings

Criterion	Points	Explanation
17. Generalizations founded		The authors generalize their findings only to the population from which they selected their sample. For example, if their population was families adopting a child from the Friends Agency from June 1, 2002, to December 1, 2002, then their generalizations technically should be made only about this sample. Do not give the point here if they generalize to other agencies or to adoptions in general.
18. Reader avoids extrapolation error		To be useful, the study's findings should apply to your own clients. This squishy criterion can be met if you judge that the observations made in the study would apply to your clients. Are they the same age, sex, race, ethnic background? Do they have the same problem type, strengths, and so on?
	Total number checked (18 possible) _____ Score = (number checked/18) × 100 _____	

Note. This form was revised based on experience with it while teaching social work internship classes at the University of Wisconsin—Eau Claire and with suggestions from Stephanie Baus, School of Social Work, Tulane University.

Exercise 8-1: Social Workers Employed in Substance Abuse Treatment Agencies: A Training Needs Assessment

Purpose

This exercise is designed to help you to gain experience applying the SRF to evaluate a study that involves survey technology. It is also to help you to gain experience deciding whether to take action based on your evaluation of a survey type of study.

Background

Occasionally, Mel Morganbesser teaches a popular graduate-level course in the School of Social Work at the University of Wisconsin—Madison: Alcohol and Other Drug Abuse (AODA). Because he has designed his course for professionals in the helping professions, Mel has tried to base his lessons on actual training needs among helping professionals who have worked with clients with AODA problems or plan to do so. Mel would like to incorporate lessons into his course that will best meet the needs of professionals who will encounter AODA problems among their clients.

Here is Mel's COPES question:

For those actually working with clients with AODA problems, what will they list as being their most pressing needs for training to be more effective and knowledgeable in their AODA work?

Instructions

Please go to INFOTRAC: www.infotrac-college.com/access.html Enter your passcode, and search for the following article: Hall, M. N., Amodeno, M., Shaffer, H. J., & Bilt, J. V. (2000). Social workers employed in substance abuse treatment agencies: A training needs assessment. *Social Work, 45*(2), 141–155. This is INFOTRAC Article A60470926.

As you read the article, keep in mind that Mel will want to assess whether Hall et al.'s needs assessment is of sufficient quality to warrant its generalizations. He will want to know if the respondent's preferences are sufficiently strong to indicate a fairly uniform agreement on top-ranked needs, and he will need to examine characteristics of subjects in the study to see if they resemble his students sufficiently to warrant applying findings to his students.

Questions

1. Why might a dedicated instructor like Mel consider the Hall et al. (2000) study an important one as a guide to planning his class?

_____

_____

2. What is your SRF Score for the Hall et al. needs assessment?

   _____

   _____

3. What are its principal strengths and weaknesses?

   _____

   _____

   _____

4. What were the high-priority areas for social worker training?

   _____

   _____

5. Did Hall et al. do a qualitative study to develop their needs-assessment measure?

   _____

   _____

6. Are respondents, as described in the study, sufficiently like those in Mel's classes to warrant extrapolating the study's findings to his students? Use the following table for your assessment.

Area for Comparison	Your Clients	Study Clients
Client Problem		
Client Strengths		
Age		
Sex		
Race		
Ethnic Background		
Your Resources Versus Study Resources for Implementing Treatment or Assessment Procedure		
Other		

Distinctions Between Qualitative and Quantitative Research

Qualitative research ". . . aspires to understand people and their social environments in ways that are as close as possible to normal human experience by studying them in their natural settings" (Tutty, Rothery, & Grinnell, 1996, p. iv). "Qualitative researchers seek a deeper truth" (Greenhalgh, 1997, p. 151) that implies understanding the meaning that underlies the complexity of human behavior.

On the other hand, *quantitative* research begins with a specific testable proposition or hypothesis, applies measures, and arrives at conclusions based on numerical data. Quantitative researchers use experimentation, surveys, and well-developed measures that have been tested for their reliability and validity. Quantitative researchers ask enumerative types of questions that ask, How many? (e.g., How many patients at Middleton Memorial VA Hospital met the CAGE criterion for alcohol abuse among a stratified random sample proportionate to the census on each of its eight wards?) What proportion? (What proportion met the CAGE criterion relative to the number surveyed on the wards?) How long? (Among those who met the CAGE criterion, for how many years have they been consuming alcohol?)

Qualitative research uses different kinds of methods and asks different kinds of questions. Qualitative researchers rely on detailed and intensive observation and in-depth interviews. Qualitative researchers ask these kinds of questions: "What is the reason? How did you experience that? What was the meaning of that?

An Example of Qualitative Research

Judith Globerman (1996) did a qualitative study of how daughters and sons-in-law experience caring for relatives with Alzheimer's disease. After describing relevant literature, Globerman posed these kinds of questions: "How do in-laws [daughters-and sons-in-law] take responsibility for their spouses' parents?" "In what ways do in-laws [daughters-and sons-in-law] describe the meaning of these experiences [i.e., affection, obligation, motives, support of a spouse]?" (pp. 37–38). Globerman's subjects were selected by convenience sample from among 60 families that had experienced a member's diagnosis of Alzheimer's disease in 1992 at a single geriatric psychiatry clinic. Thirty-eight families agreed to participate. Globerman writes: "This article is based on qualitative analyses of the 16 children-in-law interviews and the 16 interviews with their 6 husbands (the sons) and 10 wives (the daughters)." Globerman collaborated with four student interviewers, who conducted a series of 1.5 to 3-hour long interviews, who were trained in qualitative interview techniques. The interviews were transcribed entirely and analyzed for content and themes according to a systematic procedure. Globerman reviewed the interview transcripts and derived themes from them in collaboration with the interviewers, but no tests of independent inter-observer agreement were made to check on coding. The article contains numerous quotes that Globerman perceived as being representative of the study's conclusions. One principal theme concerns the "performer versus director" distinction. The daughters-in-law were characterized as directors or initiators of care to their parent-in-laws. Globerman demonstrates due caution in generalizing. She says, ". . . [T]he study's limited nonprobability sample and interpretive methodology do not allow us to make such generalizations [wider beyond the convenience sample]," p. 43. Regarding the performer versus director roles, Globerman writes,

> Involvement of sons-in-law was circumscribed like sons, but it was relational toward their wives in a way that was responsive to their partner's requests and marital needs, not reactive to the needs of the AD [Alzheimer's disease] parent-in-law. They were buffers and shock absorbers for their wives, the daughters. Daughters'-in-law experiences were gendered in that they were the kinkeepers, like daughters, but not necessarily out of love [more from duty and obligation]. (p. 43)

Why Qualitative Studies?

Arguing about whether qualitative or quantitative research is *better* is like arguing over whether a screwdriver is better than a hammer. Each serves a different function in a classification of research tools. For example, trying to use quantitative methods to explore the existential meaning of breast cancer for women newly diagnosed with it would be naïve. Using qualitative methods to study effects of treatments on women's survival in treatment for breast cancer would be equally naïve (best studied by a randomized controlled trial). Each methodology fits a niche appropriate to a particular function.

Qualitative methods can apply at a basic level to all of the five COPES question types. For example, regarding *effectiveness questions,* a qualitative study might use in-depth interviews regarding quality of life as women go through the experience of treatment for breast cancer. Then, out of such a qualitative analysis, a quantitative measure for treatment outcome might be devised that validly taps major quality of life dimensions isolated in the qualitative study. Regarding *risk-assessment questions,* a real qualitative study investigated the question, "What are the characteristics of adult female survivors of child sexual abuse who have perpetrated child sexual abuse?" (Robinson, Coady, & Tutty, 1996, p. 158). The characteristics so isolated might provide items for a risk-assessment scale that could then be measured in a quantitative study to test the scale's ability to predict future abuse. Regarding *descriptive questions,* a qualitative study might conduct in-depth interviews of cocaine abusers who have successfully stopped their abuse for over 2 years to see what factors seemed pivotal in stopping their addiction. A descriptive study could then devise a questionnaire based on those factors to quantify what proportion of cocaine abusers possess those factors in a larger and perhaps more representative sample.

Qualitative Study Quality Form

Background

Because qualitative research applies varied methods to investigate a wide range of questions (Denzin & Lincoln, 1994, p. ix), developing a universally applicable rating form stretches it a bit; still, guidelines can reflect qualitative study standards. The Qualitative Study Quality (QSQ) form is based on other qualitative study rating forms (Greenhalgh, 1997, pp. 155–162; Institute of Health Sciences, July 19, 2000); discussions of qualitative study quality (Britten, Jones, Murphy, & Stacy, 1995; Globerman, 2002; Oktay, 2002); and on discussions of standards for designing qualitative studies (Berg, 2001, pp. 15–38).

Purpose

This section is designed to teach you to compute a score that reflects the quality of a qualitative study. Higher scores indicate a stronger qualitative study. Scores range from 0 through 100. The QSQ form provides a checklist of what to look for in a qualitative study. This section will give you practice evaluating a qualitative study with the goal of applying its findings to practice.

Instructions

Please read the Explanation for each criterion on the QSQ form with the intent of applying the criteria to what you read. The form was intended to rate the quality of a qualitative study. Give one point for each check mark. Scores can range from 0 to 100. This is only an ordinal scale, meaning that a score of 10 is higher than a score of 5 but not necessarily twice as high a score. No norms exist for QSQ, nor data for its validity (other than the literature cited here), nor reliability checks for independent ratings using the form.

Table 8.2 | Qualitative Study Quality (QSQ)

Source in APA Format (American Psychological Association, 2001)

Criterion	Points (One Point for Each Criterion Checked)	Explanation
Clear About What the Author(s) Wanted to Know		
1. Importance of the study		The authors cite literature that states specifically why the qualitative study is worth doing.

Table 8.2 | Continued

Criterion	Points (One Point for Each Criterion Checked)	Explanation
2. Clarity of research question		Qualitative studies do not always begin with a very specific question, but they should begin with a general statement about what they want to know. For example, "We wanted to study abused women to better understand that experience" is too vague. One more specific question—there could be many—might be: "We conducted this study of married women, whose records at X agency showed they had been sexually abused between the ages of 6 and 16, to determine whether they thought this experience had affected their sexuality." Give credit if the authors' research question was stated specifically enough to get an answer.
3. Research question stated in writing before the study began		Give this point if the authors state specifically that they stated what they wanted to know in writing for the record (e.g., question stated in a research proposal) before they began their research. This avoids the research becoming a disorganized fishing expedition.
Appropriate Methodology		
4. Appropriate qualitative methodology type		The authors do *all three* of these: • Name a qualitative methodology (e.g., grounded theory, focus groups, in-depth interviews, participant observation, content analysis). • State specifically why they chose this methodology to answer their question. • Cite literature that defines this chosen methodology.

continued

Table 8.2 | Continued

Criterion	Points (One Point for Each Criterion Checked)	Explanation
5. Qualitative study is most appropriate methodology for question type		The study does not investigate a question that would be more effectively investigated by a quantitative study (e.g., general effectiveness of a violence-prevention program in a school, effectiveness of crisis-intervention teams to reduce effects of trauma on disaster victims, accuracy of a parole prediction scale, agreement between assessment tools for depression, frequency of preferences for county services among Hmong families within a county). Qualitative studies can seek a deeper understanding related respectively to the issues listed (e.g., focus groups among students to identify their perceptions of an ideal violence-prevention program, in-depth interviews of recipients of services of crisis-intervention teams to identify behaviors they thought helpful and not so, in-depth interviews of parolees judged to be low risk who committed another offense to determine the sequence of events preceding the offense. . .).
Sampling Procedures		
6. Location for source of sample		The authors state where they physically selected their subjects or got their records for observation. The key here is that you could go there and would know exactly where they got their observations (e.g., case records kept by Clark County Human Services clients, 14 W. Gibirdie Street . . .).
7. Time frame for selecting sample		The authors state a beginning date for when they began making their observations, and they state when they stopped making their observations or state the time frame for records.

Table 8.2 | Continued

Criterion	Points (One Point for Each Criterion Checked)	Explanation
8. Refusals and lost subjects recorded		The authors record the number of observations that they *tried* to make, and they list the number of observations that they were *able* to make. For example, they may have contacted 20 subjects to participate in a focus group and 15 accepted their invitation to participate. They may have selected 20 records for review, but only 12 could be found.
9. Reason for refusals and lost subjects recorded		In Criterion 8, the authors state specifically the reason(s) for not making attempted observations if there were any. If all observations were made as planned, then give the point for item 9.
10. Criteria for selecting sample		The authors state their criteria for selecting subjects or records for observation so specifically that you could follow their procedure confidently, knowing that you were doing so exactly as the authors did.
11. Random sample or stratified random sample		The authors state that they selected subjects or records from a larger population or list of records according to a random selection procedure of some kind, *and* they state specifically what that procedure was so clearly that you could follow the same procedure without doubt about what to do. For example, qualitative researchers might intend to generalize from Hmong elders, age 50 or older, who still do not speak English, who reside in a given city, who live with a son or daughter. Such subjects could be listed and numbered, and then a random sample could be selected for a series of translated interviews to determine what factors relate to their decision regarding learning English.

continued

Table 8.2 | Continued

Criterion	Points (One Point for Each Criterion Checked)	Explanation
Controls for Bias in Making Observations		
12. Triangulation (multiple ways to make observations)		The authors apply more than one method for making their observations to collect their data. For example, they may use an interview guide regarding a subject's perceptions of an event and they also record what the subject did at that event.
13. Inter-observer agreement		The authors do not rely on a single observer; they rely on two or more *independent* observers who observe the same behavior, code records, watch events, and so on. Independence implies that the observers do not know how the other observers are recording their observations, nor do observers change their records when they find out what the other observers have recorded.
14. Specific about procedures for evaluating inter-observer agreement		Regarding Criterion 13, the authors describe their procedure for checking inter-observer agreement so specifically that you have no doubt about how they went about the process of checking such agreement.
15. Data given in report regarding inter-observer agreement		The authors give specific data that define how well the observers agreed once their independent assessments were compared. For example, the report might state that Observer 1 and Observer 2 agreed in seven of ten cases.
16. Data-checking procedure		The authors state specifically that they checked their recorded data in some way to see if they contained errors, *and* they describe this procedure so specifically that you would know what to do to perform the same data check.
Control for Respondent Bias		
17. Respondent bias minimal		The authors state that they did something (anything) to ensure that respondents gave accurate responses or behaved normally, as respondents would have if not under observation.

Table 8.2 | Continued

Criterion	Points (One Point for Each Criterion Checked)	Explanation
Study Findings		
18. Specific findings		The authors state their findings in terms of observations made during the study, *and* you can clearly see the link between these observations and their conclusions. In other words, they do not draw conclusions that they have not supported by observations.
19. Reproducibility of findings		The authors specifically state that they made transcripts of interviews, kept coding sheets, or kept records that another researcher could examine directly to see if these data warrant the authors' conclusions.
20. Independent auditor's findings		The authors name by name an outsider, a disinterested person, who also looked at records of their observations to see whether they drew the same conclusions as did the authors.
21. Author avoids extrapolation error		Read the qualitative study's conclusions section. Look for any inferences about how the study's findings may generalize to others. Give this point if the authors avoid making a single inference that their study's findings apply to others outside the sample they studied if they did not pick their subjects by a randomized or stratified random procedure. For example, a qualitative study may have involved an in-depth interview with ten men about their experiences with prostate cancer who were picked by a convenience sample method. Give this point if the authors say: "In-depth interviews with our ten subjects showed that men *in this study.* . . . " Give no points if they make generalizing statements like this: "This study shows that men with prostate cancer. . . ."

continued

Table 8.2 | Continued

Criterion	Points (One Point for Each Criterion Checked)	Explanation
22. Reader avoids extrapolation error		To be useful, the study's findings should apply to your own clients. This squishy criterion can be met if you judge that the observations made in the study would apply to your clients. Are they the same age, sex, race, ethnic background? Do they have the same problem type, strengths, and so on?
	Total number checked (22 possible) _____ Score = (number checked/22) × 100 _____	

Exercise 8-2: A Qualitative Study of Life After Stroke

Purpose

This exercise is designed for you to gain experience applying the QSQ to evaluate a study that involves qualitative study methodology. You will also gain experience deciding whether to take action based on your evaluation of a qualitative type of study.

Background

I have had the pleasure of working with a 78-year-old woman who still works at clerical tasks at our university. She is no stranger to adversity. Her husband died young, leaving her to raise their five children alone. She never remarried. One of her children has preceded her in death. Two days ago, she was walking her dog and had a stroke. I understand from others who have visited her in the hospital that she received prompt anticoagulant treatment and has regained her speech. I will go to visit her this afternoon. Before my visit, I would like to understand her experience and to know what kinds of problems she will face to determine what we might do to support her during her recovery.

Here is my COPES question:

For elderly persons who experience a stroke, what is the experience like for them emotionally and practically?

Instructions

Please go to INFOTRAC: www.infotrac-college.com/access.html Enter your passcode, and search for the following article: Pilkington, F. B. (1999). A qualitative study of life after stroke. *Journal of Neuroscience Nursing, 31*(6), 336–347. This is INFOTRAC Article A59984478.

This study addresses an issue ideally suited for a qualitative study. It certainly holds personal interest for me. The QSQ will provide an outline for examining issues regarding how accurately the study reflects individuals studied and how well these individuals represent a wider set of mild-to-moderate stroke victims' experiences.

Questions

I went to visit the elderly woman today. Her face and neck were badly bruised by her fall, but she seemed alert and articulate. She told us of her experience without slurring her words. She had been walking her dog; leaned over to help the dog; and fell to the ground, hitting her face—unable to move her legs. She lay there conscious and unable to help herself. Within minutes, a neighbor who had seen her fall, came out to help. Another neighbor called an ambulance, and my friend was conscious the whole time in the ambulance and at the hospital during her testing there. In less than 3 hours, she was given a drug that she called "TPH"; she remained 2 days in the hospital and was at home when we visited her. She explained that, other than being a bit tired and weak, she felt fine and like herself mentally. She talked about wanting to get back to work again.

Though my elderly friend's experience does not fit the severity of stroke described in the article, the article helped me to understand what she was going through personally. Elements from the article somewhat reflected her experiences. It was frightening for her to lose control over her legs; she will live with after effects and restrictions related to her stroke, and she has surely discovered consoling relationships that give her strength. Her granddaughter was with her when we visited, and the neighborhood has rallied around her.

1. What is your QSQ score for the Pilkington article?

   _____

2. What are this qualitative study's strengths and weaknesses?

   _____

   _____

   _____

   _____

   _____

3. How many subjects served in this qualitative study?

   _____

4. How were subjects chosen for inclusion in this qualitative study?

   _____

5. Would this study help you to gain understanding of the experience of stroke and its effects on quality of life?

   _____

   _____

   _____

6. Are clients, as described in the study, sufficiently like those in your own practice to warrant extrapolating the study's findings to the client(s) at hand? Use the following table for your assessment.

Area for Comparison	Your Clients	Study Clients
Client Problem		
Client Strengths		
Age		
Sex		
Race		
Ethnic Background		
Your Resources Versus Study Resources for Implementing Treatment or Assessment Procedure		
Other		

7. If you were I, about to visit my friend who suffered her stroke, how confident do you think I should be that her experience reflects that of subjects in the Pilkington study?

   _____

   _____

In God we trust—all others must use data! **Attributed to W. Edwards Deming,** *but Brian Joiner (according to David Balsiger) says: "I don't think he ever said that, but he should have."*

Collecting Data in Practice

9

Overview

Progress to This Point

Up to this point, you have come a long way following steps outlined by Sackett et al., back cover). Initially, this text defined evidence-based practice through concept, example, and operation. Then examples of common errors in practice reasoning were demonstrated to motivate you by demonstrating potentially harmful thinking that stands in direct opposition to evidence-based practice. Hopefully, this text has strengthened your resolve to pose questions about practice in the first place and then to pose clear COPES questions. This text has only gotten you started searching efficiently, electronically, for answers to your COPES questions by applying MOLES and appropriate search terms. During your professional lifetime, the information revolution will surely carry you much farther in ways that can only be speculated about now. Chapter 5 through Chapter 8 defined how to critically appraise evidence to determine its implications for action/no action.

Why Collect Data in Practice?

- *You need to make your own observations.* The whole evidence-based process might end by just taking evidence-guided action and trusting that you have done the best you can, but what if your clients still do not benefit?

How would you ever know without collecting your own data? The lives of clients are too precious to just assume that evidence-based action has had its desired effect.

- *Just extrapolating from research to your own clients can still put them at risk.* The possibility exists that the research was fraudulent or flawed in ways not detected in your critical appraisal. The possibility exists that subjects in the research were so dissimilar from yours that study results do not apply to your clients. The possibility exists that you lack some essential element of skill or experience that was not evident from reading a research report. Such factors make it necessary, wherever possible, to make your own systematic and direct observations.

- *Your data collection need not be elaborate and time-consuming.* To the contrary, if it is, you will probably not find time to do it. Data need to be simple and related directly to what you are trying to accomplish. For example, if you are working in hard-to-place adoptions and you wonder what the experience is like for the many teenage adoptees on your caseload, you may do an in-depth qualitative interview with two or three typical adoptees recording central themes in their stories. If you are working with married couples who have communication problems, you may apply a marriage communication assessment form as a pretest and a posttest. Such data can be collected as part of practice efficiently, as examples from practice in this chapter will demonstrate.

- *The data-collection process may serve client preferences directly.* Jim Campbell (1988) surveyed 30 clients and their mental health social workers in the Duluth, Minnesota, area about whether they would prefer that their counselor apply one of three single-subject designs (i.e., B, AB, BAB) as part of mental health treatment, or would prefer that they rely on the practitioner's personal opinion to assess their progress. Campbell found that the clients preferred any of the three single-subject evaluations over their counselor's personal opinion as a treatment-evaluation procedure (according to responses on a Likert-type scale). In a more detailed analysis of the same data, Campbell (1990) found, when he compared the clients and their social workers' ratings of the same situations, that the clients placed a greater confidence in single-subject evaluation procedures than did their counselors (p. 13).

Chapter Organization

How to make direct observations by doing small studies in practice has been covered thoroughly elsewhere, particularly regarding the effectiveness of treatments. Therefore, this essential chapter is short relative to the others. This chapter gives an example of the kind of data that you might collect regarding each question type; it discuss some issues in doing each type of study and refers you to related literature. This chapter's organization, going downward, follows the far right column in Table 9.1.

Table 9.1	Question Types Relative to Their Appropriate Best Evidence and Guides to Action		
Question Type	**Appropriate Rating for Evidence**	**Evidentiary Guides to Action**	**Appropriate, Simple, Data-Collection Methods for Practice**
Effectiveness Questions: Chapter 5	Quality of Study Rating Form (QSRF)	Statistical significance, absolute risk reduction, number needed to treat, number needed to harm	Single-subject studies with repeated measures, small-group studies
Prevention Questions: Chapter 5	Quality of Study Rating Form-Prevention (QSRF-P)	Statistical significance, absolute risk reduction, number needed to treat, number needed to harm, problem reduction relative to base rate	Single-subject data regarding prevented behavior, small-group studies regarding prevented behavior
Meta-Analysis (Primarily Effectiveness Questions): Chapter 6	Multiple Evaluations for Treatment Assessment (META)	Transformations to number needed to treat, combined number needed to treat	Meta-analyses are syntheses of studies; so, by definition, meta-analysis has been omitted from this chapter. You may do a continually updated meta-analysis regarding a specific question, but they are time-consuming.
Assessment Questions and Risk-Assessment Questions: Chapter 7	Client Assessment and Risk Evaluation (CARE)	Inter-rater agreement, criterion-related validity, positive predictive value, negative predictive value	Small studies of inter-rater agreement, applying assessment/risk instruments to try them out, small prediction studies, applying an assessment measure to a few cases
Description and Qualitative Questions: Chapter 8	Survey Rating Form (SRF)	Sample means and proportions	Small client surveys regarding need for services and client satisfaction
	Qualitative Study Quality (QSQ)	Content ratings, frequencies	Small qualitative studies involving a few clients

Effectiveness: Single-Subject Studies with Repeated Measures, Small-Group Studies

Example Regarding Participation in Treatment for HIV

Jennifer Day (1999) worked at the AIDS Resource Center of Wisconsin. Jennifer tried to help her clients, who had been infected by HIV, to take their medications as prescribed. These medications can cause painful side effects and

Table 9.2 | Bill's Pill-Taking Participation by Date

Bill Took Medication on Time														
Took Medication														
Dates in July	1	2	3	4	5	6	7	8	9	10	11	12	13	14

require taking the right combination of medications at the times specified. If the client does not take the medications as prescribed, the virus can mutate quickly to overcome effects of the medication. Then the client becomes ill from opportunistic infections and dies.

Bill [all names are fictitious], one of Jennifer's HIV clients, a resident of a group home for men with mental illness, had not been taking his medication as prescribed. Jennifer was concerned that, if Bill did not conform to his drug regimen, he would suffer the consequences. Jennifer read sources on the World Wide Web including an article by Singh, Squiere, and Sirek (one that I cannot locate). Her reading suggested using a pillbox. Jennifer secured a pillbox, and she worked with the group home's resident manager to construct a chart to record Bill's pill-taking behavior. The chart simply lists medications taken by day as reflected by the contents of Bill's pillbox. The data were recorded in the format something like that given in Table 9.2. Jennifer recorded just one instance in which the medications were not taken appropriately.

Example Regarding Eye Movement Desensitization and Reprocessing for Sexual Trauma

Kristen Reinartz (1999) worked at the Chippewa County Guidance Clinic. She counseled Amy [all not true names], a woman in her late 30s, who had experienced a rape and sexual trauma earlier in life and still seemed affected by these experiences. When Kristen discussed her client with her coworkers at the clinic, they decided that the client might benefit from Eye Movement Desensitization and Reprocessing (EMDR) to overcome effects of her trauma. To define EMDR, Kristen located an article by Wilson, Becker, and Tinker (1995). EMDR applies desensitizing cognitive methods that include a set of eye movements as part of the process. Kristen posed a COPES question regarding EMDR's effectiveness, and she searched for evidence regarding the efficacy of EMDR. Kristen rated the Wilson et al. study highest giving it a score of 86 on the Quality of Study Rating Form with standardized mean differences ($ES1$) ranging from .44 to 2.07. Still skeptical, Kristen located an Impact of Event Scale that asks questions about the traumatic event's intrusiveness into the client's thoughts and avoidance thinking. Kristen planned a pretest and posttest for Amy using the Impact of Event Scale, as shown in Table 9.3. She only obtained pretest data, because the client quit attending the counseling sessions.

Table 9.3	Impact of Event Scale Score at Pretest and Posttest for a Sexually Abused Woman		
Scale of Impact of Event Scale's Score	Pretest	Posttest	Norms for Impact of Event Scale
Intrusiveness scale (scores range from 0–28)	25		Horowitz, M.J., Wilner, N. & Alvarez, W. (1979). Impact of Event Scale. *Psychosomatic Medicine,41*, 209–218.
Avoidance scale (scores range from 0–32)	30		

Example Regarding Desensitization for Discomfort Around Needles

Sarah North (1996) chose medical social work for her internship and was accepted at a local hospital, but she was a bit concerned about a potential problem there for herself—she was downright uncomfortable around syringes and needles! Consequently, she devised a desensitization-therapy program for herself based on her reading (Hamilton, 1995; Rice, 1993). Her reading suggested that she pair relaxation techniques with situations that she found successively more and more stressful, pausing at each level until she was comfortable. Her hierarchy of events is as follows:

STAGE 1 (PREPARATION INTERVENTION)

- Traveling to the needle-injection site
- Physically positioning for the injection (sitting in chair with body ready for injection)
- Observation of the nurse putting on gloves
- Conversation with the nurse regarding the injection
- Rolling up of my shirt sleeve by nurse wearing gloves
- Observation of alcohol pad and syringe on nearby table

STAGE 2 (TOUCH INTERVENTION)

- Preparation and application of alcohol pad sterilization
- Additional touch by nurse wearing gloves
- Continued conversation with nurse regarding injection
- Handling and inspection of syringe by me

STAGE 3 (POKE INTERVENTION) (PP. 2–3)

Sarah's nurse friend administered the treatment to Sarah. They took Sarah's blood pressure as an index of Sarah's level of comfort, and they recorded blood-pressure data for each stage as outlined in Figure 9.1.

The following examples demonstrate that data collection can range from relatively simple to relatively complex but should always be directly useful and practical.

Figure 9.1 | Sarah's Systolic and Diastolic Readings by Desensitization Stage

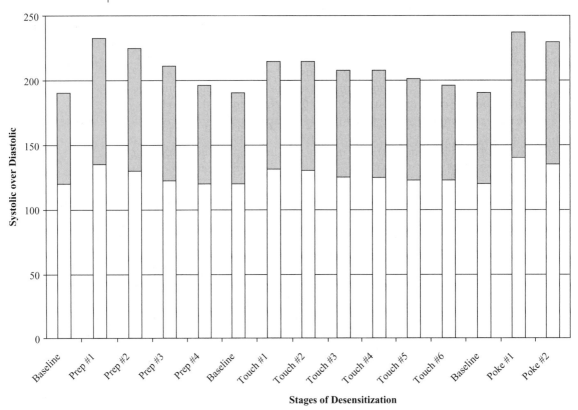

From *Evaluation of Practice Personal Single Subject Design: An Experiment in Desensitization Therapy,* by S. North, 1996, University of Wisconsin—Eau Claire. Adapted with permission.

Useful Literature Regarding How to Do Small Effectiveness Studies in Practice

- Bloom, M., Fischer, J., & Orme, J. G. (1999). *Evaluating practice: Guidelines for the accountable professional* (3rd ed.). Boston: Allyn & Bacon. [This comprehensive and practical guide to integrating single-system designs into practice includes measures (behavioral records, rating scales, questionnaires, logs), and single-subject evaluation designs (including a CASS computer program that plots and analyzes client data statistically).]
- Gambrill, E. (1997). *Social work practice: A critical thinker's guide.* New York: Oxford University Press. [Chapter 19 provides the briefest and most specific guide to evaluation of which I am aware.]
- Richards, S. B., Taylor, R. L., Ramasamy, R., & Richards, R. Y. (1999). *Single-subject research: Applications in educational and clinical settings.* San Diego: Singular. [Includes chapters on historical learning principles,

data recording, and issues in single-subject research; two thirds concern single-subject designs.]

- Tripodi, T. (1994). *A primer on single-subject design for clinical social workers.* Washington, DC: National Association of Social Workers. [Includes basic single-subject designs, statistical methods appropriate for each design, and 11 outcome measures.]

Prevention: Single-Subject Data Regarding Prevented Behavior, Small-Group Studies

Example Regarding Violence Prevention in a School

Kim Andres (2000) did her training at an elementary school of 275 students. Teachers, officials, and counseling staff at the school had become increasingly concerned about an apparent trend toward more violent behaviors among the students. Kim's office received referrals for "fights on the playground or in the gym and also bullying behavior such as pushing in the halls and tripping students" (p. 2). To combat the apparent trend, staff at the school had decided to try a Second-Step Violence-Prevention Program. Kim was given the task of implementing the Second-Step program for two half-hour sessions per month. The program presents a poster lesson that outlines a situation in a school. The lessons teach impulse control, how to express emotions appropriately, how to take the perspective of another, how to solve problems, and how to manage anger.

Though the decision had already been made to implement the Second-Step program, Kim searched the literature regarding its effectiveness before she started her training. She found a review (Frey & Sylvester, 1997), and she concluded that the best evaluation for the program was the one done by Harris (1995).

Kim devised a way to collect pretest-posttest comparison group data regarding the Second-Step program's effectiveness. She reasoned that the school's detention records could provide a clue. Electronic files at the school record the detention and reasons for it; so Kim was able to collect the data outlined in Table 9.4.

Example Concerning Preventing HIV/AIDS

Sometimes practitioners cannot collect meaningful data simply and easily regarding the outcome of prevention programs. For example, it can take 10 years for the virus that causes AIDS to cause symptoms. Also, collecting data regarding HIV can involve highly confidential information; so it can be difficult to get infection information and condom-use information from schoolchildren participating in prevention programs. In such difficult circumstances, one can still take action based on the current best evidence and hope for the best.

For example, Ann Wiederholt (1999) found herself confronted with an HIV/AIDS prevention problem. While doing her training at a regional office of the American Red Cross, Ann became concerned about the difference in the

Table 9.4 | Behavioral Referrals for Violent Behavior in Two Groups Before and After the Second-Step Program

	Behavioral Referrals Prior to Second-Step Program (12-Week Period from August 13 to October 25)	Behavioral Referrals After Second-Step Program Began in Late October (12-Week Period—minus holidays—from November 1 to March 3)
Every Sixth Student Selected from Roster of 130 in Grade 1 Through Grade 3 ($n = 20$)	10	21
Twenty Students Selected Randomly from Grade 6 Through Grade 8	3	7

rate of HIV infection in two neighboring and very similar (both rural, both almost entirely Caucasian) counties. According to the Division of Public Health in Madison, Wisconsin, one county had 44 individuals with HIV/AIDS (population 40,000), and the other had 17 with HIV/AIDS (population 45,000). Ann also noted that, according to a public health nurse's data, in the first county, minimal information was taught in the schools about safe sex and the risk of getting HIV/AIDS; in the latter, there were informative programs. Though many factors other than prevention programs might account for this difference, Ann decided to search for literature that evaluated the effectiveness of prevention programs for school-age children and to advocate for the program that followed the most effective model (assuming there is one). She reviewed several studies and decided that one by Fang, Stanton, Fiegelman, and Baldwin (1998) that used friendship groups was the strongest relative to QSRF criteria. This study's pretest-posttest design reported a significant increase in condom use among youthful participants. Ann went on to advocate for a similar program in both counties.

The reader is referred to "Useful Literature Regarding How to Do Small Effectiveness Studies in Practice."

Assessment and Risk: Small Studies of Inter-Rater Agreement, Small Criterion Validity Studies, Small Prediction Studies

Issues Regarding Assessment and Risk

Ways to collect data regarding inter-rater reliability and predictive validity were described in chapter 7 in the "Detailed Explanation for CARE Criteria" section. Ideally, data could be collected in practice that tests inter-rater reliability and predictive validity, but my experience and that of colleagues have been less than ideal so far. Typically, our practice students have stated their COPES questions to clarify their measurement need, located electronically the most reliable and valid ones (often using the Health and Psychosocial Instruments Database), and have fulfilled their data-collection requirement by applying their best measure to a few cases. Up to this point, none have had sufficient influence in an agency to get other workers to try a test of inter-rater reliability as shown in Figure 7.1. We have been able, as the example at the beginning of chapter 7 demonstrates, to gain experience applying risk-assessment measures.

Assessing Need for Discharge Planning from a Hospital

Sara Makovec (2000) worked on the Medical-Telemetry-Oncology Unit at Sacred Heart Hospital. She noted that a member of the Social Services Department saw every client before discharge. She noted also that many did not need her department's services. Evaluating each client cut into valuable staff time and unnecessarily inconvenienced persons who were sick and under stress. Sara was concerned also that hurried staff might miss persons who needed help with discharge. Sara's supervisor mentioned that the hospital had formed a Discharge-Planning Committee that intended to develop some sort of screening tool.

Sara searched for literature hoping to find an example measure to assess need for social services for discharge planning. She found discussions of the topic (Weaver & Burdi, 1992; Wertheimer & Kleinman, 1990; Williams, Greenwell, & Groom, 1992), but she found no measures that could be applied to discharge screening. Sara also called social service departments at six hospitals in the state to discuss their criteria and to see if any had a measure. None provided an adequate measure, but her discussions helped her to develop her list of needs. Sara then developed a nine-item checklist to be administered by a nurse that included items like these:

- Is the patient safe to live alone? (Is there any live-in support system?)
- Are there any home services currently being received (MOW, HHC, Supportive Care, Lifeline, social services, etc.)?. . . (Makovec, 2000, Appendix B)

Sara and a colleague administered her screening test to 61 new admissions over a week's time, finding that 23 (38%) did not need services (p. 7).

Useful Literature Regarding Risk Assessment and Assessment Studies

- Duggan, C. (Ed.). (1997). Assessing risk in the mentally disordered. *British Journal of Psychiatry, Supplement 32, 170(32)*, 1–39. [Initially discusses issues in predictive validity; later contributions give examples regarding violence, sex offenses, dangerousness, and risk to children.]
- Gibbs, L. E. (1991). *Scientific reasoning for social workers: Bridging the gap between research and practice.* New York: Merrill, an imprint of Macmillan. [Chapter 7 includes nominal inter-rater agreement and Kappa as an index of reliability, and chapter 10 includes essentials of predictive validity.]

- Kraemer, H. C. (1992). *Evaluating medical tests: Objective and quantitative guidelines.* Newbury Park, CA: Sage.

Description Questions: Small Client Surveys Regarding Need for Services and Client Satisfaction

Example Regarding Client Satisfaction with an Aphasia Caretakers' Support Group

Catherine Schmale (1999) worked on the Neurosciences Unit of Luther Hospital. Catherine developed her concern for stroke victims and their caregivers, because she worked with many during her training on the unit. She explained that stroke frequently results in aphasia, or brain damage that affects a person's ability to communicate, primarily through speech, but can also include inability to read and write. Catherine explained that nonfluent aphasia refers to slowed speech with incomplete sentences, sometimes being reduced to a small, single-word vocabulary. She explained also that individuals with fluent aphasia can speak without pauses and hesitations, but they have a noticeable inability to find the right word, sometimes inserting an inappropriate or nonsense word into their conversation. In either case, the experience can frighten and stress family caregivers who try their best to help their loved one.

Catherine was invited to attend a support group for caregivers; and, as typical of her dedication, she quickly became involved in the group. Catherine volunteered to construct and administer a client-satisfaction questionnaire to aid the group in serving its members' needs. She located several client-satisfaction questionnaires and studies, but none were specific to an aphasia support group's concerns (Johnson, 1998; Kane, Reinardy, Penrod, & Huck, 1999; Pound, Gompertz, & Ebrahim, 1993; Tebb, 1995); so she developed her own ten-item, caregiver-satisfaction questionnaire based on what she read. Her questionnaire's instructions asked respondents to mark one of five levels of agreement with ten statements, and it provided space to explain responses; so her analysis included both quantitative and qualitative data. Here are the first two of her questionnaire's items:

APHASIA GROUP
Caregiver Questionnaire

1 Strongly Agree
2 Disagree
3 Undecided
4 Agree
5 Strongly Agree

1. Through the caregivers' group I have learned more about aphasia.   1 2 3 4 5
   (Comments)
2. Through the caregivers' group I have learned new strategies
   to communicate with my loved one.   1 2 3 4 5
   (Comments)

Useful Literature Regarding How to Do Descriptive Studies in Practice

- Applebaum, R. A., Straker, J. K., & Green, S. M. (2000). *Assessing satisfaction in health and long-term care.* New York: Springer. [Author advocates for assessing client satisfaction including an outline of qualitative methods and surveys, includes references to survey instruments, and sources on the World Wide Web.]
- McKillip, J. (1987). *Need analysis: Tools for the human services and education.* Newbury Park, CA: Sage. [Gives examples of different methods for need analysis and their relative merits and provides an algorithm for identifying appropriate needs-assessment methods specific to problems.]
- Reviere, R., Berkowitz, S., Carter, C. C., & Ferguson, C. G. (1996). *Needs-assessment: A creative and practical guide for social sciences.* Washington, DC: Taylor & Francis. [Outlines needs-assessment methods for types of questions, design, sampling, and planning a needs assessment; two thirds of the book are examples of needs assessments.]
- Strasser, S., & Davis, R. M. (1991). *Measuring patient satisfaction for improved patient services.* Ann Arbor, MI: Health Administration Press. [How to plan a satisfaction survey including its measure and how to execute the survey using quantitative and qualitative analyses.]
- Wilkikn, D., Hallam, L., & Doggett, M. (1992). *Measures of need and outcome for primary health care.* Oxford: Oxford University Press. [Discusses issues in needs-assessment measurement; includes 39 measures regarding needs in mental health, social support, quality of life, disease-specific problems, and patient satisfaction.]

Qualitative Studies: Studies Involving a Close Look at a Few Clients

A Qualitative Study of Adopted Children's Reflections on Adoption

This qualitative study was more ambitious than most practitioners could manage, because it involved the cooperation of three persons: a faculty advisor, Gloria Fennell; and two students, Inger Nelson and Adriana Monti (both students were placed in adoptions agencies that heavily serve special needs adoptions). Their literature review included two qualitative studies, one titled *Kids Speak Out on Adoption* (Moroz, Churchill, & Brgant, 1993) and *How It Feels to Be Adopted* (Krementz, 1982). The purpose of their qualitative study was "to capture the adoption experience from the child's point of view and in the child's words" (Nelson, 2001, p. 4). Special needs children may have received extensive services due to a physical or emotional disability; they may have survived abuse or neglect, may be placed in transracial homes, and may be a member of a sibling group (Nelson, 2001).

To accomplish the qualitative study's purpose, the students interviewed a convenience sample of a total of 17 special needs children who had been adopted for at least 2 years. Their interview included ten open-ended questions, including, for example: "What would you like to see changed to make the adoption process better for other children?" (Nelson, 2001, p. 10), and "What was good about (what did you like) about the adoption process?" (p. 11). Both students independently coded responses into themes from transcriptions of the interviews and compared their themes without applying a systematic test of inter-rater agreement. I will not scoop them by giving their themes here, but Inger appeared excited about insights that she had learned from the study. Their data were a structured interview and a content analysis for responses to each question.

Useful Literature Regarding Doing Qualitative Research in Practice

- Berg, B. L. (1998). *Qualitative research methods for the social sciences.* Needham Heights, MA: Allyn & Bacon. [Designing qualitative research with practical guides for interviewing, focus groups, ethnographic field studies, sociometry, unobtrusive measures, oral traditions, case studies, and content analysis.]
- Crabtree, B. F., & Miller, W. L. (Eds.). (1992). *Doing qualitative research.* Newbury Park, CA: Sage. [A practical guide for doing qualitative research in health care settings with two examples from medical practice.]
- Denzin, N. K., & Lincoln, Y. S. (2000). (Eds.). *Handbook of qualitative research.* Thousand Oaks, CA: Sage. [Written by a sociologist and educational administration educator, this book provides a compilation of chapters written by experts across the qualitative study topics, including historical, philosophical, ethical, and practical chapters regarding qualitative methods.]

Summary

Even though the best evidence may support taking action in practice, study findings may not generalize to your own practice. Consequently, wherever possible, data should be collected to see if evidence-based action accomplishes what it should be accomplishing. This chapter has only given a few examples to demonstrate the types of data that may be collected regarding each of the five question types. How to collect data regarding each of these questions has been covered in much greater detail elsewhere, as the "Useful Literature" sections indicate. The next and final chapter discusses the final step of evidence-based practice: teaching others to follow the process.

Exercise 9-1: Collecting Data in Practice

Background

Some will not be in practice with access to clients; so collecting data from practice will be impossible unless you have solicited a COPES question from a practitioner (Exercise 3-2) who is willing to help you. Ideally, the data collected will be central to your mission and simple to collect. As previously stated, the specifics for how to collect and to interpret data from practice can occupy volumes, going beyond space available here.

Purpose

This exercise is designed to give you experience collecting minimal but useful data in practice.

Instructions

You may start with Table 9.1 to see which type of data will be most appropriate to your question type; then look at the related example, and read the most appropriate source in the "Useful Literature" section. Do remember not to make a production out of it, and collect data only if they will clearly answer your question.

Questions

1. Are the data that you intend to collect:
   [ ] Simple enough to collect with relative ease?
   [ ] Specific to your question?
   [ ] Worth the effort to collect (such that a finding might change your actions)?
   [ ] Available by other easier means?
   [ ] Not in violation of client rights and preferences?
2. Please record your answers in the following table.

Data-Collection Form

COPES Question
Type of COPES Question (Circle One): Effectiveness, Prevention, Assessment, Risk, Description
Research Question
Relevant Type of Data
What You Expect to Find
Method of Data Collection
Data
Finding

In a time of drastic change, it is the learners who inherit the future. The learned usually find themselves equipped to live in a world that no longer exists. **Eric Hoffer, 1973**

10 | Teaching Others

Overview

Why a chapter about teaching evidence-based practice to others? Wouldn't teaching EBP be better left to professional teachers? I am not so sure. When practitioners confront a knotty problem, when they ponder a critical question regarding client care, to whom do they generally turn? Do they call an educator, or do they walk down the hall to the office of a trusted colleague for counsel there? I think the latter. Your immediate help to colleagues may have the greater effect on life-affecting judgments and decisions. Second, EBP and the most appropriate methods for teaching it will likely find a cold reception among all but the most innovative and dedicated educators. Evidence-based practice departs from established dogma and tradition. It runs against the grain of present educational practice, much as would taking a cat by the tail and pulling the fur back up toward the head [never do that]. Consequently, this chapter includes arguments opposing EBP and how to counter them. Expect obstacles. Prepare for them. Evidence-based practice represents innovation, and innovation generally generates discomfort and resistance. Such resistance is not personal, just a normal reaction to innovation.

This chapter also discusses problem-based learning and how its application to teaching. Evidence-based practice contrasts with conventional methods for teaching about practice. Problem-based learning (small groups applying

EBP steps to real problems in practice) can stress learners who have been comfortable with didactic teaching that emphasizes knowledge and skill retention. This chapter also discusses evidence regarding the effectiveness of EBP and strategies for introducing EBP into a human service organization. Finally, this chapter includes two exercises, one concerning whether to adopt a controversial treatment, the other concerning teaching others. Box 10.1 and Box 10.2 give examples of how efforts to teach EBP to others can be informal.

| Box 10.1 | **Teaching Others in a Hospital** |

Shannon Nyhus (December 13, 2000) worked as a hospital social worker on the Telemetry/Oncology ward and four other wards at Sacred Heart Hospital for her fieldwork training. Just as she started her training, Shannon's instructor was asked to serve on a new Palliative Care Service Team. This team, ". . . composed of a physician board-certified in palliative medicine, a nurse practitioner, a chaplain/counselor and social worker. . . ," works with clients facing grave debilitating illnesses." (Palliative Care Service, n.d. p. 2). These illnesses typically include the following: "cancer, lung disease, heart disease, AIDS, end-stage organ failure, and progressive neurological disease" (p. 2).

Shannon did her EBP assignment regarding client satisfaction with palliative care to give the team feedback about their new team's performance.

Shannon administered a FAMCARE survey to the client and client's family 5 days after the client was admitted. She assured respondents that their responses would be anonymous. She told respondents that accurate information would help the team to improve the team's services, and she always left the room while respondents completed the FAMCARE survey. Shannon also arranged with the next semester's student to administer the same FAMCARE survey 60 days after Shannon's pretest (most likely after the client had died). The FAMCARE survey's items

are specific to palliative care and appear in a randomized controlled trial of palliative care (The SUPPORT Investigators, 1995), but the point here concerns Shannon's efforts to teach EBP to others.

Here is what Shannon said of her effort to teach others:

> I showed Karen, my supervisor's supervisor, my EBP assignment, and she was amazed because last semester Sara [previous student] was at Sacred Heart and had showed [sic] Randee her EBP assignment [and how its search required going through the library]. I showed Karen how Dr. Gibbs's database worked [this book's Web site]. She [Karen] was just amazed at how you did not have to go through the library and you could just punch on Web sites. (Nyhus, December 13, 2000)

> Angie, Karen, and Randee [of the Social Service Department] came the next day [after Shannon offered to demonstrate search techniques on the computer in her office]. . . . I outlined the steps of EBP and then showed them the steps in my EBP paper. . . . I used the [COPES] question for my paper for my demonstration. . . . At the very end we searched for Munchausen syndrome. We found a lot, and we needed to narrow that down; so we needed to use MOLES, and that narrowed it down to about two articles. We didn't have the articles in the hospital library. We were just playing around with it then. (S. Nyhus, personal communication, June 13, 2001)

Box 10.2	**Teaching Others in Community Work with Persons with Chronic Mental Illness**

Melissa Utech (2001) and Liz Durch (2001) did their training for practice in a county community support program serving persons with chronic mental illness. Their clients included adults and adolescents with depression, schizophrenia, developmental disabilities, alcoholism and other drug abuse, and other chronic behavioral problems. Melissa and Liz's agency applied a team approach involving nurses, social workers, psychiatrists, and direct-service workers to help clients. The team frequently faced problems communicating about the clients' performance and treatment goals. They needed a way to list client strengths and task skills. Consequently, Melissa and her supervisor, Ron Hon, posed this COPES question: "If mentally ill persons in a Community Support Program (CSP) are administered a Daily Living Activities Scale (Scott & Presmanes, 2001) or an Independent Living Skills Survey (Wallace, Liberman, Tauber, & Wallace, 2000), which will be the most valid, reliable, and easy to use?" (Utech, 2001). Liz faced an equally practical problem of great importance to the team.

The team had lost a client to suicide in the past. Consequently, David Hensley, Liz's supervisor, helped Liz to define her question. Liz's COPES question was: "If clients with chronic mental illness are administered either the Suicide Assessment Checklist, the SAD Persons Scale, or the Scale for Suicide Ideation, which will be the briefest, most inexpensive, valid, and reliable screening tool to assess risk for suicide?" (Durch, 2001)

Both Melissa and Liz did a careful job by obtaining the instruments, reviewing critical literature, and presenting their findings in a tabular review to the CSP team. The team was impressed with Liz and Melissa's thoroughness. Ron Hon (personal communication, December 14, 2001) said, "Melissa ordered the instruments from her own funds. The agency is moving toward assessment tools that are most practical, possibly for computer record keeping. The state is moving toward funding based on severity of the problem. We may adopt the Independent Living Skills Survey for the mentally ill. One of the case managers will be trying the instrument for assessments." Liz and Melissa's demonstration of on-line database searching did not go so well. They set up the computer and data projector but were thwarted by problems with access to the university's databases due to a bent cable plug and a computer worm that shut down the system (i.e., Reeezak Worm).

A Natural Resistance to Innovation Including Evidence-Based Practice

The quotation at the very beginning of this chapter carries prophetic meaning for the helping professions right now: We must become learners to adapt to the information revolution. The information revolution will come, with or without us. If we insist that our learned status entitles us to professional respect without mastering information technology, as it applies to our practice decision-making, then a consequence far more serious than loss of professional status may follow—our clients will suffer repeated error unnecessarily!

One obstacle to evidence-based practice concerns ways that this text's lessons can make you a bit of a misfit. Many of your colleagues will never have worked with a bibliographic database to gain access to the helping literature. Most will never have learned to pose answerable COPES questions. Most will never have done critical appraisal of evidence using rating forms like the QSRF, the META, and the CARE. They may wrinkle their noses and "beetle their brows" at you if you mention MOLES. Your unusual knowledge and skills will set you apart from fellow practitioners.

Naturally, if you become set apart from others by your ways of thinking, your colleagues may react differently toward you. Some may even go so far as to want to regard you sideways out of one eye as though viewing an odd duck. They might even have the urge to peck on you a bit. What can you do? The arguments and counterarguments in Table 10.1 may help you to prepare for inevitable objections to your efforts to teach and to implement evidence-based practice.

Arguments and Counterarguments Regarding Evidence-Based Practice

The arguments and counterarguments regarding evidence-based practice shown in Table 10.1 are from an earlier version of an unpublished manuscript by L. Gibbs and E. Gambrill, *Evidence-Based Practice: Counterarguments to Objections* (included with permission from *Research on Social Work Practice*). These arguments were collected from a wide variety of sources.

Table 10.1 | Arguments and Counterarguments Regarding Evidence-Based Practice

Argument Opposing EBP	Argument Supporting EBP
1. There is nothing new about evidence-based practice.	Figure 1.3 in chapter 1 suggests why social workers and psychologists might make this statement. Figure 1.3 shows how these disciplines have not yet caught onto the EBP literature; so they might be ignorant of this advance. Topics in this text are new including the following: practitioners' access to the World Wide Web, EBP databases, procedures for posing COPES questions, new search strategies including MOLES, and organizations that synthesize evidence for practitioners (the Cochrane and Campbell Collaborations).
2. Social workers are already teaching EBP in professional education programs.	If social work has not caught onto the EBP literature (see Figure 1.3), then how could its educators teach it? Secondly, new methods for teaching EBP rely on problem-based learning. Teaching EBP will require changing teaching methods. Problem-based learning involves helping students to pose and to answer questions (Boud & Feletti, 1991; Barrows, 1994).

continued

Table 10.1 | Continued

Argument Opposing EBP	Argument Supporting EBP
3. No high-quality evidence is available via electronic means that can assist practitioners.	This will be true for some COPES questions as posed by practitioners in any discipline; however, examples in this text have demonstrated useful evidence. Useful evidence will often lie outside one's own discipline's databases.
4. EBP violates the Council on Social Work Education's (CSWE) standards regarding the need to collect evaluation data regarding the effectiveness of interventions in the fieldwork course (excluding data regarding risk assessment, accuracy in assessment, prevention, qualitative data). The CSWE requires that students must collect only data regarding effectiveness. See the Curriculum Policy Statement for Degree Programs in Social Work Education, Section B5.7.9 (Council on Social Work Education, 1992).	Here are several reactions to this statement: (a) Chapter 9 discusses how data may be collected as a step in EBP. (b) Interpreting CSWE standards to mean that only data regarding effectiveness of treatment can be collected ignores other data regarding at least four equally important types of questions (see chapter 3). (c) The scientist/practitioner model for practice data collection has run into serious problems with implementation (Wakefield & Kirk, 1996). (d) The data from small evaluation studies in practice, though directly relevant to individual clients and goals set with them, are less credible than larger studies involving more subjects and greater methodological rigor that can be obtained electronically.
5. Those who teach EBP violate educational standards, because such exercises will take time and resources away from required essential lessons.	One could state this classical argument in opposition to any advance. If we did not make room for advances in the curriculum, we would still be teaching to administer high oxygen levels to premature infants (and increase the incidence of retinopathy of prematurity, a form of blindness). The "we don't have room in the curriculum" argument has been made in opposition to teaching problem-based learning (Margetson, 1991).
6. Evidence-based practice does not match what is done in other components of the curriculum. To be fair, all students and practitioners must have the same learning and the same levels of knowledge.	What if one component of the curriculum taught something untrue and potentially harmful to clients, for example, the belief that delinquent youths should be subjected to the Juvenile Awareness Program that was designed to scare the delinquency out of delinquents? This belief opposes results of a randomized controlled trial showing a 30% difference favoring controls (i.e., harmful effect) (Finckenauer, 1982, p. 135). Curriculum should be evaluated based on its merits, not whether its lessons are widely accepted.
7. Difficult and time-consuming lessons in EBP make students and practitioners uncomfortable. Most practitioners have never posed a COPES question, have never worked with a database, and do not want to learn this technology.	All change comes at a price. Is the price worth the effort? Are the potential benefits to clients worth the effort?

Table 10.1 | Continued

Argument Opposing EBP	Argument Supporting EBP
8. Evidence-based practice does not match current agency policy and practices.	Again, the question concerns what will help the agency to best serve its clients, not how to preserve traditional practices. Draw a distinction between authority-based practice (i.e., based on tradition and edict by persons in power), as opposed to EBP where the authority lies in current best evidence (Gambrill, 1999).
9. You are advocating for EBP because you want to cause trouble . . . because you like controversy . . . because you like to appear innovative . . . because you want to write a book . . . because you. . . .	Such arguments impugn motives and are irrelevant to whether EBP would benefit clients. In the first place, how could a critic know your inner motives? Can you even know yourself why you do things? Who cares? Such questions are beside the point: If clients receive evidence-based help, will they benefit more than if they do not?
10. There is *no difference* in teaching students *how to think* (methodologically for themselves as a way to answer their own practice-related questions) versus teaching students *what to think* (teaching practice as a collection of truths), because by teaching how to think you are really telling students what they must think.	This argument presents a contradiction: Event A does not equal Event Non-A. Helping practitioners to learn to pose and to answer their own COPES questions does not equal telling practitioners what practices to follow. The two approaches are worlds apart.
11. Those who teach EBP teach reverence for just another authority, in this case the authority of the researcher.	This statement demonstrates ignorance about why we have research methods. Evidence-based practice seeks to avoid blindly following authority but, instead, advocates for considering the intersect between current best evidence, practice experience, and the client's wishes. Research methods' measures and experimental designs have been developed to rule out bias as much as possible. Ideally, those who synthesize research for meta-analyses will look for all the evidence, not only confirming evidence.
12. If you look diligently enough, you can always find a study that will support your conclusion, and you can always find fault with a study that does not support your favored conclusion.	This argument demonstrates a misunderstanding for what research is about. Researchers, who revere knowing the truth, look for *disconfirming* evidence with the same vigor that they look for *confirming* evidence (a major lesson in Chapter 4). When looking for current best evidence, the EBP practitioner cares about knowing the answers related to clients, not winning a particular argument by stacking the deck.

continued

Table 10.1 | Continued

Argument Opposing EBP	Argument Supporting EBP
13. Those who question EBP, based on the preceding arguments, have not mentioned EBP's impact on clients in their arguments.	All ethical codes for all the helping professions place the client's interests first. According to the *Code of Ethics* for the National Association of Social Workers, the "Social workers' primary responsibility is to promote the well-being of clients" (National Association of Social Workers, Ethical Standards, 1997, Section 1.01). This concern for clients should have been the very first one mentioned by critics of EBP.

Methods for Teaching Evidence-Based Practice Versus Traditional Methods

In addition to knowing about opposing arguments, those who want to teach evidence-based practice to others may find it helpful to contrast traditional teaching methods with methods best suited to teach EBP. A useful contrast in learning concerns the way a sponge works compared with the way a filter works (Browne & Keeley, 1994). In traditional teaching, learning often goes on like a sponge, because the learner is expected to absorb lessons uncritically. In teaching for EBP, learning goes on like a filter, to let weaker evidence pass through the filter to retain only the best and most useful nuggets.

To aid practice decision making, evidence must pass through successively finer and finer filters at each of these stages: first a question of relevance to practice decision making must be posed; then reports of studies must pass editors' and reviewers' scrutiny; then the evidence needs to be retrieved by a practitioner; then the retriever must judge whether that evidence is of sufficient quality to guide practice; and, finally, the practitioner must decide whether the study's findings are sufficiently generalizable to the retriever's clients to warrant applying the research findings to the practice situation (Gray, 1997, p. 60).

Traditional methods for teaching practice generally seek to impart practice wisdom as a collection of facts and skills. Usually, practitioners study under the tutelage of a wise and experienced senior practitioner, who may assign readings from appropriate texts and articles. These readings generally reflect a lifetime of reflection and experience and include a mixed bag of evidence that is often anecdotal with case material to serve as illustrations. The traditional mentor demonstrates and often lectures to students who are expected to follow along. Generally, the senior practitioner, though tolerating some deviance, expects students to follow a lead and to accept the conclusions of the mentor. True, the kindly senior practitioner will accept and even encourage some questioning, but excessive questioning will be perceived as impertinence or insecurity on the learner's part. In any case, the ultimate arbiter will be the senior practitioner's experience and authority.

In contrast, those who teach evidence-based practice tend to use problem-based learning methods. The problem-based teacher *coaches* learners through a process and does not seek to impart a collection of truths to be committed to memory. This process may be called problem-based learning or practice-based learning (Boud & Feletti, 1991; Barrows, 1994). This process begins with a client-oriented question of practical significance to clients that is clearly enough stated to guide a search for evidence (e.g., COPES question).

The evidence-based-practice teacher's most important goal concerns teaching others to be efficient lifelong learners. Lifelong learning implies that it is better in the long run to teach someone to fish (look for evidence) than to feed them a fish dinner (impart information and wisdom). The learning usually takes place in a small group of eight to ten students with the coach generally demonstrating how to pose questions, to search efficiently for the best evidence, and to weigh that evidence for its practice implications. Once students have learned the process of EBP, the responsibility for learning shifts to the team members who learn to support and to question each other in the learning process. The coach rates performance not on the basis of knowledge retained but, rather, on thinking skills, including, for example, learning how to pose a specific question (Gibbs, 1991, p. 114).

How does didactic (traditional, lecture-based) versus problem-based learning affect learners? Two meta-analyses—coincidentally, done the same year—have compared the effectiveness of problem-based learning (PBL) versus traditional teaching methods for medical students. The authors of the first meta-analysis used the terms *problem-based, education,* and *learning* to search medical education literature between 1972 through 1992 (Albanese & Mitchell, 1993). My score on the META form was 10 points for the Albanese and Mitchell analysis. They recommended caution before implementing curriculum-wide conversions from traditional teaching to PBL because, though teachers and students enjoyed PBL as a method and PBL students scored as well or better than traditional students at clinical tasks, PBL is expensive in time and resources. They reported that PBL students in a few instances scored lower on basic science examinations and may have had a tendency to reason backward from a list of problems to eliminate them rather than forward from the client's information. A second meta-analysis, scoring 9 points on the META form, was more positive toward PBL (Vernon & Blake, 1993, p. 550). This review compared PBL to traditional methods in 22 studies, finding the following differences on the QSRF's *ES1* index of treatment effect size as weighted for sample size: +.55 (95% confidence interval (CI) +.40 to +.70) for student's attitudes and opinions regarding teaching method; +.28 (95% CI +.16 to .+40) for students' clinical performance; +.09 (95% CI +.06 to −.24) for factual knowledge; and +.08 (95% CI −.05 to +.21) for clinical knowledge. These comparisons all favored PBL. The only difference favoring traditional methods was that traditional students did better on a National Board of Medical Examiners test, −.18 (95% CI − 10 to −.26), a test that evaluates a lot of memory tasks.

Effects of Evidence-Based Practice on Clients

The question of whether clients fare better if served by evidence-based practitioners, versus not, concerns a vital issue. In fact, this should be the *most important issue* when deciding to adopt any new method in practice and, I hope, a question that you began to ask yourself long ago, if lessons in this text have truly taken effect.

The studies summarized here were included because they were done to determine whether evidence-based practitioners take action based on evidence and/or whether EBP clients fare better than if treated by traditionally trained practitioners. Table 10.2 summarizes results of these few studies. Column 4 gives a QSRF score that ranges from 0 to 100 (see chapter 5). Five of these eight studies concern effects of EBP training on reading habits. Two report on the practitioner's judgments about case material, and no study reports a randomized trial to compare the effect of EBP directly on clients compared with the effect of conventional practice.

Implementing Evidence-Based Practice

The preceeding evidence weakly supports the effectiveness of evidence-based practice, but research is needed regarding the relative effectiveness of EBP versus conventional authority-based methods in the helping professions regarding direct effects on clients. Still, it seems logical that applying the current best evidence to help clients would better serve clients than applying outdated weaker evidence and would be better than applying methods based on authority-based principles that rest on the sandy ground of tradition and status (Gambrill, 1999), but we cannot know without investigation. We need randomized educational trials that pit traditional practice against EBP on measures of client outcomes. No such studies could be found. Perhaps you will do one.

If you accept the weak evidence in Table 10.2 and logical arguments in this text, then how might evidence-based practice be implemented? I suggest that you obey your own conscience and implement EBP into your own practice however you feel it most appropriate to do so. Perhaps you can decide to use a better assessment tool (example in Box 10.2). You may make referrals to agencies that use the most effective methods to suit the needs of your clients. You may speak out to advocate for an effective prevention program.

You may want to go beyond your own practice and advocate that evidence-based practice be implemented on a wider scale. Your advocacy might bear more fruit if based on research regarding why and how organizations change, since implementing EBP represents a change. I had hoped to find research that evaluated factors related to implementing EBP—no such luck—but I did encounter a research-based article regarding factors associated with research-based innovation in health care settings (Kitson, Harvey, & McCormack, 1998). Kitson and her colleagues list three factors associated with innovation in health care and apply these dimensions to four case studies of research utilization. Their three dimensions are as follows: the quality and

Table 10.2 | Studies Evaluating Effects of Evidence-Based Practice on Practice

Source	Purpose	Study Design	QSRF Score	Findings
Bennett et al. (1987)	Evaluated 16 weeks of training for medical students in problem solving	Controlled trial with posttest only for 45 experimentals and 35 in comparison group	72 (This score ranges from 0 to 100 to mark better studies.)	31% difference for test of diagnostic accuracy; 12% difference for therapy decisions both favoring experimental group.
Green & Ellis (1997)	Evaluated 7-week evidence-based medicine (EBM) curriculum for second- and third-year medicine residents	Pretest-posttest for 26 experimentals and comparison group	72	Experimentals turned to an original study to help patient more often ($p < .04$).
Landry, Pangaro, Kroenke, Lucey, & Herbers (1994)	Evaluated two 90-minute seminars on reading habits regarding patient care	Pretest-posttest on 65 seminar participants and 81 comparison medicine students	42	No difference in number of articles cited in patient workups.
Linzer, Brown, Frazier, DeLong, & Siegel (1988)	Evaluated five one-hour training sessions for Journal club on hospital staff	Randomly assigned medical interns to training or to control	54	Trained group said they changed the way they incorporated literature into practice ($p < .02$).
Linzer, Delong, & Hupart (1987)	Evaluated effect of EBP team leader on Team 1 ($n = 42$) vs. Team 2 without EBM leader ($n = 43$)	Randomly assigned EBM team leader to one of two teams (Team 1)	66	Team 1 members read fewer articles ($p < .02$) but no significant differences in completeness nor in methodological reading.
Riegelman (1986)	Evaluated effect of 12 hours of lecture and 4 hours of seminar on 118 medical students	Pretest-posttest design	62	53% and 54% difference in reading habits favoring fourth-year students over first-year students in two comparisons.
Stewart, Hillman, Donovan, & Tanli (1997)	Constructed EBP guidelines for endoscopic sinus surgery at an academic center in Houston, Texas	Patients not randomly assigned to guideline-based ($n = 50$) or non-guideline-based ($n = 41$)	44	Only statistically significant difference was that the guideline-based were readmitted to hospital less frequently than non-guideline-based treated group.
Shin, Haynes & Johnston (1993)	Compared effect of entire EBM program with traditional education on willingness to accept harmful intervention	Treatment group and comparison groups were graduates of two programs ($n = 41$ vs. $n = 41$) from 1974–1985	62	Evidence-based-medicine graduates taught by problem-solving method were less likely to use less-ineffective treatment for high blood pressure.

Note. The search for this evidence was conducted by Kay McBride. She included only studies that evaluated effects of training on practitioner's use of evidence in practice decisions or effects on client behavior. These arguments come from an earlier version of a manuscript: Gibbs, L., & Gambrill, E. (Unpublished). *Evidence-based practice:* Counterarguments to objections, to appear in *Research on Social Work Practice,* Reprinted with permission.

applicability of the evidence, the context or organizational environment into which the research is to be placed, and the process of implementing change (p. 149). Suggestions that follow are from Kitson et al. (1998, p. 151), who state that their, ". . . framework has limited construct and face validity and has been set out to stimulate debate in this important but complex area" (p. 158). They suggest that their three dimensions are not linear (i.e., happening one after the other) but, rather, need to be considered simultaneously.

SUGGESTIONS FOR IMPLEMENTING EVIDENCE-BASED PRACTICE

Consider the quality and applicability of evidence.

- The research evidence strongly supports an innovation (randomized controlled trials, meta-analyses).
- The research evidence consistently supports clinical experience within the organization.
- Clients' preferences are considered in partnership with them.

Consider the context or organizational environment.

- The agency's culture values learning, is client centered, has high morale, and supports continuing education.
- The agency's leaders have clear roles, value effective teamwork, have a clear organizational structure, and provide strong leadership.
- The agency uses internal measures that provide an internal audit and feedback with peer review.

Consider the process of implementing change (i.e., facilitators or opinion leaders who are insiders who will implement the change).

- Facilitators' characteristics include that they have the respect, empathy, authenticity, and credibility to implement change.
- Facilitators have access to authority and have the legitimate role of innovator who can negotiate change.
- Facilitators have an effective interpersonal style that is flexible and that wins consistent support.

Summary

In summary then, if you want to implement evidence-based practice into an agency, basing your approach on these ideas of Kitson and her colleagues (1998), begin by finding strong research that concerns an important, current, and perplexing practice question. Ideally, you might pick a time when members of the agency genuinely do not know what to do but strong research supports an answer. Pick a question initially that would be fairly consistent with practitioners' impressions about what may be true. Try to include clients in the whole process. Assess your agency to see how open to change it may be. Include in your assessment whether the agency values learning and places the welfare of its clients first. Ideally, the research should have clear and important implications for clients. Assess whether your agency's leaders value teamwork and whether they have sufficient power and credibility to support EBP as an innovation. Without support from agency leaders, the effort may fail. Assess whether the agency has an ongoing process of evaluation that might incorporate indicators of the impact of some EBP-supported procedure. Finally, of great importance to your success, determine whether the agency has a facilitator (possibly you) who might carry the ball to implement the change within the agency as a respected insider. This facilitator should have the respect of persons within the agency based on integrity and empathy for others. The facilitator should be respected by those in authority within the agency and should logically be considered the one who might bring innovation to the agency. The facilitator should have an effective interpersonal style that would win consistent support long enough to implement the change. This facilitator should fully understand EBP and share your commitment to bringing EBP to the agency.

Projections into the Future

True prediction means predictors must climb out on a limb and hand someone behind them a saw. Predictions must precede the event predicted to have any credibility. For the record then, here are some predictions made on March 16th, 2002 regarding evidence-based practice. If you consider these predictions valid, then they may help you to prepare yourself for future trends and to plan your own learning. My reasons for making these predictions accompany each one:

- As the basis for the first prediction, please examine Figure 1.3 in chapter 1. These trends toward evidence-based practice will continue upward in citations to evidence-based literature for several years, particularly in helping professions new to the topic—including social work and psychology. The term *evidence-based practice* will become a stylish word.
- This increased popularity of *evidence-based practice* will generate interest among authors who may not take sufficient time to read the excellent EBP literature thoroughly enough to understand how the *process* works (e.g., Sackett, Straus, Richardson, Rosenberg, & Haynes, 2000) and who may not have practical experience with the *process* before they write about it. Misinterpretations will include the idea that EBP is a set of practice guidelines or standards and that it is just another form of the scientist/practitioner model.
- The World Wide Web will strengthen as a tool for busy practitioners who learn to use it efficiently. The Web will soon carry trillions of bits of information per second as light switches are perfected (Stix, 2001, p. 81). *The Semantic Web* (Berners-Lee, Hendler, & Lassila, 2001), an advance that will rival the Web itself in its importance, will allow practitioners to answer highly specific questions and to stay current with question-related evidence. This means it will be easier to stay current with COPES types of

questions. Direct, portable access to databases will become more reliable and inexpensive.

- In 1455, Johannes Gutenberg invented the printing press with movable type; he made consistent high-resolution printing available. I predict that the impact of electronic communication and information will have as much impact on us in the helping professions. Electronic media will replace books in many contexts (Levy, 2000, 96–97). New E-books, or electronic books, have already been produced, but their resolution falls short of a printed page. According to Levy, most of the pieces of the electronic puzzle are already in place: ". . . fast chips, long-lasting batteries, capacious disk drives and the Internet." (p. 96). Only a screen that gives resolution as clear as a printed page and high-speed wireless bandwidth that can quickly load E-books remain as obstacles to wide acceptance. Levy projects that by 2003 E-book devices weighing less than a pound and costing $100 will be available; and, for $900, E-books with high-resolution magazine quality images will become widely available. Levy projects that by 2009 readers will subscribe to their favorite book author directly, and by 2012 the market for pulpwood that produces paper will crash.

- For this next prediction, I will go far out on a limb. Ideally, the applied social sciences will develop collaborations like the Cochrane Collaboration (see this book's Web site). The Campbell Collaboration may fill this gap. To serve effectively as guides for human service practice, these collaborations will need to start with COPES questions solicited from active practitioners. These collaborations will need to be *apolitical*, revering only truthful answers to COPES questions, using structured protocols for synthesizing literature (e.g., metaxis, *www.metaxis.com*) and honestly stating limitations when evidence is insufficient to guide decision making. Of course, by definition, COPES questions will be selected representatively based on client need to reflect a widespread need of many clients.

One Final Word of Advice

A word about courage seems most fitting here. Courage comes in different styles and levels. My uncle, William Carey, had courage. It was only after his death, as we stood around his casket to talk, that we discovered why he could be buried at Arlington National Cemetery. We discovered after his death that he had been awarded the Bronze Star for bravery in battle during World War II. He had never told his wife when he returned home from Europe after the war, nor did he tell any of his children. We discovered that, as his health failed and he knew of his impending death, he had researched his service record to find the least costly and troublesome way to arrange for his funeral and burial. He had risked his life and limb for an ideal.

If you intend to follow lifelong learning as an evidence-based practitioner, you will need courage too, but a more persistent, decades-long, day-by-day, career-long dedication, where you may face isolation, derision, and possibly censure for your ideals. You will need courage, because your thinking will ring unfamiliar to authority-based practitioners' ears. Authority-based practitioners will have answers, where you will have questions. They will react quickly with knee-jerk reflexes, where you will need time to search for evidence and to ponder on it. They will reason backward from a favored conclusion to find only supporting evidence, while you will look forward actively seeking disconfirming evidence along with evidence that confirms your beliefs. They will follow the crowd and bask in its warm approval, while you will be an independent thinker sometimes standing alone in the cold. They will respect status and power, while you will revere whatever is best for clients through knowing the best evidence.

Courage comes from a sense of inner purpose. When you face your testing, it may help you to remember why we get into the helping professions in the first place. It is not for personal fortune. It is not for personal status. It is not for personal power. It is to benefit our clients! Your struggle is worth the effort for them. When tested, I turn to memories of my Uncle Bill and those like him, as you too can think of truly brave people. Have courage. Take heart!

> The well-fed defenders of illusion loll in unthreatened ease on their battlements. They haven't even heard a shout of derision for a generation now. It would be in the worst of taste. But far below their mighty bastions—faint yet cheering—the attentive ear can catch the jolly clink of the sapper's chisel. (From *The Natural History of Nonsense* by Bergen Evans, 1958, p. 4)

Exercise 10-1 Teaching Others

Background

This exercise is designed to help you to teach principles of evidence-based practice to other practitioners. Your experience may help others.

Purpose

This exercise is to give you experience demonstrating evidence-based practice.

Instructions

Become personally as competent at evidence-based practice as you can, and approach others when the time is most opportune. Wait until a quandary arises (some question of central importance), then follow the process yourself to find an answer. If you find useful evidence, then suggest to others that you may have something useful to them, and demonstrate your search having already made yourself familiar with the topic. If some become interested in the process, focus your efforts on training them to do their own searches, possibly sharing this book with them.

Questions

Before you try to demonstrate evidence-based practice, consider these questions:

1. Have you:
   [ ] Developed sufficient skill that you can demonstrate the process of EBP?
   [ ] Picked a topic of importance to others whom you may teach?
   [ ] Sufficient rapport with your colleagues that they may listen to you?
   [ ] Picked a topic to search that, if you find strong evidence, could possibly lead to action?
   [ ] Formulated a clear COPES question that accurately reflects colleagues' and clients' concern?
   [ ] Conducted a search ahead of time before trying to demonstrate the process?
   [ ] Made sure that the necessary equipment and databases will function efficiently? (So far, this has been a key problem.)
   [ ] Prepared as well as you can for the inevitable questions, problems, objections?

2. What happened as you tried to demonstrate the process of evidence-based practice?

   _____

   _____

   _____

   _____

   _____

   _____

   _____

   _____

3. What did you learn from your teaching experience?

   _____

   _____

   _____

   _____

   _____

Exercise 10-2 A Decision Regarding Whether to Apply Recovered-Memory Therapy

Background

As a counselor in an outpatient mental health facility who frequently counsels adult women, you encounter the argument that women should make an effort to recall repressed memories of prior sex abuse (regardless of whether they have any memory of such abuse), using a technique called recovered-memory therapy, to overcome the long-term effects of the abuse. The following argument was constructed as a composite of ideas from two books regarding later effects of repressed memories of child sex abuse on adults (Bass & Davis, 1988; Blume, 1990).

> Many women who have experienced sex abuse do not recall that abuse, but experience symptoms nevertheless. These classical symptoms can include, for example, any of the following: ". . . fear of being alone in the dark. . . nightmares, swallowing and gagging sensitivity, repugnance to water on one's face when bathing or swimming. . . poor body image. . . gastrointestinal problems; gynecological disorders (including spontaneous vaginal infections); headaches; arthritis or joint pain. . . eating disorders, drug or alcohol abuse (or total abstinence). . . suicidal thoughts. . . depression. . . adult nervousness over being watched or surprised; feeling watched; startle response. . . guilt, shame; low self-esteem. . . high risk taking ('daring the fates'); inability to take risks. . ." and much more. (Blume, 1990, The Incest Survivors' Aftereffects Checklist, p. xviii)

Advocates for recovered-memory therapy believe that the abuse may include sexual intercourse but can include ". . . a father showing pornographic pictures to a small child, a babysitter or anyone in a position of trust handling a child inappropriately, an adult fondling a child, an older brother forcing his sister to undress" (Blume, 1990, p. 8).

Advocates believe that most women having these symptoms have no recollection of prior sex abuse but must be helped to recall their abuse through numerous methods, including support groups (Blume, 1990, p. 95). To help in the process of remembering and dealing with the experience, the therapist may apply several techniques, including the following: self-help groups (Blume, 1990, p. 271); therapist-run groups (p. 274); couples therapy; sex therapy; assertiveness training (p. 275); hypnosis (p. 279); and body work (massage therapy and newer types of manipulation that help to unlock memories of childhood trauma) (p. 279).

Remembering constitutes one step in the stages of healing. Ultimately, the final stage in the healing process is "resolution and moving on." In this phase "Your feelings and perspectives will stabilize. You will come to terms with your abuser and other family members. While you won't erase your history, you will make deep and lasting changes in your life. Having gained awareness, compassion, and power through healing, you will have the opportunity to work toward a better world" (Bass & Davis, 1988, p. 59).

Purpose

This exercise is designed to place you in a realistic situation. This exercise will give you practice in evidence-based decision making.

Instructions

Imagine that you are in practice and other practitioners are urging you to consider adopting recovered-memory therapy.

Question

1. Would you refer any clients to someone who specializes in recovered-memory therapy for sexual abuse syndrome? (Apply all of the skills that you have learned from this text.)

Exercise 10-3: A Decision Regarding Whether to Adopt Whole Language or Phonics to Teach Basic Reading Skills to Children

Background

Assume that you are a new principal who heads a school that serves children from kindergarten through fifth grade. A debate has raged for several years among the school's teachers about how to best teach basic reading skills competency to children in the lower grades. One camp advocates for whole language, the other equally committed to phonics as a way to teach basic reading skills most effectively. You have faith in rational-data-based thought as a way to settle a debate.

Instructions

Please pose a related COPES question and follow EBP steps to answer your question.

Questions

1. Please state your COPES question.

_____

_____

2. Please summarize your search strategy, current best evidence, and state what you think should be done based on your assessment of the evidence.

References

Abraham, I. L., & Schultz, S. (1984). The "law of small numbers": An unexpected and incidental replication. *The Journal of Psychology, 117,* 183–188.

Acosta, O., & Toro, P. A. (2000). Let's ask the homeless people themselves: A needs assessment based on a probability sample of adults [1]. *American Journal of Community Psychology, 28*(13). 343–366.

Adams, K. (1997). A rationale for information literacy. EDTE 590 Information Literacy, Group Projects, Millersville University. Retrieved March 12, 2000, from www.millersv.edu/~mwarmkes/EDTE590/jkmration2.html

Ahmed, T., & Silagy, C. (1995). The move towards evidence-based medicine. *Medical Journal of Australia, 163*(2), 60–61.

Albanese, M. A., & Mitchell, S. (1993). Problem-based learning: A review of literature on its outcomes and implementation issues. *Academic Medicine, 68*(1), 51–81.

Alternative therapy. (1986). British Medical Association. London: Chameleon.

American Psychological Association. (2001). *Ethical principles of psychologists and code of conduct,* Draft 6, The Code of Ethics Project Task Force. (Available from the ANA Center for Ethics and Human Rights, 600 Maryland Avenue SW, Suite 100W, Washington, DC 20024)

Anderson, C. A. (1983). Abstract and concrete data in the perseverance of social theories: When weak data lead to unshakable beliefs. *Journal of Experimental Social Psychology, 19,* 93–108.

Andres, K. (2000). *Evaluation of the effectiveness of Violence Prevention Curriculum.* University of Wisconsin–Eau Claire.

Antman, E. M., Lau, J., Kupelnick, B., Mosteller, F., & Chalmers, T. C. (1992). A comparison of results of meta-analyses of randomized controlled trials and recommendations of clinical experts. Treatments for myocardial infarction. *Journal of the American Medical Association (JAMA), 268*(2), 240–248.

Armstrong, E. (1998, November 17). *On the need for evidence-based medicine.* Power Point Presentation. Continuing Medical Education, Luther Hospital, Eau Claire, WI.

Armstrong, E. (1999). The well-built clinical question: The key to finding the best evidence efficiently. *Wisconsin Medical Journal, 98*(2), 25–28.

Armstrong, E. (2001). *Review of: Evidence-based practice for the helping professions: A practical guide with integrated multimedia.* Lehigh Valley Family Practice Residency Program, Allentown, PA.

Babbie, E. R. (1973). *Survey research methods.* Belmont, CA: Wadsworth.

Bainbridge, W. S. (1989). *Survey research: A computer-assisted introduction.* Belmont, CA: Wadsworth.

Baird, C., & Wagner, D. (2000). The relative validity of actuarial- and consensus-based risk assessment systems. *Child and Youth Services Review, 22*(11/12), 839–871.

Bandolier Home Page. (February 28, 2002). www.jr2.ox.ac.uk/bandolier/.Pain Research Centre, Oxford University, UK.

Barrett, S. (1993). The truth-seekers. In S. Barrett & W. T. Jarvis (Eds.), *The health robbers.* Buffalo, NY: Prometheus.

Barrows, H. S. (1988). *The tutorial process* (Rev. ed.). Springfield, IL: Southern Illinois University School of Medicine.

Barrows, H. S. (1994). *Practice-based learning.* Springfield, IL: Southern Illinois University School of Medicine.

Bass, E., & Davis, L. (1988). *The courage to heal: A guide for women survivors of child sexual abuse.* New York: Harper & Row.

Bennett, K. J., Sackett, D. L., Haynes, R. B., Neufeld, V. R., Tugwell, P., & Roberts, R. (1987). A controlled trial of teaching critical appraisal of the clinical literature to medical students. *Journal of the American Medical Association, 257*(18), 2451–2454.

Berg, B. (2001). *Qualitative research methods for the social sciences.* Boston: Allyn & Bacon.

Berkowitz, C. D. (1993). Doing our own housekeeping: A mandate for quality improvement. *Journal of Child Sexual Abuse, 2*(3), 99–101.

Berners-Lee, T., Hendler, J., & Lassila, O. (2001). The semantic web. *Scientific American, 285*(5), 35–43.

Berra, Y. (1998). *The Yogi book: "I really didn't say everything I said!"* New York: Workman.

Bishop, D. J., Giles, C. R., & Das, S. R. (2001). The rise of optical switching. *Scientific American, 284*(1), 88–94.

Bloom, M. (1975). Information science in the education of social work students. *Journal of Education for Social Work, 11,* 30–35.

Bloom, M. (1995). The great philosophy of science war. *Social Work Research, 19*(1), 19–23.

Bloom, M., Fischer, J., & Orme, J. G. (1999). *Evaluating practice: Guidelines for the accountable professional* (3rd ed.). Boston: Allyn & Bacon.

Bloomfield, J. (1999). *Evidence-based practice paper: Assessing dementia.* University of Wisconsin–Eau Claire.

Blume, E. S. (1990). *Secret survivors: Uncovering incest and its aftereffects in women.* New York: John Wiley.

Blythe, J. (1993). Assessing nurses' information needs in the work environment. *Bulletin of the Medical Library Association. 81*(4), 433–435.

Booth, A., & Madge, B. (1998). Finding the evidence. In T. Bury & J. Mead (Eds.). *Evidence-based health care: A practical guide for therapists.* Oxford: Butterworth-Heinemann.

Boud, D., & Feletti, G. (Eds.). (1991). *The challenge of problem-based learning.* London: Kogan Page.

Briggs, N. M. (2000). *Validation therapy for dementia.* Cochrane Library, 1–19 [a meta-analysis]. Retrieved April 21, 2000, from the www.library.com

Britten, N., Jones, R., Murphy, E., & Stacy, R. (1995). Qualitative research methods in general primary care. *Family Practice, 12*(1), 104–114.

Brown, W. A. (1998). The placebo effect. *Scientific American, 278*(1), 90–95.

Browne, M. N., & Keeley, S. M. (1994). *Asking the right questions: A guide to critical thinking* (4th ed.). Englewood Cliffs, NJ: Prentice-Hall.

Buckingham, J., Fishor, B., & Saunders, D. (2000). *Worksheet for using a systematic review.* EBM Tool Kit, Retrieved September 22, 2000, from www.med.ualberta.ca/ebm/overview.htm

Bunyan, L. E., & Lutz, E. M. (1991). Marketing the hospital library to nurses. *Bulletin of the Medical Library Association, 79*(2), 223–225.

California woman earns "welfare queen" title. (1981, March 12). *Jet, 59*, 8.

Campbell, J. A. (1988). Client acceptance of single-system evaluation procedures. *Social Work Research and Abstracts, 24*(2), 21–22.

Campbell, J. A. (1990). Ability of practitioners to estimate client acceptance of single-subject evaluation procedures. *Social Work, 35*, 9–14.

Candell, M. (2001). *Sex offender recidivism: Evidence-based practice exercise.* University of Wisconsin–Eau Claire.

Chalmers, T.C., Smith H., Blackburn, N., Silverman, B. Schroeder, B., Reitman, D., & Ambroz, A. (1981). A method for assessing the quality of a randomized control trial. *Controlled Clinical Trials, 2* (1), 31–49.

Chambers, B. R., You, R. X., & Donnan, G. A. (2000). *Carotid endarterectomy for asymptomatic carotid stenosis.* Cochrane Library, Cochrane Database of Systematic Reviews, 1, no page #, available electronically by subscription.

Chambless, D. L., & Hollon, S. D. (1998). Defining empirically supported therapies. *Journal of Consulting and Clinical Psychology, 66*, 7–19.

Chambliss, C., & Doughty, R. J. (1994). *Parental response to the Lovaas treatment of childhood autism.* (ERIC Document Reproduction Service No. ED370340)

Charlton, B. G., Hopayian, K., D'Amico, R., Deeks, J. J., & Moore, A. (1999). Number needed to treat derived from meta-analysis. *British Medical Journal, 319*(7218), 1199–1200. Retrieved from INFOTRAC.

Chase, S. (1956). *Guides to straight thinking.* New York: Harper & Row.

Cialdini, R. B. (2001). The science of persuasion. *Scientific American, 284*(2), 76–81.

Cochrane Collaboration. Cockrane Library Home page. www.cochrane.org/.

Cohen, J. (1977). Statistical power analysis for the behavioral sciences. (Rev. ed). New York: Academic Press.

Cohen, J. (1988). *Statistical power analysis for the behavioral sciences.* Hillsdale, NJ: Lawrence Erlbaum Associates.

Cook, D. J., Mulrow, C. D., & Haynes, R. B. (1997). Systematic reviews: Synthesis of evidence for clinical decisions. *Annals of Internal Medicine, 126*(5), 376–380.

Cook, T. D., & Campbell, D. T. (1979). *Quasi-experimentation: Design and analysis issues for field settings.* Boston: Houghton Mifflin.

Cooper, H. M. (1984). *The integrative research review: A systematic approach.* Applied Social Research Methods Series, 2. Beverly Hills, CA: Sage.

Cordell, W. H. (1999). Number needed to treat (NNT). *Annals of Emergency Medicine, 33*(4), 433–436.

Corr, C. A. (2000). What do we know about grieving children and adolescents? In K. J. Doka (Ed.), *Living with grief.* Washington, DC: Hospice Foundation of America.

Cotrane, E.L. (2000). At-Risk African American Male Youth Effectiveness of Mentorship, University of Wisconsin–Eau Claire.

Council on Social Work Education. (1992). Curriculum Policy Statement for baccalaureate and master's degree programs in Social Work education. Alexandria, VA: Council on Social Work Education.

Council on Social Work Education. (June 24, 1994). Council on Social Work Education Curriculum Policy Statement for Baccalaureate Degree Programs in Social Work Education [A document]. Retrieved February 18, 2001, from www.cswe.org/bswcps.htm

Council on Social Work Education. (June 24, 1994). Council on Social Work Education Curriculum Policy Statement for Master's Degree Programs in Social Work Education [A document]. Retrieved February 18, 2001, from www.cswe.org/mswcps.htm

Council on Social Work Education. (2001). *Educational policy and accreditation standards.* 1725 Duke St., Suite 4500, Alexandria, VA. Retrieved November 19, 2001, from www.cswe.org

Cousins, P. S., Fischer, J., Glisson, C., & Kameoka, V. (1986). The effects of physical attractiveness and verbal expressiveness on clinical judgments. *Journal of Social Service Research, 8*(4), 59–74.

Czaja, R., & Blair, J. (1996). *Designing surveys: A guide to decisions and procedures.* Thousand Oaks, CA: Pine Forge.

Davis, D., O'Brien, M. A., Freemantle, N., Wolf, F. M., Mazmanian, P., & Taylor-Vaisey, A. (1999). Impact of formal continuing medical education. *JAMA, 282*(9), 867–874.

Davis, J. (2000). *Coerced alcohol treatment.* Internship Seminar Paper, Department of Social Work, University of Wisconsin–Eau Claire.

Dawes, R. M. (1994). *House of cards: Psychology and psychotherapy built on myth.* New York: The Free Press.

Dawes, R. M., Faust, D., & Meehl, P. E. (1989). Clinical versus actuarial judgment. *Science, 243,* 1668–1673.

Day, J. (1999). *Evidence-based practice.* University of Wisconsin–Eau Claire.

Delay won in Medicare-pay rules fight. (1998, September). *NASW News, 43*(8), 1.

Denzin, N. K., & Lincoln, Y. S. (Eds.). (1994). *Handbook of qualitative research.* Thousand Oaks, CA: Sage.

Detlefsen, M., McCarty, D. C., & Bacon, J. D. (1999). *Logic from A to Z.* London: Routledge.

Detsky, S. S., Naylor, C. D., O'Rourke, K., McGeer, A., & L'Abbe, K. L. (1992). Incorporating variations in the quality of individual randomized trials into meta-analysis. *Journal of Clinical Epidemiology, 45*(3), 255–261.

Devereaux, P. J. (2000). How do the outcomes of patients treated within randomized controlled trials compare with those of similar patients treated outside these trials? *Evidence Based Health Care Newsletter, 20,* 4. Also available from hiru.mcmaster.ca/ebm/trout

Du Bois, T. J. (1998). *Evidence-based practice: The prediction/risk assessment of suicide.* University of Wisconsin–Eau Claire.

Dunkin, M. J. (1996). Types of errors in synthesizing research in education. *Review of Educational Research, 66*(2), 87–97.

Durlak, J. A., & Wells, A. M. (1997). Primary Prevention mental health programs for children and adolescents: A meta-analytic review. American Journal of Community Psychology, 25(2), 115–153.

Duquette, A., Kerouac, S., Sandhu, B., Ducharme, F., & Saulnier, P. (1995). *International Journal of Nursing Studies, 32*(5), 443–456.

Durch, E. A. (2001). *Suicide risk assessment: An evidence-based approach.* University of Wisconsin–Eau Claire.

Eau Claire County Department of Human Services. (n. d.). *Mission statement.* Eau Claire, WI.

Emrick, C. D. (1975). Review of psychologically oriented treatment of alcoholism II. The relative effectiveness of different treatment approaches and the effectiveness of treatment versus no treatment. *Journal of Studies on Alcohol, 36,* 88–108.

Engel, S. M. (1990). *With good reason: An introduction to informal fallacies.* New York: St. Martin's Press.

Evans, B. (1958). *The natural history of nonsense.* New York: Vintage.

Evidence-Based Medicine Working Group. (1992, November 4). Evidence-based medicine. A new approach to teaching the practice of medicine. *Journal of the American Medical Association, 268*(17), 2420–2425.

Faerber, M. (Ed.). (2000). *Gale directory of databases.* Farmington Hills, MI: Gale Group.

Family Support Administration. (1984). *Quality control, Aid to Families with Dependent Children, detailed statistical tables, findings.* Washington, DC: U.S. Department of Health and Human Services.

Fang, X., Stanton, B., Li, X., Feigelman, S., & Baldwin, R. (1998). Similarities in sexual activity and condom use among friends within groups before and after a risk-reduction intervention. *Youth and Society, 29*(4), 431–450.

Finckenauer, J. O. (1982). *Scared straight! And the panacea phenomenon.* Englewood Cliffs, NJ: Prentice-Hall.

Fischer, J. (1978). *Effective casework practice: An eclectic approach.* New York: McGraw-Hill.

Fox, G. N. (1993, March 10). Evidence-based medicine: A new paradigm for the patient. *Journal of the American Medical Association, 269*(10), 1253.

Frasca, M. A., Dorsch, J. L., Aldag, J. C., & Christiansen, R. G. (1992). A multidisciplinary approach to information management and critical appraisal instruction: A controlled study. *Bulletin of the Medical Library Association, 80*(1), 23–28.

Frey, K., & Sylvester, L. (1997). *Research on the Second Step program: Do student behaviors and attitudes improve? What do teachers think of the program?* Seattle, WA: Committee for Children. (ERIC Document Reproduction Service No. ED 426143)

Friedland, D. J., Go, A. S., Davoren, J. B., Shlipak, M. G., Bent, S. W., Subak, L. L., & Mendelson, T. (1999). *Evidence-based medicine: A framework for clinical practice.* Stamford, CN: Appleton & Lange.

Furukawa, T. A. (1999). From effect size into number needed to treat. *Lancet, 353*(9165), 1. (full-text article from EpPrint@epnet.com)

Galen, R. S., & Gambino, S. R. (1975). *Beyond normality: The predictive value and efficiency of medical diagnosis.* New York: John Wiley.

Gambrill, E. (1997). *Social work practice: A critical thinker's guide.* New York: Oxford University Press.

Gambrill, E. (1999). Evidence-based practice: An alternative to authority-based practice. *Families in Society: Journal of Contemporary Human Services, 80*(4), 341–350.

Gehlbach, S. H., Bobula, J. A., & Dickinson, J. C. (1980). Teaching residents to read the medical literature. *Journal of Medical Education, 55,* 362–365.

Gibbs, L. (1990). Using online databases to guide research and practice. In R. Reinoehl & T. Hanna (Eds.), *Computer literacy in human services* (pp. 97–116). New York: Haworth Press.

Gibbs. L. (1991). *Scientific reasoning for social workers: Bridging the gap between research and practice.* New York: Macmillan.

Gibbs, L. (2002). Assessing risk in social work practice: Essential elements. In A. Roberts & J. Greene (Eds.), *Social worker's desk reference.* New York: Oxford University Press.

Gibbs, L., & Gambrill, E. (2002). *Arguments opposing evidence-based practice.* Unpublished manuscript.

Gibbs, L., & Gambrill, E. (1999). *Critical thinking for social workers: Exercises for the helping profession(s).** Thousand Oaks, CA: Pine Forge. [*The title left off the (s) on the first 2000 copies printed negating our request to make the book interdisciplinary.]

Gibbs, L., Gambrill, E., Blakemore, J., Begun, A., Keniston, A., Peden, B., et al. (1995). A measure of critical thinking about practice. *Research on Social Work Practice. 5*(2), 193–204.

Gibbs, L. E. (1989). Quality of Study Rating Form: An instrument for synthesizing evaluation studies. *Journal of Social Work Education, 25*(1), 55–67.

Gibbs, L. E., & Johnson, D. J. (1983). Computer assisted clinical decision making. *Journal of Social Service Research, 6*(3/4), 119–132.

Giguere, M., & Lewis, M. (1994). The interdisciplary team component of case management: A positive experience. *CONA* (Canadian Orthopedics Nurses' Associaiton), *16*(3), 17–21.

Gilovich, T. (1991). *How we know what isn't so.* New York: The Free Press.

Gingerich, W. J. (1984). Generalizing single-case evaluation from classroom to practice setting. *Journal of Education for Social Work, 20*(1), 74–82.

Glass, G. V., & Kliegel, R. M. (1983). An apology for research integration in the study of psychotherapy. *Journal of Consulting and Clinical Psychology, 51*(1), 31(table).

Glass, G. V., McGaw, B., & Smith, M. L. (1981). *Meta-analysis in social research.* Beverly Hills, CA: Sage.

Globerman, J. (1996). Motivations to care: Daughters- and sons-in-law caring for relatives with Alzhemer's disease. *Family Relations, 45,* 37–45.

Globerman, J. (2002). *Notes for MSW students*. School of Social Work, University of Toronto, Toronto, Ontario M5S 1A1.

Goldner, E. M., & Bilsker, D. (1995). Evidence-based psychiatry. *Canadian Journal of Psychiatry, 40*, 97–101.

Gomory, T. (1999). Programs of assertive community treatment (PACT): A critical review. *Ethical Human Sciences and Services, 1*(2), 147–163.

Gottshalk, R., Davidson, W. S., Mayer, J., & Gensheimer, L. K. (1987). Behavioral approaches with juvenile offenders: A meta-analysis of long-term treatment efficacy. In E. K. Morris & C. J. Braukman (Eds.), *Behavioral approaches to crime and delinquency: A handbook of application, research, and concepts*. New York: Plenum.

Govier, T. (1995). *A practical study of argument*. Belmont, CA: Wadsworth.

Gray, J. A. M. (1997). *Evidence-based healthcare*. New York: Churchill Livingstone.

Green, M. L. & Ellis, P. J. (1997). Impact of an evidence-based medicine curriculum based on adult learning theory. *Journal of General Internal Medicine, 12*, 742–750.

Greenhalgh, T. (1997). *How to read a paper*. London: BMJ Publishing Group.

Greenhalgh, T., & Donald, A. (2000). *Evidence based health care workbook: Understanding research for individual and group learning*. London: BMJ Publishing Group.

Gresham, F., & MacMillan, D. (1997). Denial and defensiveness in the place of fact and reason: Rejoinder to Smith and Lovaas. *Behavioral Disorders, 22*(4), 219–230.

Grinnell, R. M. (1978). *Social work research and evaluation*. Itasca, IL: F. E. Peacock.

Grinnell, R. M. (1997). *Social work research and evaluation: Quantitative and qualitative approaches*. Itasca: IL: F. E. Peacock.

Grove, W., & Meehl, P. (1996). Comparative efficiency of informal (subjective, impressionistic) and formal (mechanical, algorithmic) prediction procedures: The clinical-statistical controversy. *Psychology, Public Policy, and Law, 2*, 293–323.

Gula, R. J. (1979). *Nonsense: How to overcome it*. New York: Stein & Day.

Hamill, R., Nisbett, R. E., & Wilson, T. D. (1980). Insensitivity to sample bias: Generalizing from atypical cases. *Journal of Personality and Social Psychology, 39*(4), 578–589.

Hamilton, J. G. (1995). Needle phobia: A neglected diagnosis. *Journal of Family Practice, 41*(2), 169–175.

Hanson, R. K. (1998). What do we know about sex offender risk assessment? *Psychology, Public Policy and Law, 4*(1/2), 50–72.

Harris, I. M. (1995). *Teachers' response to conflict in selected Milwaukee schools*. San Francisco, CA: Annual Meeting of the American Educational Research Association. (ERIC Document Reproduction Service No. ED 393855)

Hause, E. (1999). *Restraint reduction: Examining the risks of falls*. University of Wisconsin–Eau Claire.

Haynes, R. B., Sackett, D. L., Gray, J. M., Cook, D. J., & Guyatt, G. H. (1996b). Transferring evidence from research to practice: 1. The role of clinical care research evidence in clinical decisions. *ACP Journal Club, 125*(3), A14–A16.

Haynes, R. B., Sackett, D. L., Gray, J. M. A., Cook, D. J., & Guyatt, G. H. (1996a). *Evidence-Based Medicine, 1*(7), 196–197.

Haynes, R. B., Wilczynski, N., McKibbon, K. A., Walker, C. J., & Sinclair, J. C. (1994). Developing optimal search strategies for detecting clinically sound studies in MEDLINE. *Journal of the American Medical Informatics Association, 1*(6), 447–458.

Hays, W. L. (1981). *Statistics* (3rd ed.). New York: Holt, Rinehart, & Winston.

Hedges, L. V. (1984). Advances in statistical methods for meta-analysis. In W. H. Yeaton & P. M. Wortman (Eds.), *New directions for program evaluation. Vol. 24. Issues in data synthesis* (pp. 25–42). San Francisco: Jossey-Bass.

Hedges, L. V., & Olkin, I. (1985). *Statistical methods for meta-analysis*. Orlando, FL: Academic Press.

Heinemann, G. D., Farrell, M. P., Schmitt, M. H. (1994). Groupthink theory and research: Implications for decision making in geriatric health care teams. *Educational Gerontology, 20*(1), 71–85.

Helland, J. (2001). *Nursing home influences: Patients' preferences.* University of Wisconsin–Eau Claire.

Heller, R. F. & Peach, H. (1984). Evaluation of a new course to teach the principles and clinical applications of epidemiology to medical students. *International Journal of Epidemiology, 13*(4), 533–537.

Hellerslia, R. (2000). *Evaluating my practice.* Department of Social Work, University of Wisconsin–Eau Claire.

Herbert, V. (1983). Special report on quackery: Nine ways to spot a quack. *Health, 15*(10), 39–41.

Hilley, C. M., & Morley, C. J. (1994). Evaluation of government's campaign to reduce risk of cot death. *BMJ, 309,* 703–704.

Hobbs, N., et al. (1995). The economic and psychological burdens associated with Lovaas treatment for autism. (ERIC Document Reproduction Service No. ED381975)

Hoffer, E. (1973). Reflections on the human condition. In R. Andrews (Ed.), *Columbia dictionary of quotations* (1993). New York: Columbia University Press.

Holden, G., Rosenberg, G., & Weissman, A. (1996, April). Degrees of specification in the dissemination of meta-analysis [202 lines]. STAT- L Digest [stat-1@vml.mcgill.ca], 4/11–12/96, Special Issue.

Horowitz, M., Wilner, N., & Alvarez, W. Impact of Event Scale: A measure of subjective stress. *Psychosomatic Medicine, 41*(3), 209–218.

Howard, M. O., & Jenson, J. M. (1999). Clinical practice guidelines: Should social work develop them? *Research on Social Work Practice, 9*(3), 283–301.

Iles, P., & Auluck, R. (1990). Team building, inter-agency team development and social work practice. *British Journal of Social Work, 20,* 151–164.

Individuals with Disabilities Act (IDEA), Amendments of 1997, H.R. 5, Sec. 614(a)–(d).

Institute of Health Sciences. (July 19, 2000). Critical appraisal skills programme: 10 questions to help make sense of qualitative research. Institute of Health Sciences, Old Road, Headington, Oxford, UK, OX3 7LF. Retrieved May 15, 2001, from www.public-health.org.uk/casp/qualitative.html

International Council of Nurses. (2000). *Code of ethics for nurses* www.icn.ch/icncode.pdf

Ioannidis, J. P., Cappelleri, J. C., & Lau, J. (1998). Issues in comparions between meta-analyses and large trials. *Journal of the American Medical Association, 279*(14), 1089–1093.

Ioannidis, J. P. A., & Lau, J. (1998). Can quality of clinical trials and meta-analyses be quantified? *Lancet, 352*(9128), 590–591.

James, L. S., & Lanman, J. T. (1976). History of oxygen therapy and retrolental foibroplasia. *Pediatrics, 57*(4), 589–642.

Janis, I. L. (1971, November). Groupthink. *Psychology Today, 5,* 43–46, 74–76.

Janis, I. L. (1982). *Groupthink: Psychological studies of policy decisions and fiascoes* (2nd ed.). Boston: Houghton Mifflin.

Jarboe, G. R., & McDaniel, C. D. (1985). Influence patterns and determinant attributes in nursing home choice situations. *Journal of Healthcare Marketing, 5*(3), 19–30.

Jarvis, W. (1987). Chiropractic: A skeptical view. *The Skeptical Inquirer, 12*(1), 47–55.

Jarvis, W. T., & Barrett, S. (1993). How quackery sells. In S. Barrett & W. T. Jarvis (Eds.), *The health robbers: A close look at quackery in America.* Buffalo, NY: Prometheus Books.

Jayaratne, S. (1990). Clinical significance: Problems and new developments. In L. Videka-Sherman & W. Reid (Eds.), *Advances in clinical social work research.* (pp. 271–296). Silver Spring, MD: NASW Press.

Jemmott, J. B., Jemmott, L. S., Fong, G. T., & McCaffree, K. (1999). Reducing HIV Risk-associated behavior among African American adolescents: Testing the generality of intervention effects. *American Journal of Community Psychology, 27*(2), 161–187.

Jensen, J. (2000). *Client satisfaction survey.* Department of Social Work, University of Wisconsin–Eau Claire.

Jeste, D. V., & Wyatt, R. J. (1981). Changing epidemiology of tardive dyskinesia: An overview. *American Journal of Psychiatry, 138*(3), 297–309.

Johnson, P. (1998). Rural stroke caregivers: A qualitative study of the positive and negative response to the caregiver role. *Topics in Stroke Rehabilitation, 5*(3), 51–68.

Johnson, S. M., Kurtz, M. E., Tomlinson, T., & Howe, K. R. (1986). Students' stereotypes of patients as barriers to clinical decision making. *Journal of Medical Education, 61*(9), 727–735.

Juni, P., Witschi, A., Bloch, R., & Egger, M. (1999). The hazards of scoring the quality of clinical trials for meta-analysis. *JAMA, 282*(11), 1054–1060.

Kadushin, A., & Kadushin, G. (1997). *The social work interview* (4th ed.). New York: Columbia University.

Kane, R., Reinardy, J., Penrod, J., & Huck, S. (1999). After the hospitalization is over: A different perspective on family care of older people. *Journal of Gerontological Social Work, 31*(1/2), 119–141.

Karger, H. J., & Levine, J. (1999). *The Internet and technology for the human services.* New York: Longman.

Kassirer, J. P., & Kopelman, R. I. (1991). *Learning clinical reasoning.* Baltimore: Williams & Wilkins.

Kirk, S. A. (1979). Understanding research utilization in social work. In A. Rubin & A. Rosenblatt (Eds.), *Sourcebook on research utilization.* New York: Council on Social Work Education.

Kirk, S. A. (1990). Research utilization: The substructure of belief. In L. Videka-Sherman & W. J. Reid (Eds.), *Advances in clinical social work research* (pp. 233–250). Washington, DC: NASW Press. [Article that documents how little social workers use research in their practice.]

Kirk, S. A., & Berger, R. M. (1993). Improving research writing. *Social Work Research and Abstracts, 29*(4), 3–4.

Kirk, S. A., & Penka, C. E. (1992). Research utilization in MSW education: A decade of progress? In A. J. Grasso, & I. Epstein (Eds.), *Research utilization in the social services: Innovations for practice and administration.* New York: Haworth.

Kirst-Ashman, K. K., & Hull, G. H. (1999). *Understanding generalist practice* (2nd ed.). Chicago: Nelson-Hall.

Kitchens, J. M., & Pfeifer, M. P. (1989). Teaching residents to read the medical literature. *Journal of General Internal Medicine, 4,* 384–387.

Kitson, A., Harvey, G., & McCormack, B. (1998). Enabling the implementation of evidence-based practice: A conceptual framework. *Quality in Health Care, 7,* 149–158.

Klassen, D., & O'Connor, W. A. (1989). Assessing the risk of violence in released mental patients: A cross-validation study. *Psychological Assessment, 1*(2), 75–81.

Klec, T., Pearce, K., & Carson, P. K. (2000). Improving the positive predictive value of screening for developmental language disorder. *Journal of Speech, Language, and Hearing Research, 43*(4), 821–833.

Klein, W. C., & Bloom, M. (1995). Practice wisdom. *Social Work, 40*(6), 799–808. (EBSCOhost Full Display, pp. 1–10.)

Kopfstein, R. (1994). Inservice education for interdisciplinary teamwork: Training and evaluating teams. (ERIC Document Reproduction Service No. ED376666)

Krementz, J. (1982). *How it feels to be adopted.* New York: Alfred A. Knopf.

Kurtz, M. E., Johnson, S. M., & Rice, S. (1989). Students' clinical assessments: Are they affected by stereotyping? *Journal of Social Work Education, 25*(1), 3–12.

Lancaster, T., & Stead, L. F. (2001a). *Individual behavioural counselling for smoking cessation* (Cochrane Review). In: The Cochrane Library, Issue 1, 2000. Oxford: Update Software.

Lancaster, T., & Stead, L. F. (2001b). *Self-help interventions for smoking cessation* (Cochrane Review). In: The Cochrane Library, Issue 1, 2000. Oxford: Update Software.

Landry, F. J., Pangaro, L., Kroenke, K., Lucey, C., & Herbers, J. (1994). A controlled trial of a seminar to improve medical student attitudes toward, knowledge about, and use of the medical literature. *Journal of General Internal Medicine, 9,* 436–439.

Lastrucci, C. L. (1967). *The scientific approach: Basic principles of scientific method.* Cambridge, MA: Schenkman.

Lau, J., Ioannidis, J. P. A., & Schmid, C. H. (1997). Quantitative synthesis in systematic reviews. *Annals of Internal Medicine, 127,* 820–826. Retrieved from www.acponline.org/journals/annals01nov97/quantsyn.htm

LeCroy, C. W., & Tolman, R. M. (1991). Single-system design use of behavior therapists: Implications for social work. *Journal of Social Service Research, 14*(1/2), 45–56.

Leeson, H. (2000). *Evidence-based practice (EBP) exercise.* Department of Social Work, University of Wisconsin–Eau Claire.

Lefering, R., & Neugebauer, E. (1997). Problems of randomized controlled trials (RCT) in surgery. *Nonrandomized Comparative Clinical Studies—Proceedings of a Conference held in Heidelberg,* April 10–11, 1997. Available from R. Lefering & E. Neugebauer, Biochemical and Experimental Division, Second Department of Surgery, University of Cologne, Ostmerheimer Str. 200, D-51109 Cologne, Germany. Retrieved February 15, 1998, from symposion.com/nrccs/lefering.htm

Levy, S. (2000). It's time to turn the last page. *Newsweek, 134*(26), 96–97.

Lidz, C. W., Mulvey, E. P., & Gardner, W. (1993). The accuracy of predictions of violence to others. *JAMA, 269*(8), 1007–1011.

Lilienfeld, S. O., Wood, J. M., & Garb, H. N. (2001). What's wrong with this picture? *Scientific American, 284*(5), 81–87.

Linzer, M., Brown, J. T., Frazier, L. M., DeLong, E. R., & Siegel, W. C. (1988). Impact of a medical journal club on house-staff reading habits, knowledge, and critical appraisal skills. *Journal of the American Medical Association, 260*(17), 2537–2541.

Linzer, M., DeLong, E. R., & Hupart, K. H. (1987). A comparison of two formats for teaching critical reading skills in a medical journal club. *Journal of Medical Education, 62,* 690–692.

Lipsey, M. W. (1992). The effect of treatment on juvenile delinquents: Results from meta-analysis. In F. Losel, D. Bender, & Bliesener, T. (Eds.), *Psychology and law.* Berlin: Walter de Gruyter.

Lovaas, O. I. (1987). Behavioral treatment and normal educational and intellectual functioning in young autistic children. *Journal of Consulting and Clinical Psychology, 55*(1), 3–9.

Lynch, C. (1997). Searching the Internet. *Scientific American, 276*(3), 52–56.

Lyons, P., Doueck, H. J., & Wodarski, J. S. (1996). Risk assessment for child protective services: A review of the empirical literature on instrument performance. *Social Work Research, 20*(3), 143–154.

M2 Communications, Ltd., M2 PRESSWIRE. (2000). Internet speed smashed: KPNQwest and Alcatel quadruple top speed for data transfer. Retrieved October 2, 2000, from www.mailto:lexis-nexis@prod.lexis-nexis.com (A press release)

Maisel, R., & Persell, C. H. (1996). *How sampling works.* Thousand Oaks, CA: Pine Forge.

Makovec, S. (2000). *Improving discharge planning.* University of Wisconsin–Eau Claire.

Mann, C. C. (1994). Can meta-analysis make policy? *Science, 266*(11), 960–962.

Margetson, D. (1991). Why is problem-based learning a challenge? In D. Boud & G. Feletti (Eds.), *The challenge of problem-based learning.* New York: St. Martin's Press.

Marino, R., Green, R. G., & Young, E. (1998). Beyond the scientist-practitioner model's failure: Social workers' participation in agency-based research activities. *Social Work Research, 22*(3), 188–192.

Marshall, J. G. (1992). The impact of the hospital library on clinical decision making: The Rochester study. *Bulletin of the Medical Library Association, 80,* 169–178.

McCain, G., & Segal, E. M. (1988). *The game of science.* Pacific Grove, CA: Brooks/Cole.

McKechnie, J. L. (1983). *Webster's new universal unabridged dictionary* (2nd ed.). New York: Simon & Schuster Division of Gulf & Western Corporation.

McKibbon, A., Eady, A., & Marks, S. (1999). *PDQ Evidence-based principles and practice.* Hamilton, UK: B. C. Decker.

McKibbon, K. A. (1999). Finding answers to well-built questions. *Evidence-Based Medicine, 4*(6), 164–167.

Miller, N. S., & Flaherty, J. A. (2000). Effectiveness of coerced addiction treatment (alternative consequences): A review of clinical research. *Journal of Substance Abuse Treatment, 18,* 9–16.

Miller, R. W. (1985, March). The voice of the quack. [HHS Publication No. (FDA) 85-4196]. Rockville, MD: Department of Health and Human Services, Public Health Services, Food and Drug Administration, Office of Public Affairs.

Moher, D., & Olkin, I. (1995). Meta-analysis of randomized controlled trials: A concern for standards. *JAMA, 274*(24), 1962–1964.

Moher, D., Jadad, A. R., Nichol, G., Penman, M., Tugwell, P., & Walsh, S. (1995). Assessing the quality of randomized controlled trials: An annotated bibliography of scales and checklists. *Controlled Clinical Trials, 16*, 62–73.

Montgomery, R. J. V., & Borgatta, E. F. (1989). The effects of alternative support strategies on family caregiving. *The Grontologist, 29*(4), 457–464.

Montgomery, S. (2000). *Evidence-based practice assignment: Caregiver knowledge of dementia.* Unpublished paper, University of Wisconsin–Eau Claire.

Moore, B. N., & Parker, R. (1986). *Critical thinking: Evaluating claims and arguments in everyday life.* Palo Alto, CA: Mayfield.

Morgan, W. K. (1994, October 1). Evidence-based care writings: gobbledegook. *Canadian Medical Association Journal, 151*(7), 916–918.

Moriarty, P. M. (1998). Relative risk reduction versus number needed to treat as measures of lipid-lowering trial results. *American Journal of Cardiology, 82*, 505–507.

Moroz, K. J., Churchill, F., & Brgant, G. J. (Eds.). (1993). *Kids speak out on adoption: A book by adopted children in Vermont.* Waterbury, VT: Vermont Adoption Project.

Mulrow, C. D. (1994). Rationale for systematic reviews. *British Medical Journal, 309*, 597–599.

Myers, L. (November 10, 2000). 24-Telcom. Eau Claire, WI.

National Association of Social Workers. (January 1, 1997). *Code of ethics.* Silver Spring, MD: NASW Press.

National Association of Social Workers. (1999). *Code of ethics* (A document). Retrieved February 16, 2001, from www.naswdc.org/Code/ethics.htm

Nehring, C. (1999). *Evidence-based practice exercise: Teen living skills group.* University of Wisconsin–Eau Claire.

Nelson, I. (2001). *Kids' reflections on adoption: A follow-up study.* University of Wisconsin–Eau Claire.

(The) New international Webster's concise dictionary of the English language. (1997). Naples, FL: Trident Press International.

Newcomer, R., Yordi, C., DuNah, R., Fox, P., & Wilkinson, A. (1999). Effects of the Medicare Alzheimer's Disease Demonstration on caregiver burden and depression. *Health Services Research, 34*(3), 669–689.

Nony, P., Cucherat, M., Haugh, M. C., & Boissel, J. P. (1997). Standardization of terminology in meta-analysis: A proposal for working definitions. *Fundamentals of Clinical Pharmacology, 11*, 481–493.

Nordholm, D. L. A. (1980). Beautiful patients are good patients: Evidence for the physical attractiveness stereotype in first impressions of patients. *Social Science and Medicine, 14A*, 81–83.

Norman, G. R., & Schmidt, G. H. (1992). The psychological basis of problem-based learning: A review of the evidence. *Academic Medicine, 67*(9), 557–565.

Norman, G. R., & Shannon, S. L. (1998). Effectiveness of instruction in critical appraisal (evidence-based medicine) skills: A critical appraisal. *Canadian Medical Association Journal, 158*(2), 177–181.

North, S. (1996). *Evaluation of practice personal single subject design: An experiment in desensitization therapy.* University of Wisconsin–Eau Claire.

Nyhus, S. (December 13, 2000). *EBP assignment: Oral presentation.* University of Wisconsin–Eau Claire.

Oktay, J. S. (2002). Standards for quality in qualitative research: Discussion and exemplar. In A. Roberts & J. Greene (Eds.), *Social worker's desk reference.* New York: Oxford University Press.

O'Loughlin, F., & Webb, M. (1997). Controlled assessment of alcoholics admitted involuntarily to a general psychiatric hospital. *Irish Journal of Psychological Medicine, 13*(4), 140–143.

Oliver, D., Britton, M., Seed, P., Martin, F. C., & Hooper, A. H. (1997). Development and evaluation of evidence based risk assessment tool (STRATIFY) to predict which elderly patients will fall: Case-Control and cohort studies. *British Medical Journal. 315*(7115), 1049–1054.

Oskamp, S. (1982). Overconfidence in case-study judgments. In D. Kahneman, P. Slovic, & A. Tversky (Eds.), *Judgment under uncertainty: Heuristics and biases* (pp. 287–293). Cambridge: Cambridge University Press.

Ostwald, S., Hepburn, K. W., Caron, W., Burns, T., & Mantell, R. (1999). Reducing caregiver burden: A randomized psychoeducational intervention for caregivers of persons with dementia. *The Gerontologist, 39*(3), 299–309.

Oxman, A. D., & Guyatt, G. H. (1993). The Science of reviewing research. *Annals of the New York Academy of Science, 703,* 125–133

Oxman, A. D., Sackett, D. L, & Guyatt, G. H. (1993, November 3). Users' guides to the medical literature. I. How to get started. *Journal of the American Medical Association, 270*(17), 2093–2095.

Penka, C. E., & Kirk, S. A. (1991). Practitioner involvement in clinical evaluation. *Social Work, 36*(6), 513–518.

Perry, A. (2000). *The clock drawing test.* University of Wisconsin–Eau Claire.

Rayner, K., Poorman, Foorman, B., Perfetti, C. A. Pesetsky, D., & Seidenberg, M. S. (2002). How should reading be taught. *Scientific American, 286*(3), 84–91.

Poulin, J. E., Walter, C. A., & Walker, J. L. (1994). Interdisciplinary team membership: A survey of gerontological social workers. *Journal of Gerontological Social Work, 22*(1/2), 93–107.

Pound, P., Gompertz, P., Ebrahim, S. (1993). Development and results of a questionnaire to measure caregiver satisfaction after stroke. *Epidemiology and Community Health, 47,* 500–505.

Price, D. J. deSolla. (1963). *Little science, big science.* New York: Columbia University Press.

Proudfoot, J., Guest, P., Carson, J., Dunn, G., & Gray, J. (1997). Effect of cognitive behavioral training in job-finding among long-term unemployed people. *Lancet, 350*(907), 96–100.

Quinsey, V. L., Harris, G. T., Rice, M. E., & Cormier, C. A. (1998). *Violent offenders: Appraising and managing risk.* Washington, DC: American Psychological Association.

Radack, K. L., & Valanis, B. (1986). Teaching critical appraisal and application of medical literature to clinical problem-solving. *Journal of Medical Education, 61,* 329–331.

Rafuse, J. (1994, May 1). Evidence-based medicine means MDs must develop new skills, attitudes, CMA conference told. *Canadian Medical Association Journal, 150*(9), 1479–1481.

Redig, J. M. (1998). *Evidence-based practice exercise: Features of effective hospital discharge planning.* University of Wisconsin–Eau Claire.

Reduction of HIV transmission from mother to infant. (1994). *Canadian Medical Association Journal, 151*(5), 583–585.

Reid, W. (2001). The scientific and empirical foundations of clinical practice. In H. E. Briggs & K. Corcoran (Eds.), *Social work practice: Treating common client problems.* Chicago: Lyceum.

Reid, W. J. (1995). Research overview. In *Encyclopedia of social work, 2* (pp. 2040–2054). Washington, DC: NASW.

Reinartz, K. (1999). *Evidence-based practice exercise: An evaluation of the effectiveness of eye movement desensitization and reprocessing (EMDR).* University of Wisconsin–Eau Claire.

Rice, L. J. (1993). Needle phobia: An anesthesiologist's perspective. *Journal of Pediatrics, 122*(5 Pt. 2), 9–13.

Richards, S. B., Taylor, R. L., Ramasamy, R., & Richards, R. Y. (1999). *Single-subject research: Applications in educational and clinical settings.* San Diego: Singular.

Richardson, S. W. (1998). Ask, and ye shall retrieve. *Evidence-Based Medicine, 3,* 100–101.

Richardson, S. W., Wilson, M. C., Nishikawa, J., & Hayward, R. S. A. (1995). The well-built clinical question: a key to evidence-based decisions. *ACP Journal Club, 123,* A12–A13.

Riegelman, R. K. (1986). Effects of teaching first-year medical students skills to read medical literature. *Journal of Medical Education, 61,* 454–460.

Robinson, L., Coady, N., & Tutty, L. M. (1996). Females who sexually abuse children. In L. M. Tutty, M. Rothery, & R. M. Grinnell (Eds.), *Qualitative research for social workers.* Boston: Allyn & Bacon.

Rose, S., Bisson, J., & Wesseley, S. (2002). Psychological debriefing for preventing post-traumatic stress disorder (PTSD). (Cochrane Review). In the Cochrane Library, Issue 1, 2002; Update Software.

Rosen, A. (1994). Knowledge use in direct practice. *Social Service Review, 68*(4), 561–577.

Rosenthal, R. (1984). *Applied social research series, Vol. 6: Meta-analytic procedures for social research.* Beverly Hills, CA: Sage.

Rosenthal, R., & Rosnow, R. L. (1975). *The volunteer subject.* New York: Wiley.

Rosenthal, R., & Rubin, V. B. (1982). A simple, general-purpose display of magnitude of experimental effect. *Journal of Educational Psychology, 74*(2), 166–168.

Rubin, A. (1992). Education for research utilization in BSW programs. In A. J. Grasso & I. Epstein (Eds.), *Research utilization in the social services: Innovations for practice and administration.* New York: Haworth.

Rubin, A., & Babbie, E. (1997). *Research methods for social work* (3rd ed.). Pacific Grove, CA: Brooks/Cole.

Rubin, I. M., Plovnick, M. S., & Fry, R. E. (1975). *Improving the coordination of care: A program for health team development.* Cambridge, MA: Ballinger.

Rudd, M. G., Viney, L. L., & Preston, C. A. (1999). The grief experienced by spousal caregivers of dementia patients: The role of place of care of patient and gender of caregiver. *International Journal of Aging and Human Development, 48*(3), 217–240.

Sackett, D. L., & Rosenberg, W. M. C. (1995). On the need for evidence-based medicine. *Health Economics, 4,* 249–254.

Sackett, D. L., Richardson, W. S., Rosenberg, W., & Haynes, R. B. (1997). *Evidence-based medicine: How to practice & teach EBM.* New York: Churchill-Livingstone.

Sackett, D. L., Rosenberg, W. M. C., Gray, J. A. M., & Haynes, R. B., & Richardson, W. S. (1996). Evidence-based medicine: What it is and what it isn't. *British Medical Journal, 312,* 71–72.

Sackett, D. L., Straus, S. E., Richardson, W. S., Rosenberg, W., & Haynes, R. B. (1997). *Evidence-based medicine: How to practice and teach EBM* (2nd ed.). Edinburgh: Churchill Livingstone.

Sackett, D. L., Straus, S. E., Richardson, W. S., Rosenberg, W., & Haynes, R. B. (2000). *Evidence-based medicine: How to practice and teach EBM* (2nd ed.). Edinburgh: Churchill Livingstone.

Sacred Heart Hospital Palliative Care Service [brochure]. (Distributed by Sacred Heart Hospital, 900 West Clairemont Ave., Eau Claire, WI 54701)

Saleebey, D. (1992). *The strengths perspective in social work practice.* New York: Longman.

Sands, R. G. (1989). The social worker joins the team: A look at the socialization process. *Social Work in Health Care, 14*(2), 1–15.

Scheithauer, K. (1999). *Assessing risk of returning to the community.* University of Wisconsin–Eau Claire.

Schamale, C. P. (1999). *Aphasia group: Caregiver satisfaction.* University of Wisconsin–Eau Claire.

Schneider, A. (1999). Assessing risk of returning to the community. University of Wisconsin-Eau Claire.

Schwarzer, R. (n.d.). *Meta: Program for secondary data analysis.* (Available from National Collegiate Software, Duke University Press, 6697 College Station, Durham, NC 27708)

Scott, R. L., & Presmanes, W. S. (2001). Reliability and validity of the Daily Living Activities Scale: A functional assessment measure for severe mental disorders. *Research on Social Work Practice, 11,* 373–389.

Seidl, F. W. (1980). Making research relevant to practitioners. In *The Future of Social Work Research* D. Fanshel (ed.). Washington, DC, National Association of Social Workers, p. 53.

Shah, A., Herbert, R., Lewis, S., Mahendran, R., Platt, J., & Bhattacharyya, B. (1997). Screening for depression among acutely ill geriatric inpatients with a short geriatric depression scale. *Age and Aging. 26*(3), 217–223.

Shaughnessy, A., & Slawson, D. (Revision 1997). Worksheet for articles about treatment. School of Medicine, University of Virginia.

Shaw, I., & Shaw, A. (1997). Game plans, buzzes, and sheer luck: Doing well in social work. *Social Work Research, 21*(2), 69–79.

Sheras, P. L. (2000). Grief and traumatic loss: What schools need to know and do. In K. J. Doka (Ed.), *Living with grief.* Washington, DC: Hospice Foundation of America.

She's known as Chicago's "welfare queen." (1978, July 3). *U.S. News & World Report, 84,* 28.

Shin, J. H., Haynes, R. B., & Johnston, M. E. (1993). Effect of problem-based, self-directed undergraduate education on life-long learning. *Canadian Medical Association Journal, 148*(6), 969–976.

Shumway—Cook, A., Bauer, S., & Woollacott, M. (2000). Predicting the probability for falls in community-dwelling older adults using the Timed Up & Go Test. *Physical Therapy, 80*(9), 896–903.

Silagy, C., Mant, D., Fowler, G. & Lancaster, T. (2001). Nicotine replacement therapy for smoking cessation (Cochrane Review). In: The Cochrane Library, Issue 1, 2001. Oxford: Update Software.

Slaby, A. E., Goldberg, R. J., & Wallace, S. R. (1983). Interdisciplinary team approach to emergency psychiatric care. *Psychosomatics, 24*(7), 627–637.

Slawson, D. C., & Shaughnessy, A. F. (1997). Obtaining useful information from experf based sources. *British Medical Journal, 314,* 948–949.

Smith, T., Eikeseth, S., Klevstrand, M., & Lovaas, O. (1997). Intensive behavioral treatment for preschoolers with severe mental retardation and pervasive developmental disorder. *American Journal of Mental Retardation, 102*(3), 238–249.

Spector, A., Orrell, S. A., Davies, S., & Woods, R. T. (2000a). *Reminiscence therapy for dementia* (Cochrane Review). Cochrane Library, 1–16 [a meta-analysis]. Retrieved January 23, 2001, from www.cochranelibrary.com

Spector, A., Orrell, S. A., Davies, S., & Woods, B. (2000b). *Reality orientation for dementia* (Cochrane Review). Cochrane Library, 1–16 [a meta-analysis]. Retrieved April 21, 2000, from www.cochrane/library/.com

Spiers, P. S., & Guntheroth, W. G. (1994). Recommendations to avoid the prone sleeping position and recent statistics for sudden infant death syndrome in the United States. *Archives of Pediatric and Adolescent Medicine, 14*(2), 141–146.

Stamm, S. (2000). *Assessing shaken baby syndrome.* University of Wisconsin–Eau Claire.

Stern, K. (1995). Clinical guidelines and negligence liability. In M. Deighan & S. Hitch (Eds.), *Clinical effectiveness from guidelines to cost effective practice.* Brentwood: Earlybrave Publications.

Stix, G. (2001). The triumph of the light. *Scientific American, 284*(1), 81–86.

Stocks, J. T. (1998). Recovered memory therapy: A dubious practice technique. *Social Work, 43*(5), 423–436.

Stuart, M. G., Hillman, E. J., Donovan, D. T., Tanli, H. H. (1997). The effects of a practice guideline on endoscopic sinus surgery at an academic center. *American Journal of Rhinology , 11*(2), 161–165.

(The) SUPPORT Investigators. (1995). A controlled trial to improve care for seriously ill hospitalized patients. *JAMA, 274*(20), 1591–1598.

Svik, D. (1999). *Working with the mentally ill in a hospital setting: Patient participation, multidisciplinary teams, and the mentally ill.* University of Wisconsin–Eau Claire.

Swets, J. A., Dawes, R. M., & Monahan, J. (2000a). Better decisions through science. *Scientific American, 283*(4), 82–87.

Tebb, S. (1995). An aid to empowerment: A caregiver well-being scale. *Health and Social Work, 20*(2), 87–92.

Test, M. A., & Stein, L. I. (1977). A community approach to the chronically disabled patient. *Social Policy, 8*(1), 8–16.

Thibado, R. (1998). *Evidence-based practice assignment.* University of Wisconsin–Eau Claire.

Timmermans, D. (1996). Lost for words? Using verbal terms to express uncertainty. *Making Better Decisions* (an experimental newsletter by E. Gambrill and L. Gibbs, University of Wisconsin–Eau Claire), *3*(2), 2, 4–5.

Toner, J. A., Miller, P., & Gurland, B. J. (1994). Conceptual, theoretical, and practical approaches to development of interdisciplinary teams: A transactional model. *Educational Gerontology, 20*(1), 53–69.

Toseland, R. W., & Rossiter, C. M. (1989). Group interventions to support family caregivers: A review and analysis. *The Gerontologist, 29*(4), 438–448.

Treatment of Attention-Deficit/Hyperactivity Disorder. Summary, Evidence Report/Technology Assessment: Number 11. AHCPR Publication No. 99-E017, December 1999, Agency for Health Care Policy and Research, Rockville, MD. Available from www.ahrq.gov/clinic/adhdsum.htm

Tripodi, T. (1994). A primer on *single-subject design for clinical social workers.* Washington, DC: National Association of Social Workers.

Tritchler, D. (1999). Modeling study quality in meta-analysis. *Statistics in Medicine, 18,* 2135–2145.

Troy, J. A. (2000). *Problems with reunifying children in foster care with their families.* University of Wisconsin–Eau Claire.

Tversky, A., & Kahneman, D. (1971). Belief in the "law of small numbers." *Psychological Bulletin, 76,* 105–110.

Tversky, A., & Kahneman, D. (1974). Judgment under uncertainty: Heuristics and biases. *Science, 185,* 1124–1131.

Tversky, A., & Kahneman, D. (1982). Judgment under uncertainty: Heuristics and biases. In D. Kahneman, P. Slovic, & A. Tversky (Eds.), *Judgment under uncertainty: Heuristics and biases.* Cambridge: Cambridge University Press.

Utech, M. (2001). *An assessment of activities of daily living (ADL): Measuring the ADL of mentally ill persons in a community support program.* University of Wisconsin–Eau Claire.

Varlejs, J. (Ed.). (1990). *Information literacy: Learning how to learn.* Jefferson, North Carolina and London: McFarland and Company, Inc.

Vernon, D. T. A., & Blake, R. L. (1993). Does problem-based learning work? A meta-analysis of evaluative research. *Academic Medicine, 68*(7), 550–563.

Vertosick, F. T. (1998). First, do *no* harm. *Discover, 19*(7), 106–111.

Wakefield, J. C., & Kirk, S. A. (1996). Unscientific thinking about scientific practice: Evaluating the scientist-practitioner model. *Social Work Research, 20*(2), 83–95.

Walker, R. J., & Pomeroy, E. C. (1996). Depression or grief? The experience of caregivers of people with dementia. *Health & Social Work, 21*(4), 247–254.

Wallace, C. J., Liberman, R. P., Tauber, R., & Wallace, J. (2000). The Independent Living Skills Survey: A comprehensive measure of the community functioning of severely and persistently mentally ill individuals. *Schizophrenia Bulletin, 26,* 631–658.

Walsh, D. C., Hingson, R. W., Merrigan, D. M., & Levenson, S. M. (1992). Treating the employed alcoholic: Which interventions work? *Alcohol Health and Research World, 16*(2), 140–148.

Weaver, F. M., & Burdi, M. (1992). Developing a model of discharge planning based on patient characteristics. *Journal of Aging and Health, 4*(3), 440–452.

Weber, J. J. (1999). *Racial orientation in children.* University of Wisconsin–Eau Claire.

Webster's new twentieth century dictionary (2nd ed.). (1983). New York: Simon & Schuster Division of Gulf & Western Corporation.

Weick, A., Rapp, C., Sullivan, W. P., & Kisthardt, W. (1989). A strengths perspective for social work practice. *Social Work, 34*(4), 350–354.

Welch, G. J. (1983). Will graduates use single-subject designs to evaluate their casework practice? *Journal of Education for Social Work, 19*(2), 42–47.

Wertheimer, D. S., & Kleinman, L. S. (1990). A model for interdisciplinary discharge planning in a university hospital. *The Gerontologist, 30*(6), 837–840.

Wiederholt, A. (1999). *What is the most effective way to educate youth about HIV/AIDS?* University of Wisconsin–Eau Claire.

Williams, E. I., Greenwell, J., & Groom, L. M. (1992). Characteristics of patients aged 75 years and over who are discharged from hospital without district nursing support. *Journal of Public Health Medicine, 14*(3), 321–327.

Wilner, D. M., Greathouse, V. L., Wilton, R. J., Ershoff, D. H., Foster, K. E., & Hetherington, R. W. (1976). The custom research database in the analysis and transfer of information. *Evaluation, 3,* 11–14.

Wilson, A., & Henry, D. A. (1992). 10. Meta-analysis Part 2: Assessing the quality of published meta-analyses. *The Medical Journal of Australia, 156*(3), 173–187.

Wilson, T., & Rachman, S. (1983). Meta-analysis and evaluation of psychologic outcome: Limitations and liabilities. *Journal of Consulting and Clinical Psychology. 51*(1), 54–64.

Wilson, S. A., Becker, L. A., & Tinker, R. H. (1995). Eye movement desensitization and reprocessing (EMDR) treatment for psychologically traumatized individuals. *Journal of Consulting and Clinical Psychology, 63*(6), 928–937.

Wilson, S. J., & Lipsey, M. W. (2000). Wilderness challenge programs for delinquent youth: A meta-analysis of outcome evaluations. *Evaluation and Program Planning, 23,* 1–12.

Winitzky, N., Sheridan, S., Crow, N., Welch, M., & Kennedy, C. (1995). Interdisciplinary collaboration: Variations on a theme. *Journal of Teacher Education, 46*(2), 109–119.

Witkin, S. L. (1996). If empirical practice is the answer, then what is the question? *Social Work Research, 20*(2), 69–76.

Witkin, S. L. (2001). The measurement of things. *Social Work, 46*(2), 101–104.

Wong, J. H., Findlay, J. M., & Suarez-Almazor, M. E. (1997). Regional performance of carotid endarterectomy. *Stroke, 28*(5), 891–898.

Wong, J. H., Lubkey, T. B., Suarez-Almazor, M. E., & Findlay, J. M. (1999). *Stroke, 30,* 12–15.

Wood, J. (1998). *Gang prevention: The best evidence.* University of Wisconsin-Eau Claire.

Woolf, S. H. (1992, May). Practice guidelines: A new reality in medicine. I. Recent developments. *Archives of Internal Medicine, 150*(9), 1811–1819.

Woolf, S. H. (1992). Practice guidelines, a new reality in medicine II. Methods of developing guidelines. *Archives of Internal Medicine, 152* (5), 946–952.

Zarit, S. H., Reever, K. E., & Bach-Peterson, J. (1980). Relatives of the impaired elderly: Correlates of feelings of burden. *The Gerontologist 20* (6), 649–655.

Zenz, J. H. (1999). *Brief Psychiatric Rating Scale: A suicide assessment.* University of Wisconsin–Eau Claire.

Zlotnik, J. L., McCroskey, J., Gardner, S., de Gibaja, M. G., Taylor, H. P., George, J., et al. (1999). *Myths and opportunities: An examination of the impact of discipline-specific accreditation on interprofessional education.* Alexandria, VA: Council on Social Work Education.

Index